The Free System Corollary

The Free System Corollary

Responding to Abductive Problems of Evil

Peter J. Morgan

WIPF & STOCK · Eugene, Oregon

THE FREE SYSTEM COROLLARY
Responding to Abductive Problems of Evil

Copyright © 2019 Peter J. Morgan. All rights reserved. Except for brief quotations in critical publications or reviews, no part of this book may be reproduced in any manner without prior written permission from the publisher. Write: Permissions, Wipf and Stock Publishers, 199 W. 8th Ave., Suite 3, Eugene, OR 97401.

Wipf & Stock
An Imprint of Wipf and Stock Publishers
199 W. 8th Ave., Suite 3
Eugene, OR 97401

www.wipfandstock.com

PAPERBACK ISBN: 978-1-5326-8620-7
HARDCOVER ISBN: 978-1-5326-8621-4
EBOOK ISBN: 978-1-5326-8622-1

Manufactured in the U.S.A.

This book is dedicated to my children. May you ever be able to hear the voice of God in the midst of the storm.

We theists should view our theism, while grounded in the past, as also dynamic, and as needing better specifications as we learn more and more, individually and communally, about ourselves and the world we live in, so as to refine theism into its best and truest versions.

—Stephen Wykstra

"Skeptical Theism, Abductive Atheology, and Theory Reasoning," 163

Contents

Acknowledgments | xi
Abbreviations | xii

Chapter 1: Introduction | 1
    Why the Problem of Evil? 1
    A Daily Does of Abduction 3
    The Work Ahead 5
        A Glimpse at Free Systems 5
        A Word on Limitations 6
    Method of Approach 8
        Chapter Divisions 8
        Chapter Summaries 9
    Conclusion 12

Chapter 2: Considerations of the Good | 13
    The Call of Moral Obligation toward the Good 13
    Significant Freedom toward Choosing the Good 19
    Does God's Good Nature Eliminate His Freedom? 23
    Conclusions 28

Chapter 3: Natural Law | 30
    Rational Karmic Morality? 30
    Natural Law and Divine Humility 33
    Spiritual Complacency 37
    Conclusions 41

Chapter 4: The Free Will Defense | 43
    J. L. Mackie   43
        Causation and Teleological Reality   43
        Metaphysical Double Vision   46
    Alvin Plantinga   51
        Properly Basic Belief & Rationality   51
        The Free Will Defense   54
    Conclusions   58

Chapter 5: The Expanded Free Will Defense | 59
    Bruce Russell   59
        Experience as the Foundation of Justification   59
        The Flexibility of Greater Amounts of Good   62
    Peter van Inwagen   67
        Moral Lines in the Sand   67
        Regularity and the Expanded Free Will Defense   69
    Conclusions   74

Chapter 6: Inculpable Nonbelief | 76
    Paul Draper   76
        The Hypothesis of Indifference   76
        Biologically Gratuitous Pain   80
    Daniel Howard-Snyder   84
        Inscrutable Evil   84
        Inculpable Non-Belief   87
    Conclusions   91

Chapter 7: Skeptical Theism | 92
    Stephen Wykstra   92
        CORNEA   92
    William Rowe   95
        A Trolley Ride to Obscurity   95
    Conclusions   99

Chapter 8: The Free System Corollary | 101
    The Free System Corollary Defined   103
        William Alston and Theodical Suggestions   104
        Theodical Suggestions as Applied to the FSC   105
    The Necessioty of a Free System for Free Will   106
        The Nature of Free Will   106
        Regularity/Consistency as Part of a Free System   110
        The Potential for Oppression   112
    Free Will in a Free System   116
        Individual Responsibility for Moral Actions   116
        Prayer as an Act of Free Will   118
        What Should Be Expected   122
    Challenges to the Free System Corollary   127
        Miracles and Regularity   127
        The Linchpin of Free Will   129
        Are We Still on Rowe's Trolley?   132
    Conclusions   135

Chapter 9: Applying the Free System Corollary | 137
    Addressing a Particular Case of Natural Evil   138
        A Free System Corollary Account of an Instance of Natural Evil   138
        The Free System Corollary in Comparison with Naturalism, Part 1   142
    Addressing a Particular Case of Moral Evil   146
        A Free System Corollary Account of an Instance of Moral Evil   146
        The Free System Corollary in Comparison with Naturalism, Part 2   149
    Conclusions   153

Chapter 10: Conclusion | 155

Bibliography | 163

Acknowledgments

I would like to thank Dr. Edward Martin, Dr. Daniel Mitchell, and Dr. David Beck of Liberty University for their assistance and support throughout the drafting of this text. Also, my wife, Ann-Marie, deserves special thanks for her many hours of patient listening and support as I worked through various hurdles in this long journey. Lastly, I would also like to thank the team at Wipf and Stock for their helpfulness and patience throughout this process. Thank you all.

Abbreviations

APOE	Abductive Problem of Evil
DH	Divine Hiddenness
E1	The death of a fawn, Bambi, in a forest fire
E2	The rape/murder of a 5-year-old girl
EFWD	Expanded Free Will Defense
FSC	Free System Corollary to Free Will Defenses
FW*	Free will is a fundamental good for all of humanity
FW1	The thesis that an individual's free will is not more important than avoiding intense evil
FWD	Free Will Defense
G	A wholly good and loving all-powerful God
[g]	An all-powerful being understood with no other preconceptions
HI	Hypothesis of Indifference
INB	Inculpable Non-Belief
J	Justification for good
MDV	Metaphysical Double Vision
ME*	There exists a valid reason(s) for why G would allow intense moral evil
ME1	G is incompatible with the existence of intense moral evil, therefore G does not exist
MO	Moral Obligation
O	Observations of pleasure, pain, and suffering in humans and animals
POE	Problem of Evil
TWD	Transworld Depravity

1

Introduction

Why the Problem of Evil?

IN AND OF ITSELF, the Problem of Evil (POE) is not new to the realm of philosophy and theology. However, the POE is no less important today for its historical presence. There are at least two reasons why this discussion continues to be had between theists[1] and non-theists:[2] (1) applicability and (2) ceaseless change.

The general question of the POE, "How can a wholly good God allow evil to take place?" is a question that is imminently applicable to theistic belief in a God that is supremely good. Horrors exist in the daily lives of people in communities around the world. The severe illness of a child, starvation, loss of family, and so many more examples of pain and suffering can be easily found. Factoring in the atrocities that occur during war, and the frequencies of wars, the amount of suffering that takes place is hard to ignore. Thus, the POE is timelessly applicable to any who would claim to believe in a wholly good God. However, it is not merely the applicability of the POE that continues to make it relevant for today. Theologians for centuries have given explanations for the great number of occurrences of evil in this world. The POE persists not only because of its applicability but new answers need to be given because of its capacity for ceaseless change.

Evidence for the ceaseless change of the POE can be found in the various arguments and discussions that have been had in the twentieth century and beginning of the twenty-first century, let alone the centuries prior. This is not

---

1. While there are theists who hold to other gods, the Judeo-Christian God is a supreme example of a fully omnipotent, omniscient, loving, and good God. Therefore, any theistic references in this paper should be understood as referring to the God of the Bible.

2. Here, "non-theist(s)" refers to that general group of people who believe that there is no God or that if there is a God it is impossible to know of that God's existence and who hold that all realities of life are purely naturalistic in nature with no supernatural influence that can be detected or proved.

to say that theistic answers to the POE were not adequate, but the POE is ever changing in that new perspectives on what constitutes evil have a tendency to change and/or become more nuanced. Therefore, with each theistic response to the POE it is possible for a refined statement/challenge of the POE to be formulated. This does not necessarily invalidate the answers previously given, but it does beg for additional/more complete responses.

For much of the history of the POE, a predominate (deductive) question was the logical compatibility of the existence of evil with an omnipotent, omniscient, and wholly good God (G). Today, the emphasis of the POE has shifted from logical compatibility to plausibility. A strong voice in non-theistic philosophical writings is Bruce Russell, and he encapsulates the current focus on the POE when he states, "Hence, any hypothesis that implies that this was not nearly certain would be improbable on what we know. And if a hypothesis is improbable on what we know, it cannot serve as an adequate defense of theism."[3] Here, Russell is referring to his argument that G has a moral obligation to stop at least one more instance of evil because it is in G's power to do so, and doing so will not decrease the amount of good in the world. Russell is making an evidential argument. This evidential argument is inductive in nature in that it seeks to reveal a general truth about the existence of G from particular instances of suffering, but it is also abductive in that it argues for an inference to G's nonexistence. This abduction is an inference to the best explanation on what is known of the situation of the POE, and while induction may do a lot of the foot work it is abduction that is the closing argument of non-theists such as Russell.

In making his abductive case, Russell asserts that any defense of theism will need to provide a plausible explanation for the POE that is superior to that of the non-theist. Russell states, "A defense requires that theism be conjoined with a hypothesis to explain the pattern of suffering there is and if that hypothesis is improbable on what we know, then the conjunction of theism and that hypothesis will also be improbable on that background knowledge."[4] The logical compatibility of the existence of G and evil is of minor concern for these kinds of non-theistic arguments; for theism to win the day an argument is needed that more abductively accounts for the amount of intense evil that is present in the world than non-theistic arguments.

---

3. Russell, "Defenseless," 203.
4. Russell, "Defenseless," 203.

A Daily Dose of Abduction

Non-theistic arguments from the POE, such as the one briefly introduced above, place a challenge before the theist to provide a more plausible explanation for the state of affairs that are present in this world. This is a challenge that should not be ignored by theists, for though inductive and deductive reasoning are used in daily life, it is abduction that plays a significant role in living life.

David Baggett describes abduction as an inference to the best explanation which is similar to induction in that a conclusion is not guaranteed but still warranted.[5] Whereas inductive reasoning brings one to a generalized conclusion, abduction winnows the generality toward a specific explanation for an observed phenomenon, "in a way at once plausible, instinctive, and economical."[6] Baggett states, "The inference does not settle the matter, but produces new opportunities to subject the explanation to critical scrutiny to assess its effectiveness at providing further explanation of additional observations."[7] Abduction seeks a more personal/specific explanation for the states of affairs that are observed in this world than induction provides. Baggett additionally observes that Charles Sanders Peirce, who characterized abduction in the late nineteenth and early twentieth centuries, "noted that all of us tend to infer explanations; we hypothesize in efforts to explain various phenomena we encounter."[8] Not only does abduction seek for possible explanations that are more specific than induction but abduction is a common element of human existence.

Every day, millions of people commute to work. Regardless of their specific routines, each person believes that the process of boarding a train, driving a car, etc., will be as mundane as it has been for the overwhelming majority of previous days. Rarely, if ever, are thoughts given to the specific mortal dangers that lurk at every mile marker; if every other day has gone well then it is probable, since nothing else has changed, that this day will go well too. There are many potential explanations for this inductive feeling of security ranging from a belief in God's protection to the superiority of one's driving skills to the reliability of the make and model of one's car. Whenever someone draws a conclusion as to the probable reason for their safe commute they are moving from induction to abduction. The commuter need not dwell on the explanation for safety for long for it to be an abductive thought.

---

5. Baggett, *God & Cosmos*, 15.
6. Baggett, *God & Cosmos*, 15.
7. Baggett, *God & Cosmos*, 15.
8. Baggett, *God & Cosmos*, 14.

For example, even in the instant someone sees their car and briefly revels in purchasing a reliable vehicle that person has moved from the induction of belief in a safe commute toward an abductive justification for that belief. This same consideration of probability can be extended to virtually every aspect of routine life.[9] This reality of human life makes abductive arguments from the POE worthy of attention.

For the reasons mentioned above, any argument on the POE that utilizes an abductive approach would be highly relatable to those living in a world in which evil exists. The significance of this observation for the theist resides in the non-theist's confidence that no theistic defense can be more probable than that of the non-theist for explaining why there are the amounts and kinds of evils that exist in this world. While this author cannot speak as to the motivations/reasons for the non-theistic confidence of philosophers such as William Rowe, J. L. Mackie, Bruce Russell, and Paul Draper, there does appear to be a consistent tendency for the non-theist to use specific evidences (such as a fawn dying in a forest fire and the abuse/murder of a five-year-old girl) in support of their account of the POE. Theistic philosophers such as Alvin Plantinga, Peter van Inwagen, and Stephen Wykstra do provide compelling defenses, but they appear reluctant to apply their theistic defense toward the specific evidences used by non-theists. Given that non-theists are willing to evoke specific instances of natural and moral evil in their arguments, the reticence of the theists to do likewise can place them at a disadvantage in arguing for the plausibility of theism over against non-theism.

The significance of defenses, such as Plantinga's Free Will Defense, that show the logical compatibility of G with intense evil should not be taken lightly. However, the evidential arguments from evil made by non-theists are insufficiently answered by theists if theistic defenses cannot be applied to specific cases of intense evil. Indeed, non-theists not only make their logical cases but they do so in a manner that can be and is applied to the real-life observations. Therefore, a theistic defense of the POE that can answer Russell's aforementioned challenge of probability needs to address specific instances of intense evil. This is an important task, for if theism is unable to produce a defense that is not only logical but capable of addressing the same evidences used by non-theists in a more probable way, then theism is hard-pressed to show its truthfulness to a world that thinks in probabilistic terms

---

9. This author recognizes that he cannot possibly know what thoughts are in the minds of every person, but given personal experience and dialogue with others, there exists no set of data that leads this author to the conclusion that such abductive thoughts, in general, are not the norm.

INTRODUCTION   5

on a daily basis. Fortunately, the work done by Plantinga, van Inwagen, and Wykstra provide a solid foundation for just such a defense.

The Work Ahead

The issue regarding the POE that has been briefly described above can be summarized by the question, "Can theism abductively account for specific instances of intense evil better than naturalism?"[10] Therefore, this book will present a theistic defense which, on what is known, accounts for the amounts and kinds of intense evils that are in this world more fully than naturalism. This will be accomplished through building upon the Free Will Defense, the Expanded Free Will Defense, and Skeptical Theism by more fully considering what is needed in order for free will to operate properly and the implications that this has for the POE.

A Glimpse at Free Systems

In light of the challenges posed by the APOE above, considerations of the implications of systems of regularity for free creatures will provide valuable theodical suggestions,[11] for addressing the APOE.[12] In short, the free will that exists within humanity requires systems of regularity in which to operate. Within systems of regularity[13] laws/rules (e.g., gravity) are a good in that they allow for consistent interaction between the free will of human agents and the physical world in which they live. Observing this regularity in relation to instances of intense evil will give rise to theodical suggestions that can correlate with existing defenses, such as the Free Will Defense, Expanded Free Will Defense, and Skeptical Theism. This Free System Corollary to Free Will Defenses is understood as follows:

> Free System Corollary $(FSC)_{df}$ = Theodical suggestions, born from the conjunction of free will and the systems needed for free will to be actualized provide plausible explanations, that

---

10. Here, naturalism is understood as any accounting of reality that does not allow for God or any other supernatural entity in its telling. In short, naturalism is a nontheistic explanation for reality.

11. The term "theodical suggestions" refers to utilizing theodicies to make a list of conceivable reasons that God would have for permitting evil.

12. Alston, "Inductive Argument from Evil," 103.

13. The use of the term "regularity" here is meant to be in line with that of van Inwagen's.

could be true for all we know, in response to specific instances of intense evil.

In other words, there are more factors involved in a given situation that are accessible to human knowledge than what appear on only an account of human free will. This is not to say that the FSC will open the human mind to all that is involved in a given situation. Rather, the FSC asserts that there is more that can be known, and once those factors are considered the evidence makes theism abductively plausible.

While the FSC is a natural offshoot of natural law and free will (and therefore, free will defenses) it is also a natural extension of Skeptical Theism. When delving into the implications of a free system, what appears is a world that is far more intricate than it may otherwise appear to be. Just as humanity simultaneously increased its knowledge of the universe and was humbled by the vastness of the unknown through the exploration of outer space so too does the FSC contribute to understanding what is within and beyond human ken. The FSC is a theistic defense that speaks to limitations of human knowledge, yet it has the ability to offer plausible explanations for why God allows specific instances of evil to occur through examinations of free will and systems of regularity.

A Word on Limitations

The task taken up here to answer the APOE is not without its limitations, and great care has been exercised to preserve the integrity of this discussion. Acknowledging these limitations affords some level of accountability for the author and an understanding of the author's perspective.

Perhaps the most prominent limitation of this paper involves concepts of the good. Is evil needed in order for good to exist? Does the goodness of an infinitely moral God eliminate his freedom? Questions such as these will be addressed in the next chapter, but it is possible that some would desire greater detail. Indeed, more detail is possible but is beyond the scope of this work.

An additional limitation of this project revolves around its understanding of intense evil. In this paper, intense evil is to be understood as events, natural and/or moral, which appear to be so void of good that it is challenging to understand why someone would allow such an event to happen if it were in his/her power to prevent it. The assumption here is that this understanding of intense evil is assumed to be conceivable in a universal sense, that is, intense evil as described above is something that every person in control of his or her faculties should be able to recognize when it happens. However, a comprehensive list of intense evils will not be produced as each instance of intense evil is in some way unique from other instances, which makes such a list logistically challenging, if not humanly impossible, to exhaustively compile. In sum, this book understands intense evil to have a quality that is recognizable when it happens but is difficult to quantify given the great number of unique experiences that each person has.

Another limitation that exists here involves the sheer volume of work that has been done on the POE over the centuries. Part of the approach taken here is to seriously engage with several authors regarding their explanations for the POE. However, a full treatment of every philosopher/theologian who has spoken on the POE is beyond the space allowed for here. By highlighting some of the works of Plantinga, Mackie, van Inwagen, Russell, Howard-Snyder, Draper, Wykstra, and Rowe it is the intention to offer a fair representative position of both theists and non-theists in regard to the POE and the APOE specifically. Undoubtedly, some would prefer the consideration of other authors in addition to, or in place of, these, but there are limits as to how much material can be covered adequately in a single treatise, and the authors that will be discussed here are respected in their field.

Similar to the limitation of work on the POE is the limitation on addressing instances of intense evil. Addressing every single instance of intense evil that is and has been present in this world is a monumental task that would likely require more time and resources than one person could utilize in a lifetime. This paper addresses an instance of intense natural evil and an instance of intense moral evil. Limiting the discussion to two instances of intense evil is sufficient for this discussion for two reasons. First, there is a limit to how long this work can be. Second, the instances that will be used are those that are commonly upheld by non-theists as examples that are fatal to theism. Addressing these two instances of intense evil is appropriate for an abductive defense of theism. Further discussions on other instances of evil are topics for other papers, should the need for such discussions be warranted.

An additional limitation that should be mentioned here involves the logical coexistence of G with evil. No section of this paper will be entirely devoted to this issue for at least two reasons. First, the amount of space required to make an argument for the logical coexistence of G and evil would be another work in and of itself. Second, claims of the illogical coexistence of G and evil are not emphasized by the APOE. For example, prominent non-theistic philosopher William Rowe admits that there is no logical inconsistency between G and evil and cites Plantinga's works as a clear basis for this claim.[14] Therefore, the question of the logical coexistence of G and evil are given no

---

14. Rowe, "Problem of Evil," 126n1.

further consideration for the purposes of this present project, aside for how it may pertain to better understanding Plantinga's FWD.

Finally, there is an assumption with this work that should be briefly discussed. Earlier, it was expressed that abduction is present in every day of every person's life. This is, of course, an abductive inference based upon personal experience/observation. Given the number of safety/reliability assumptions people make each day, it seems likely that people regularly think in abductive terms. Since proving this assumption could be a topic for another paper, a full discourse on the abductive habits of human populations will not be had here. However, this assumption is not a defeater for this present project. The abductive evidential challenge by non-theists on the POE has already been made. Furthermore, this abductive assumption was used to support the importance of addressing the APOE; it is not necessary for the applicability of the FSC in response to the APOE. Therefore, any disagreement regarding this assumption does not undermine the purpose of this work.

Despite the limitations presented here, there remains a solid foundation for moving forward in this discussion. By briefly discussing these limitations the reader is in a better position to understand the choices made in the content of this project. Limitations are a natural part of discussing a specific topic and may serve as an introduction to future work.

Method of Approach

Chapter Divisions

The chapter divisions here are designed to lay a logically progressive foundation which not only shows the need for but also the rationale behind the FSC. Chapter 1, being an introductory chapter, highlights, in general terms, the abductive challenge presented by non-theists in regards to the POE. Chapter 2 continues laying the foundation by giving attention to considerations of the good for human and divine actions. Chapter 3, with its emphasis on natural law, gives an account of how nature is basically understood in relation to G. By emphasizing the works of C. S. Lewis, Bruce Reichenbach, and William Rowe, these chapters provide a foundational understanding of the theistic underpinnings/perspectives of this paper. These chapters establish a foundation for the more specific POE issues discussed in the following chapters.

Chapter 4 discusses Plantinga's use of free will in his FWD of the POE and the challenges that are posed by Mackie for the validity of Plantinga's assertions. Chapter 5 continues the discussion of free will being a theistic defense in light of van Inwagen's EFWD, which as the name implies builds off of Plantinga's FWD. Just as Mackie was used as a counterpoint to Plantinga, Russell is examined for his non-theistic challenges to the EFWD. While the FSC is a continuation of the FWD and the EFWD, evidential arguments from evil that make abductive claims (APOE) essentially ask, albeit by implication, where this wholly good God (G) is in the midst of intense evil. Therefore, chapter 6 discusses Howard-Snyder's theistic thoughts regarding Inculpable Non-Belief (INB) and how Draper's Hypothesis of Indifference (HI) poses a non-theistic challenge to theism. Similarly, chapter 7 engages with Wykstra's Skeptical Theism (CORNEA), which emphasizes the limits of human knowledge in understanding why God acts as he does, and Rowe's challenge that Skeptical Theism opens the door not just for unknown goods but unknown evils as well.

With the preceding chapters in place, chapter 8 makes the case for the FSC, and chapter 9 applies the FSC to two specific instances of intense evils that are commonly used by non-theists as a defeater for theism. Finally, chapter 10 offers concluding thoughts on the potential that the FSC has for being the best explanation based upon what is known for answering the APOE.

Chapter Summaries

Of course, this book can be read from cover to cover, but it is likely that there will be those who wish to focus on a particular aspect of this discussion. Below contains a summary of each chapter so that the reader can be strategic in their reading plan.

In the event that the reader has skipped ahead to this section, chapter 1 summarizes the POE including what is referred to here as the abductive problem from evil (APOE): the assertion that naturalism offers a more probable explanation for instances of intense evil than does theism (belief in a wholly good, loving, and powerful God [G]). Though non-theistic arguments on the POE are commonly referred to as evidential arguments, due to their use of specific cases of intense suffering, they are essentially abductive in nature in that they claim that the inference to the best explanation of intense evil(s) is naturalism. This present chapter explains the problem at hand, why it is important, and will propose a theistic response to the APOE. Also foundational to the task of this book is chapter 2's discussion on the good.

Chapter 2 includes discussions on C. S. Lewis's understanding of the roles of moral obligation and free will in relation to performing good acts. Additionally, William Rowe's assertion that God's perfectly good nature eliminates significant freedom for God will be examined. Building from the discussions of chapter 2, chapter 3 addresses concepts in Natural Law in light of C. S. Lewis and Bruce Reichenbach. Central to this chapter is an understanding the relationship between God and this world and evaluation of the peculiar ability of suffering to have a positive effect upon individual spiritual growth. However, though God's relationship with this world does impact how this world operates, this chapter makes the case that the soul-making properties of suffering are real albeit a secondary, rather than a primary, design of suffering. Though chapter 2 and chapter 3 are brief (in relation to the material each addresses) these discussions help to define the parameters by which the APOE is addressed in the remainder of the paper.

Chapter 4 analyses Plantinga's Free Will Defense and Mackie's causally determined worldview. This chapter pays special attention to Plantinga's idea of trans-world depravity and his perspective on free will. Similarly, Mackie's teleological worldview is considered along with his explanation for why it appears that humanity has free will even though free will does not exist (metaphysical double vision). By the end of this chapter, it is argued that Plantinga's work is extremely valuable for theism but that it could be more robust in its treatment of natural evil. Furthermore, Mackie's causal arguments are shown to be lacking in their explanatory power for human reality, but it is also pointed out that the causal system that he highlights deserves due diligence by theists.

Following the discussion of Plantinga and Mackie, chapter 5 discusses regularity in light of Peter van Inwagen and Bruce Russell. Foundational to van Inwagen's Expanded Free Will Defense (which is an expansion upon Plantinga's FWD) is the concept of regularity as a good. Van Inwagen asserts that the regularity of pain and suffering in evolution brought about the good of sentience, which is essential for being made in the image of God. Furthermore, for van Inwagen, irregularity is a sign of the presence of evil in the world (for without regularity there would be chaos). Russell is more than willing to engage van Inwagen in terms of regularity, and he argues stridently that if God did exist regularity would not be compromised if a particular case of intense evil were thwarted by God's hand. While van Inwagen makes good logical arguments against the plasticity of Russell's use of regularity, he seems to be unwilling to apply the EFWD to a specific real-world case. Thus, it would seem that Russell has a practical, if not purely logical, advantage, but as chapters 8 and 9 discuss, the FSC is capable of bridging the gap between van Inwagen's EFWD and a specific case of intense evil.

Chapter 6 addresses the issue of God's apparent absence in the suffering that is part of intense evil and how that seems to run contrary to God's goodness. This is accomplished by analyzing Daniel Howard-Snyder's argument for Inculpable Non-Belief (INB) born from divine hiddenness (DH) and Paul Draper's Hypothesis of Indifference (HI). Draper argues that the HI better accounts for the way sufferings are experienced than does theism, whereas Howard-Snyder argues for theism but concludes that DH can account for some people having INB (i.e., it is not their fault that they do not believe in God). Of course, Draper's non-theism and Howard-Snyder's views on INB are problematic for a traditional theistic belief in God. However, the FSC not only accounts for the objections in the HI but it also accounts for DH in a way that does not require INB to be a reality.

Chapter 7 concludes the overview of theistic/non-theistic defenses of the APOE by addressing Skeptical Theism. Stephen Wykstra's CORNEA (Condition of Reasonable Epistemic Access), which was a response to William Rowe's evidential argument from evil, is examined. Additionally, Rowe's challenge to CORNEA, that CORNEA's plea to limitations of human knowledge of the good can be applied to evil as well, is discussed. Rowe's critique of CORNEA highlights a potentially harmful ramification to the theistic argument. However, an argument is made for the ability of moral obligation to serve as a governor on Rowe's critique.

Chapter 8 puts forth the case for the Free System Corollary to Free Will Defenses. In discussing the implications of systems of regularity for free will beings, the world in which humanity lives is seen to be much more intricate than it may seem at first. Systems of regularity are essential for beings possessing free will to live out that free will, and if God were to not make it so he would become an oppressor. Not only is there a relationship between free will and systems of regularity, which has implications for natural and moral evil, the considerations of free will within systems of regularity entail a great deal of responsibility for moral actions on the part of free will persons. Included in this responsibility is the concept of prayer as an act of free will that can allow God to intervene in human affairs without violating free will and systems of regularity. In the end, the FSC offers additional information/perspectives which complement/supplement the theistic defenses discussed in this paper.

Chapter 9 argues that the FSC provides a more complete picture of how free will beings live their lives in this world and how it is also capable of addressing specific cases of intense natural evil (a fawn burning to death alone in a forest fire) and moral evil (the abuse and murder of a five-year-old girl). This is a defense, not a theodicy that seeks to have the answers for why every good/evil thing happens the way that it does. Here, the application of theodical suggestions as a defense seeks to show a *possible* reason for why God would allow an instance of intense evil to happen. Furthermore, the FSC offers a plausible explanation for the way things are more satisfactorily than naturalism. Finally, chapter 10 serves as a conclusion by highlighting the concepts and conclusions presented in this paper.

Conclusion

Two important theistic defenses, the FWD and the EFWD, provide valuable thought in defense of theism but are insufficient for addressing specific cases of intense evil, as the non-theistic naturalistic evidential/abductive arguments from the POE (APOE) are want to do. However, theodical suggestions from systems of regularity, as a necessary part of living out a free will existence, provide a theistic defense that correlates with free will defenses and more fully accounts for the existence of good and intense evil. Furthermore, the FSC will be applied to specific cases of intense natural and moral evil. Through the application of the FSC to these specific cases, the argument is made that theism offers better potential explanations than naturalism for intense evil based on what is known of human reality.

2

Considerations of the Good

DISCUSSIONS ON THE POE are, in essence, discussions on the absence, apparent or otherwise, of the good. Since the good encompasses moral obligation, free will, and ultimately whether or not G is responsible for a given action, it is fitting that this book should contain at least a brief analysis of the good. Of particular interest are perspectives of the good that involve moral obligations and how those interact with free will, and thereby free will defenses. This chapter will consider theistic and non-theistic perspectives on moral obligation, define free will, and consider whether or not G's perfectly good nature renders him unworthy of praise for good actions. This will provide a foundation for discussions to come on how the FSC helps to address abductive arguments from the POE (APOE).

The Call of Moral Obligation toward the Good

MO is a unique aspect of humanity in that it is persistent, yet it can be ignored. Renowned theist C. S. Lewis astutely observes, "He [humanity] cannot disobey those laws which he shares with other things [like gravity]; but the law which is peculiar to his human nature, the law he does not share with animals or vegetables or inorganic things, is the one he can disobey if he chooses."[1] Humanity simultaneously possesses an obligation to do good and the ability to ignore this sense of morality. Therefore, it is no surprise that perspectives on the nature of this moral obligation (MO) also vary in their understanding of human existence. Theists and non-theists both recognize the existence of MO, and both seek to provide an accounting for its presence in human life. This section discusses MO in terms of instinct versus obligation, relative morality, and MO as evidence of G. Though other authors will be considered, Lewis (theist) and Richard Joyce (non-theist) will be the

---

1. Lewis, *Mere Christianity*, 5.

focus of attention here as their respective insights offer a fair representation of theistic and non-theistic thoughts on MO.[2]

In addition to calling one toward right action, MO is ever present. Regardless of the society in question, and however depraved one might view that society, a sense of MO can be found. In regard to the persistent presence of MO Lewis states, "Human beings, all over the earth, have this curious idea that they ought to behave in a certain way, and cannot really get rid of it . . . [additionally] they do not in fact behave in that way. They know the Law of Nature; they break it. These two facts are the foundation of all clear thinking about ourselves and the universe we live in."[3] By and large, people instinctually know there is right and wrong, yet it would seem that there is a consistent tendency in humanity to ignore that instinct and do otherwise. However, that call toward doing what is right remains.[4] Is it possible for this tenacity to be explained purely in instinctual terms? Lewis addresses the claim that MO may be little more than a herd instinct, that it is societal pressure toward not/doing certain actions that directs human instinct toward a perception of MO, when he states, "But feeling a desire to help is quite different from feeling that you ought to help whether you want to or not."[5] Here, Lewis highlights an important distinction in discussions of MO: instinct is related to but separate from obligation.

Recognizing beauty, fight or flight, blinking, etc., are all examples of instinct, and while one may instinctually know the right thing to do in a given situation there exists something more fundamental: obligation. Obligation can be seen when one's instinct motivates them toward one action but there is a compulsion to do another. Lewis states, "But clearly we are not acting *from* instinct when we set about making an instinct stronger than it is. The thing that says to you, 'Your herd instinct is asleep. Wake it up,'

---

2. There are many quality voices on discussion of MO representing theistic and non-theistic viewpoints that will not be discussed here. The topic of MO is vast in philosophical literature, and the constraints of this present project do not allow for addressing every philosopher who has contributed to this subject. However, it is the opinion of this author that Lewis and Joyce are representative of their respective theistic and non-theistic camps, and it is fitting to utilize these authors as such.

3. Lewis, *Mere Christianity*, 8.

4. There are, of course, cases in which someone may suffer from a neurological defect in which determining right and wrong becomes more difficult, and it is possible to "sear" one's conscience so that it becomes easier and easier to not do what is right. However, in each of these cases their remains the observance of MO in others and/or remnants of that conscience, however quiet. Therefore, it is fair to say that the call toward doing good remains a constant of human existence.

5. Lewis, *Mere Christianity*, 9.

cannot itself *be* the herd instinct."[6] Furthermore, Lewis states, "The Moral Law tells us the tune we have to play: our instincts are merely the keys."[7] Here, Lewis identifies instincts as being tools toward reaching an end, an end that is guided by Moral Law (moral obligation). MO is something prior to instinct, and it makes use of instinct, but it is not in and of itself instinct. The existence of MO points toward something more basic in the making of humanity. For Lewis, and others such as John E. Hare and Robert Merrihew Adams, this amounts to evidence for the existence of G.

Lewis observes that what can be observed "on our own steam" gives humanity two evidences for God. Lewis states, "One is that the universe He has made. . . . The other bit of evidence is that Moral Law which He has put into our minds . . . it is inside information. You find out more about God from the Moral Law than from the universe in general just as you find out more about a man by listening to his conversation than by looking at a house he has built."[8] What Lewis is observing here is the peculiar reality that humanity has a tendency to not do what it should despite the presence of MO. Lewis sees Moral Law (i.e., MO) as evidence for how G intended humanity to operate. This discrepancy between ought and action, between standard and performance, has been noticed by John E. Hare to represent not only evidence for G but also evidence for humanity's need for G. Hare states, "We humans are limited in our impartiality and in our information, and can therefore only approximate to full-fledged moral judgment."[9] Not only does humanity often fail to live up to MO, but Hare observes that humanity is incapable of living up to / fully comprehending the scope and import of MO. Hare states, "Morality, in its full critical form, is, first, something I ought to be practicing; second, something for which my natural capacities are inadequate (except by approximation); and, third, something that I should treat as the command of some other at least possible being who is practicing it."[10] For Hare, MO is in fact a moral gap, a chasm with standards of morality on one side and human insufficiency on the other. The existence of G best explains this gap, for naturalism is ill equipped to explain the existence of this feeling of ought that cannot be satisfied by human power alone. G created the moral gap, and it is only G who can help humanity to traverse the distance.

---

6. Lewis, *Mere Christianity*, 10.
7. Lewis, *Mere Christianity*, 10.
8. Lewis, *Mere Christianity*, 29.
9. Hare, *Moral Gap*, 22.
10. Hare, *Moral Gap*, 23.

Similar to Hare, Robert Merrihew Adams recognizes that theism does provide a more robust explanation for the existence of MO. Adams echoes the idea that G is the source of MO when he states, "If we suppose that God directly or indirectly causes human beings to regard as excellent approximately those things that are Godlike in the relevant way, it follows that there is a causal and explanatory connection between facts of excellence and beliefs that we may regard as justified about excellence, and hence that it is in general no accident that such beliefs are correct when they are."[11] Just as there is something of the artist in a painting, G, as creator of the universe has left an imprint of MO on the lives of humanity. Not only does this explain why it is that MO exists (especially in the lives of those creatures who are capable of higher moral reasoning), but it also explains why fallible humanity seems to be quite incapable of living up to this standard on their own. These theistic explanations for MO are not without their challengers. Though theists believe MO points toward the divine there are those who view it as little more than a by-product of naturalism.

While naturalistic accountings of the POE will be discussed more thoroughly in later chapters, for the purposes of this present discussion on MO the naturalistic axiological considerations of Richard Joyce will be considered. Joyce is a moral ethicist who recognizes the commanding presence of MO in human life and attempts to account for it naturalistically. At first glance, it may appear that Joyce is in agreement with Lewis about the inability of naturalism to account for MO when he states, "I have reiterated the question of why facts about evolution provide persons with reasons, why they ground 'ought' statements—and it should be clear that my answer is: 'They don't.'"[12] Joyce affirms that naturalism cannot account for the strong presence of MO in human life, but that is not to say that he does not espouse a naturalistic explanation for our perception of MO. In reference to MO, Joyce states, "All the work is being done by the fact that my upbringing has provided me with certain attitudes and traits that are now actively operative—and these attitudes would ground 'ought' statements even if they had nothing to do with evolution."[13] The sociological factors that are present in one's life (such as family, tradition, social convention, etc.) provide a foundation for perceptions of MO. Joyce conducts his axiological work not merely in terms of theism and non-theism but in terms of moral and non-moral explanations for axiological obligations. The significance of this distinction is profound for discussions of what it means to be good

---

11. Adams, *Finite and Infinite Goods*, 70.
12. Joyce, *Myth of Morality*, 152.
13. Joyce, *Myth of Morality*, 152.

or for something to be good. It is possible for a theist and a non-theist to be in agreement about the importance of MO in human life (they would, of course, disagree as to its source). Joyce, on the other hand, calls into question the reality of MO. In reference to moral and non-moral explanatory frameworks, Joyce states, "The latter [non-moral] is superior in that it explains everything that the former [moral] does, but is simpler, more intelligible, testable, and, most importantly, avoids any mysterious items."[14] Essentially, Joyce is arguing that both moral and non-moral frameworks can account for MO but since non-moral frameworks (i.e., that there are no necessarily absolute moral obligations) are simpler they are therefore more accurate. Serious considerations of "mysterious items" are being avoided by Joyce which reflects an *a priori* assumption against what is commonly called the supernatural. For Joyce, the idea of deity being a source for MO is absurd because of his naturalistic commitments.

Joyce recognizes the power MO has in human life but as a naturalist he does not find theistic explanations for MO to be compelling. In a thought experiment designed to identify the best possible naturalistic explanation for MO, Joyce considers someone who eats dinner alone in front of a television. The man is aware of social etiquette, but since he is alone he chooses to ignore it and eat in a less than savory manner. Joyce compares etiquette to MO to see if social demands for certain behavior can satisfactorily explain the strength of the existence of MO in human life. Joyce finds the etiquette example too weak when he states, "Such a value system is . . . surely too wimpy to be mistaken for morality. Moral thinking has a function . . . and deliberations in terms simply of what we want and need will not suffice."[15] Joyce recognizes that naturalistic attempts to account for MO in terms of social convention fall short of being able to account for the strength (what he calls "practical clout") of MO in human life, and practical clout needs to be accounted for. After deliberating about various ways in which one might attempt to account for this aspect of morality naturalistically Joyce states, "I conclude that practical clout really is a core desideratum of any moral theory, and that no form of moral naturalism can satisfy it. So much the worse for moral naturalism."[16] After admitting to the inability for naturalism to account for the import MO has in human existence, one might reasonably infer that Joyce has no choice but to surrender his naturalistic project and embrace some sort of theism as the most likely explanation for MO, but Joyce still has at least one more naturalistic angle to consider.

14. Joyce, *Myth of Morality*, 168.
15. Joyce, *Evolution of Morality*, 208.
16. Joyce, *Evolution of Morality*, 209.

In *The Evolution of Morality*, Joyce concludes his arguments by considering the implications of Darwinian evolution for morality and the reaction people had to these results. Joyce states, "The only honest and dignified course is to acknowledge what the evidence and our best theorizing indicate and deal with the practical consequences."[17] What Joyce is referring to here is what he sees as being the proper conclusion from his analysis of morality: MO is real but it is born out of the processes of evolution. As a result of the birth of MO from evolution, MO does possess practical application that has been ingrained into humanity for generations, but this also means that while the existence of MO may never cease what is entailed by MO can change over the course of time.

Lewis, though he was not a proponent of moral relativism, does admit that there can be an appearance of a change in morality. In response to a claim that morality changes with time, Lewis states, "It may be a great advance in knowledge not to believe in witches: there is no moral advance in not executing them when you do not think that they are there."[18] In other words, the morality of executing a witch is sound (because of the evil they bring) but such action differs from the determination of the witch's existence. A particular example of moral application may no longer be practiced but the basic moral principle behind it remains. As a more modern example, capital punishment for murders is no longer the assumed practice as it once was in history. Today, many people call for life in prison instead of execution. Not killing a murderer is drastically different from killing them, but the basic moral principle that those who kill an innocent person should be punished remains.

Whether one is a theist, a non-theist, a moral realist, or a moral relativist, it is agreed that MO calls one toward that which is good. Of course, there is significant difference between how Lewis and Joyce, for example, interact with and view MO. Theories of MO, such as Joyce's, which *a priori* eliminate considerations of the supernatural/spiritual are weaker in that while they claim to provide a more streamlined accounting of MO they in fact do the opposite for at least two reasons. First, for as long as recorded history, and continuing to the present day, people have expressed experiences with the spiritual, and these testimonies should not be taken lightly. That is not to say that every claimed experience is legitimate, but such a body of evidence should not be dismissed out of hand. Second, in accounting for MO one has the task of determining how it is that MO has such a strong influence on human life. Statements like, "It is necessarily

---

17. Joyce, *Evolution of Morality*, 229–30.
18. Lewis, *Mere Christianity*, 15.

wrong to torture children for fun," would seem to be widely upheld as being true. How then can naturalism account for such a universal sense of necessary morality? An application of Joyce's thoughts to this statement would indicate that he would conclude that this statement is not "necessary," not universally applicable throughout time and space. Yet, this falls short of the truth that this statement bears witness to in MO. Theism, on the other hand, offers a fuller accounting of MO, assuming one is willing to consider the existence of the spiritual. Therefore, throughout the course of this book, it will be seen whether theism can support the weight of a reality in which MO calls humanity toward that which is good while simultaneously great evils occur. Part and parcel with that discussion of the POE is a consideration of humanity's freedom to choose that which is good.

Significant Freedom toward Choosing the Good

Morality implies the existence of choice. Institutions of higher learning across the country require students to take at least one class in ethics. In the workplace there will arise situations in which a moral decision will need to be made, and these schools rightly want their students to be prepared to make sound decisions. An ethical/moral situation would not be a "situation" if the person(s) involved had no choice in their actions. In simplest terms, the choices involved with the application of MO involve that which is good and that which is evil. The freedom one has to obey/disregard MO is directly related to free will, and therefore free will defenses, including the FSC.

In describing the relationship between good and evil, William Hasker states, "Evil is seen as 'privation of good,' as the absence of some good state of affairs that would reasonably be expected to obtain."[19] Where evil exists there once was potential for good. This reality of the nature of good and evil reinforces the notion that humanity possesses free will, the ability to choose freely. In regard to free will defenses such as Plantinga's (more of which will be said in later chapters), Hasker states, "[If] God has chosen to create persons with libertarian free will and to allow them to exercise that freedom. Then it may well be the case that in important respects how things go in the world, and many things that affect the world's goodness, will depend on the way those free creatures decide."[20] Here, Hasker highlights a key concept in free will defenses: the responsibility of individual moral agents for good and evil acts. MO exists as a form of guidance/accountability for humanity to know how to choose good over evil. Humanity would not have free will if

19. Hasker, *Triumph of God over Evil*, 75.
20. Hasker, *Triumph of God over Evil*, 77–78.

there were no real possibility of ever choosing evil over good. Therefore, free will entails the potentiality of overriding/ignoring MO and acting otherwise. As was mentioned above, Hare recognizes the existence of MO and human fallibility as a chasm that cannot be crossed by human will alone. Fallible humanity is unable to always do good. This relationship between humanity and MO points humanity toward God. For, why would humanity naturally create/evolve standards it could not live up to? Therefore, humanity is in need of divine help. Lewis states, "God may be more than moral goodness: He is not less. . . . The moral law may exist to be transcended: but there is no transcending it for those who have not first admitted its claims upon them, and then tried with all their strength to meet that claim, and fairly and squarely faced the fact of their failure."[21] MO calls humanity toward standards of good and is thus a means of accountability.

MO as accountability affords all persons involved with, or observing, a moral action a means of evaluating said action. Thus, MO serves as a standard for conduct that points to how events should go, and it is a means by which those who fail to live up to its standards may be judged. Bruce Reichenbach states, "Obligations are standards for evaluating persons and thus create accountability on the part of the subject. . . . If I ought to do something and would be held accountable if I didn't do it, I can do it."[22] By nature of being an obligation, MO entails the ability for the agents under its influence to be able to choose a right or wrong action. Additionally, the nature of obligation results in MO being a source of accountability. Indeed, as will be seen, many philosophers engaged in discussions of the POE attempt to use an understanding of good and evil circumstances as a means of judging the compatibly of a good and loving god with how good and evil are understood to exist. For this present discussion, however, the nature of MO is understood to be one that entails choice and accountability on the part of human agents. Of course, this implies an acknowledgement of the existence of free will.

Free will, thus far described as the ability to make moral choices, is a subject that has garnered much discussion in philosophical literature for many centuries. It would seem that humanity lives in a world that has a determined/causal nature (e.g., loud noises causing an avalanche, the moon orbits the earth which causes the tides to ebb and flow, etc.), yet humanity, it would seem, possesses the ability to make independent choices/actions. Debates in the philosophical literature have given birth to many terms with many variations on those terms to describe this seemingly contradictory

---

21. Lewis, *Problem of Pain*, 586.
22. Reichenbach, *Epistemic Obligations*, 115.

evidence of free will and causal reality. Peter van Inwagen, in offering his perspective on the issue, takes great care to cull the excessive and needlessly delineated terms that have come to be common place in philosophical circles. The reason for this pruning of philosophical terms resides in the redundancy of meanings that have developed over time. Therefore, van Inwagen seeks to streamline discussions on free will. Toward that end, van Inwagen asserts that the terms "the free will thesis," "determinism," "compatibilism," and "incompatibilism" are sufficient for discussions of free will.[23] Van Inwagen understands these terms as follows: the free will thesis—the ability to "perform that act and the ability to refrain from performing that act";[24] determinism—"the thesis that the past and the laws of nature together determine, at every moment, a unique future";[25] compatibilism—"the thesis that determinism and the free-will thesis could both be true";[26] and incompatibilism—"the denial of compatibilism."[27] While there will undoubtedly be those who would wish to delineate these terms differently, on the whole van Inwagen presents a clear summation of the most relevant terms in free will discussions. The paper takes van Inwagen's words to heart when he states, "If you think that some term you will use has been given an adequate definition in the philosophical literature, repeat that definition."[28] Therefore, this book chooses to adopt van Inwagen's definition of the terms determinism, compatibilism, and incompatibilism. However, while this work is largely in agreement with his definition of free will there are some clarifications that should be made.

In an attempt to follow van Inwagen's advice about definitions, it should be noted that Richard Swinburne offers some concepts that are worth mentioning here along with van Inwagen. In his work *Mind, Brain, and Free Will*, Swinburne defines the principle of credulity as that principle which states, "Things are probably the way they seem to be in the absence of counter-evidence."[29] This principle of credulity, the affirmation that humanity possesses trustworthy truth tracking abilities (provided, of course, that new evidence should be considered), lends support to Swinburne's definition of free will rather than van Inwagen's. Swinburne states, "I shall in future write of an agent having 'free will' insofar as the agent

---

23. Van Inwagen, "How to Think about the Problem of Free Will," 331.
24. Van Inwagen, "How to Think about the Problem of Free Will," 329.
25. Van Inwagen, "How to Think about the Problem of Free Will," 330.
26. Van Inwagen, "How to Think about the Problem of Free Will," 330.
27. Van Inwagen, "How to Think about the Problem of Free Will," 330.
28. Van Inwagen, "How to Think about the Problem of Free Will," 328.
29. Swinburne, *Mind, Brain, and Free Will*, 201.

acts intentionally without their intentions being fully determined by prior causes."[30] The reason for preference to Swinburne over van Inwagen in this case has little to do with the words in van Inwagen's definition and more to do with van Inwagen's conclusions regarding determinism and free will. Van Inwagen states, "Reason has convinced me that free will is incompatible with determinism."[31] It should not be misconstrued from this brief treatment that van Inwagen arrives at this incompatibilist view lightly. On the contrary, he gives great thought in his discussion of determinism and free will. However, the principle of credulity would seem to apply when it is observed that there are a great many things in this life that are causally affected. Therefore, this definition of free will is proposed which makes use of van Inwagen's and Swinburne's definitions:

> Free Will$_{df}$ = the ability to intentionally perform, or refrain from performing, an act without that intention being fully determined by prior causes.

It is asserted here that this definition of free will aligns with the principle of credulity. There would be no discussions on the nature/existence of free will if there were not some ubiquitous evidence for its reality manifest in the normal course of human events. Indeed, even determinists speak of the illusion of free will (as will be seen in later discussions on J. L. Mackie). Furthermore, certain natural events (e.g., a volcanic eruption spewing lava and affecting the surrounding terrain) have a causal quality to them. So, even if the term "free will" were to cease from all spoken and written language, the concept of free will would continue in the hearts and minds of people around the world, and this would be found alongside causal evidences. Since, it would seem, this definition passes the principle of credulity, and it has good company in its origins with Swinburne, the term "free will" will be understood in this paper as to conform with the above definition, unless otherwise noted.[32]

Free will and MO are two concepts that can be found throughout humanity. Given their relevance to actions, both good and evil (in terms of ability and quality), and given that this work seeks to provide a theistic

---

30. Swinburne, *Mind, Brain, and Free Will*, 202.

31. Van Inwagen, "How to Think," 336.

32. There have been and will likely continue to be arguments for determinism, compatibilism, free will, and incompatibilism. As has been mentioned above, there is much that has been written on this subject and the debate is not over. This book recognizes that not all avenues regarding the interaction between free will and determinism have been addressed here. However, given that the purpose of this book is discussion on the APOE, further discussions on the various issues surrounding free will are subjects for another paper except as they may warrant interaction with content to come.

response to the APOE, there arises a question posed by non-theists that is pertinent to this present discussion. The question is, "Does God's good nature eliminate his freedom?" This is a claim made by non-theists, such as William Rowe, that takes aim at the worthiness of G to receive devotion. Arguing that the APOE does not disprove the existence of G while not proving that G is praiseworthy for his good deeds would be a Pyrrhic victory. For, what good is it to prove that G exists only to find that the G that remains is nothing more than an omnipotent automaton? Therefore, this question of praiseworthiness should be addressed before continuing on to discussions of natural law in chapter 3, and it is the main focus of this next section.

Does God's Good Nature Eliminate His Freedom?

Thus far, MO and free will have been discussed as being part of what it means to be human, but it should not be assumed that these traits are possessed by G. In humanity, MO entails the ability to have a sense of right and wrong and free will the ability to choose to do or refrain from doing. Aside from challenges to the existence of MO and free will, the intersection of MO and free will in human life poses no real challenges in terms of actuality. In other words, it is not difficult to conceive of a fallible human struggling with moral choices. However, what if someone were perfect in goodness? Would such a being have free will, the ability to choose to do good, or would that being only be free in the sense of being able to choose between good options of equal goodness? Non-theistic philosopher William Rowe seems to think that G, being perfectly good, cannot help but to do good, and since G cannot do otherwise he is not praiseworthy for his good actions. Rowe states, "He [G] had no role at all in bringing about his having the perfect nature he has. And it is that perfect nature that precludes his ever choosing to do less than the best. . . . It appears that only if God is in some way causally responsible for his own perfect nature can we be justified in morally praising God for the perfect acts required by his essential nature."[33] Here, Rowe is not espousing a belief in G, rather, he is saying that if G does indeed exist then there is no need to be concerned about praising him for his deeds. For Rowe, G's goodness eliminates his freedom, and therefore, G is not praiseworthy. A key component to Rowe's argument is his concept of will.

Rowe's concept of free will is greatly influenced by John Locke and Thomas Reid. Though he sees Reid as being closer to the truth regarding free will than Locke, it is Locke that helps to point the way toward some necessary yet subtle distinctions in discussions of free will. In "Two Concepts of

---

33. Rowe, *Can God Be Free?*, 150.

Freedom," Rowe engages with Lockean notions of free will via a thought experiment involving a person sitting on a chair in a room. At various incarnations of the experiment, the individual sits or stands while under the influence of drugs and mind control machines. The purpose of these thought experiments is to flesh out some shortcomings of Locke's approach to free will. Rowe summarizes Locke when he states, "A free act, says Locke, is not just a voluntary act. An act is free if it is voluntary *and* it is true that had you willed to do otherwise you would have been able to do otherwise."[34] An application of this view of free will would find that the paralyzed person who does not want to stand is not truly free in their determination to sit since they had no ability to do otherwise. However, through the aforementioned thought experiments, Rowe shows it is possible to have will but to still not be free.

Rowe notes that a problem with Locke's account of freedom to will can be seen if the subject in the chair is under the influence of a machine that manipulates the subject so that he wills to not stand up. Rowe highlights Locke's inadequate understanding of free will when he states, "It is not sufficient that you have the power to do otherwise *if* you so will; it must also be true that you have the power to will to do otherwise. Freedom that is worth the name, therefore, must include power *to will*, not simply power *to do if we will*."[35] Since it is possible that Lockean freedom can be manipulated by outside forces that alter the will of the individual, Rowe finds Locke's conclusions deficient in their ability to account for the realities of free will. Though he does not think that Reid has all of the answers either, he does think that Reid is much closer to the truth.

As opposed to the idea of freedom having to do with willing to do otherwise, Reid focuses on the cause of the will. Rowe states, "Reid believes that freedom is a *power*, a power over the determinations of our will."[36] For Rowe, this concept of "power over the determinations of our will" does not entail an infinite regress of causal events leading up to an action. Rather, the will to do, or not do, originates with the moral agent. Rowe states, "When an agent causes his action there is some event (an act of will, perhaps) that the agent causes without bringing about any other event as a means to producing it."[37] For Rowe, freedom to will entails that the initial cause of a will to act/not act originates with the individual moral agent without any other necessary prior causes. Here, Rowe's understanding of free will implies a concept of moral responsibility as well. Rowe states, "If the agent caused his

---

34. Rowe, "Two Concepts of Freedom," 45.
35. Rowe, "Two Concepts of Freedom," 47.
36. Rowe, "Two Concepts of Freedom," 52.
37. Rowe, "Two Concepts of Freedom," 55.

volition, having the power not to cause it, he may be both free and responsible. And if the agent caused his volition, having the power not to cause it, his volition and action cannot have been causally necessitated by events and circumstances that antedated the exercise of his causal power."[38] The capacity of a moral agent to will is directly proportional to the agent's moral responsibility, and it is on this concept that Rowe bases his argument for G's lack of praiseworthiness.

One does not praise someone for blinking. Blinking is a natural automatic response to outside stimulation. If one blinks one is functioning properly. However, if one is able to blink in time to the national anthem that person may be worthy of some praise for exercising their will to control their blinking. Rowe states, "Actions for which we are morally responsible are among those which we do as a result of willing (deciding, choosing) to do them."[39] Doing something that comes naturally, that requires no effort of will, is not something that is worthy of ascribing responsibility. Rowe identifies two criteria which must be satisfied for an agent to have willed something to happen, for there to be the potential for moral responsibility. Rowe states, "An agent causing of a volition to act occurs in a rational person when two conditions obtain: first, that person is free to cause (not-cause) a volition to act, as he thinks best; and second, the person exercises his power to cause that volition."[40] It is with this first criterion, being free to cause, that Rowe finds an objection with theistic understandings of human relationship with G.

As part of his argument that G (should he exist) is not worthy of praise for what humanity would perceive as morally good actions, Rowe devises a thought experiment involving a man with a broken leg on a hospital bed. The man is unable to get up from his bed, has no bed pan/catheter, and has no one who to hear his calls for help. As a result, despite holding his bladder in as long as he can, the man urinates in his bed. To this, Rowe states, "Is he *blameworthy* for urinating in his bed? Of course not, no more than God is *thankworthy* for his good act that his nature necessitates that he do. Each is such that given his nature he cannot do otherwise in the situation he is in."[41] Here is seen the potency of Rowe's argument that God is not praiseworthy for his good actions and its implications for the POE. Rowe is taking concepts of free will and MO and applying them to a perfectly good being, and his conclusion is that if such a being exists he should not be praised for his

38. Rowe, "Causing and Being Responsible," 158.
39. Rowe, "Responsibility," 244.
40. Rowe, "Free Will, Moral Responsibility, and the Problem of 'Oomph,'" 311.
41. Rowe, "Response to: Divine Responsibility," 38.

acts, for G could not have done otherwise. Rowe states, "God is not morally responsible for possessing the properties of omnipotence, omniscience, and perfect goodness. He always had and always will have those properties."[42] The theistic understanding of the basis for MO, being based on G's perfect nature, entails, according to Rowe, that G cannot do anything but what we would perceive to be good. Since he cannot do anything but that which is good G is not free to choose between good and evil actions. Therefore, according to Rowe's understanding of will and responsibility, G is not worthy of praise for doing good deeds. Rowe states, "It makes no sense to thank that being [G] for doing an act that, given his necessary properties, he is incapable of refraining from doing. For he is not responsible for the fact that he exists and necessarily possesses those properties."[43] If G cannot will to do otherwise then G bears no responsibility for any moral action, and if G bears no moral responsibility then he is not worthy of praise. This argument by Rowe, if accurate, is damning for theistic arguments for the POE, for even if the theist can prove the existence of G in the face of evil the G that remains is one which is not worthy of praise. However, there are other aspects to the relationship between G, his nature, and MO/responsibility that should be considered before one accepts Rowe's arguments.

Reichenbach identifies goodness as being rooted in actions, intentions, and dispositions. Reichenbach states, "This use of 'good' invokes the ethical sense. Herein God is good, not necessarily or essentially, but because of what he does, intends, and is disposed to do. And he is perfectly good because he always does, intends, and is disposed to do good acts."[44] Here, Reichenbach sees G as being good because he is the embodiment of goodness, and his actions are good because they originate from the source of all ethical standards of goodness. G is not disqualified from being praiseworthy because of his good nature; determinations of ethical worth (i.e., potentiality for praiseworthiness) are rooted in action and intention not nature. This perspective, while helpful for determining moral responsibility, is not as helpful in addressing Rowe as it may seem on the surface. At first look, it would appear that this argumentation bypasses the objection that G's perfectly good nature necessitates good action. However, the language of "intends" and "disposed to do" has a striking similarity to the ability to "will" in Rowe's case. Reichenbach is correct when he states, "The moral law has reality in him [God], and in effect is instantiated in the world by him in

---

42. Rowe, "Response to: Divine Responsibility," 44–45.
43. Rowe, "Response to: Divine Responsibility," 47–48.
44. Reichenbach, "Why Is God Good?," 66.

his creative act."[45] MO does have its origins in the person and work of G, but that is partly Rowe's objection. Although it makes logical sense that G would be the originator of all that is good, because G is perfectly good humanity may have freedom to choose the good, but G remains constrained by his own nature. Another perspective is needed for addressing Rowe's claim of G not being praiseworthy.

In summarizing Rowe's arguments from *Can God Be Free*, Hasker notes, "Rowe concedes that God may not be obligated to choose the best; perhaps some divine choices fall into the category of supererogatory acts rather than obligations. . . . A morally unsurpassable being will be unsurpassable in his acts of supererogation as well as in his fulfilment of obligations, so it still follows that a morally unsurpassable God will always choose the best."[46] Hasker's primary concern in this particular article is to engage Rowe on the level of possible worlds. While possible worlds has a rich history in philosophical discourse, and the scope of this present project does not allow for engaging in that discussion, the reason this quote from Hasker is mentioned is for its identification of Rowe's accounting for supererogatory acts. Hasker notes that Rowe accounts for supererogatory acts as not being a possible exception to the standard rule of always doing good because G would always do the best supererogatory act available to him. However, one does not need to engage in a discussion of best possible worlds in order to address Rowe's argument against praiseworthiness; supererogatory actions are sufficient.

At the core of Rowe's argument against G's praiseworthiness is the idea that G has no moral responsibility since he essentially has no choice in doing any action except, perhaps, between equally good choices. In essence, G's MO is qualitatively different from that of humanity's in that G is obligated to do that which is good to such a degree that he has no choice. C. Stephen Evans, in speaking on MO, states, "Although moral obligations are aimed at the good, they are not reducible to the good. An act might be good to do, even the best act a person could possibly do in some situation, without necessarily being a moral obligation."[47] Supererogatory acts, by their very nature, are beyond MO but are still considered to be good. Rowe, as was mentioned above, does not view supererogatory actions to be significantly different from any other good action committed by G, for he cannot help but do otherwise. However, because supererogatory actions are beyond the realm of MO, meaning that they are not required for morally good persons

---

45. Reichenbach, "Why Is God Good?," 64.
46. Hasker, "Can God Be Free?," 456.
47. Evans, *God and Moral Obligation*, 27.

to perform, they do offer a category of good actions for which G can be praiseworthy. The trick, if there is one, is to discern which actions G performs in human life that are indeed supererogatory.

In Christian terms, the person and work of Jesus Christ qualifies as a supererogatory act. The creator of the universe was under no obligation to offer those creatures who had sinned against him a means of restoration. It would have been good (i.e., just) for humanity to have suffered the consequences of its actions against G. However, the death, burial, and resurrection of Jesus constitute a supererogatory act in that it went above and beyond what was required by MO. So, while G is perfectly good and only does that which is good, it is possible for G to do good acts that are beyond what is required. There is no disagreement here with Rowe that when G performs a supererogatory act it will be a good act. Nevertheless, there is disagreement with Rowe as to the obligation G has to perform a supererogatory act in the first place. Since supererogatory acts are by their nature voluntary, and under no moral obligation to be performed, they constitute a category of actions for which even a perfectly good being is not obligated to perform. A supererogatory act is an act not necessitated by one's nature. Indeed, though any supererogatory act instantiated by G will be good because of his nature, the supererogatory act is in and of itself not necessary. Therefore, it is possible for G to be praiseworthy, at the very least, for supererogatory actions.[48]

Conclusions

For all the diversity that exists between every culture and each person within said culture, MO is a ubiquitous reality of human existence. MO calls one toward right action, yet humanity consistently lacks in its ability to live up to these standards. This amounts to a moral gap that cannot be crossed by human will alone. Indeed, this paper agrees with the theistic position that this MO points one toward G. Non-theists, such as Joyce, make compelling arguments for naturalistic reasons for MO, but in the end these naturalistic accounts fall short of explaining the persistence of MO. Another aspect of human reality that coincides with MO is free will. Free will is a real facet of humanity, not merely an illusion. However, some non-theists, such as Rowe, have argued that the existence of a morally

---

48. This book should not be misunderstood as arguing that the person and work of Jesus is the only example of supererogatory action by G. Indeed, many of the good works of G observable by humanity could be, in fact, supererogatory. Of course, such a bold claim will need to be argued for in another paper. However, for the purposes of this present project, it is sufficient to show that at least one significant act of goodness performed by G is/was supererogatory.

perfect being such as G, should he exist, would entail such a supreme form of goodness that free will would be overridden for G. Since G could only do good G would not be free, and, therefore, G would not be worthy of praise. Nevertheless, supererogatory actions constitute a class of good actions that are not required, even for a perfectly good being. Therefore, it is on the level of supererogatory actions, at the very least, that G is praiseworthy for his good deeds. The morally good G who gave humanity MO not only expects humanity to live up to his moral standards but he himself is worthy of praise for his good actions. Having given a basic account of the good, free will, and MO, this discussion now turns toward another foundational topic for a theistic defense of the APOE: natural law.

3

Natural Law

THIS CHAPTER WILL CONTINUE laying the foundation for a discussion on the APOE by briefly considering natural law, how moral principles that are naturally known should guide human conduct. Throughout nature one witnesses an apparent rationality for how the world operates. The rationality of the world provides clues not only for the existence of G but also for how it is that G could allow creation to operate as it does. In addition to contemplations on rationality, natural law indicates that G humbles himself for the benefit of humanity even as the evils that are seen in this world help to direct oneself away from a path of spiritual complacency. As these chapters progress, non-theistic accounts of evils and how nature operates will be discussed and considered, and a more thorough theistic accounting of natural evil will culminate in chapters 8 and 9. Admittedly, this chapter is theistic in nature, but in so being it establishes a baseline for how natural law is to be understood in the remainder of this project.

Rational Karmic Morality?

While there are still aspects of nature that are difficult to explain and/or anticipate (such as the seemingly random movement of quantum particles), the universe remains rationally consistent. Everything from the most advanced jetliner to the most archaic plowing tool rely upon the ability of someone to logically observe, evaluate, and anticipate how certain objects and materials will react with one another. Causality and the ability to rationally identify causal relationships is essential to everyday life. Bruce Reichenbach states, "Without such a basic assumption [of causal principles] scientific and metaphysical analysis of reality would be impossible. . . . If it be denied, then these other endeavors likewise become impossible, a state of affairs which few individuals would accept."[1] Consistent causal principles

---

1. Reichenbach, "Cosmological Argument," 188.

allow humanity to operate rationally in the universe. Indeed, the rationality of the universe is at the center of Bruce Reichenbach's philosophy of natural evil and how this relates to G.

Causation is ubiquitous in nature and can explain much of what happens in day-to-day life, but there is a question of its ability to explain matters of morality, especially as it relates to the strong sense of MO that is present in human life. However, this does not preclude the potential for there being a perspective on causation that can account for the willful actions of an individual agent. For Reichenbach, karma is a potential means of accounting for morality via a means akin to causation. This is not to say that Reichenbach endorses karma, but he does view it as worthy of evaluation/consideration given its attention in many world religions. As such, karma offers a perspective on causal relationships and moral actions that should be evaluated.

The main difference between universal causation and karma, Reichenbach notes, is that universal causation is concerned with all action whereas karma is concerned also with intent.[2] In other words, that which determines choice has a causal relationship with karma. Reichenbach states, "If we have certain passions or desires for the object or the fruit of the action, the action has karmic consequences; failure to have desires for the fruits obstructs the formation of karmic consequences."[3] The law of karma being considered by Reichenbach entails not just a simple cause-and-effect relationship but also intent, for within intention one finds an invaluable consideration for morality. In short, karma is the "application of the law of universal causation to moral causation."[4] To reiterate, Reichenbach is not endorsing karma, rather he recognizes potential to understand moral actions in a causal way. More specifically, Reichenbach is evaluating karma to see if it can withstand the pressures required of it in the POE. Namely, can karma account for morality in a way that can provide a causal means of accounting for MO and/or can it provide some explanation for why G would allow natural evils to take place?

Reichenbach takes issue with a naturalistic (i.e., non-spiritual) understanding of karma in terms of feasibility. In reference to karma, Reichenbach states, "We have no scale which correlates the amount of pleasure and pain to be received with the moral quality of the act performed. And even were we provided with one, it would be difficult if not impossible to carry out the relevant calculations. Pleasure and pain are notoriously difficult to quantify

---

2. Reichenbach, "Law of Karma," 399.
3. Reichenbach, "Law of Karma," 400.
4. Reichenbach, "Law of Karma," 400.

accurately."[5] Here, Reichenbach is referring to the possible means by which karma could causally effect moral repercussions for wrong actions through energies known as karmic residues. Theoretically, this would result in a karmic influence akin to how human action can impact the environment; right or wrong action would result in an eventual consequence appropriate to that action though the effect might not manifest itself immediately. However, Reichenbach states, "In short, the naturalistic explanation of the implementation of precise moral calculations through the intermediating agency of the environment is inadequate."[6] Metaphysical qualities involved in a moral decision, such as intention, are difficult if not impossible to correlate to a causal relationship. Karma, being an agentless force, cannot be supported by naturalistic explanations, for they cannot offer sufficient grounding for the qualitative aspects of moral decision making and its consequences. This, however, does not necessarily preclude a divine use of karma.

In sum, Reichenbach finds karma lacking in its ability to be a causal law that naturalistically dispenses consequences for moral actions, and this is due to karma's inability to adequately account for aspects of moral decision making, such as intention, that are qualitative rather than quantitative in nature. While karma may not be a suitable naturalistic explanation for why evils exist there remains the possibility that karma is a divine tool. Reichenbach states, "Since unconscious things generally do not move except when caused by an agent ... and since the law of karma is an unintelligent and unconscious law, there must be a conscious God who knows the merits and demerits which persons have earned by their actions, and who functions as an instrumental cause in helping individuals reap their appropriate fruits."[7] Although karma cannot fully account for all the repercussions of moral agents, it is possible that it is a means by which G can reward or discipline moral behavior. If karma is a tool used by G then natural evils have an explanation for their existence: human moral agency results in consequences carried out by karma, and guided by G, through the environment. However, the implications of karma being used in this way are troubling for theists.

There are two ways in which karma may be used by G. First, G may instantiate karma which then bears the responsibility of rewarding moral actions appropriately. Second, G directly controls karma. In the first instance, natural evils can be explained in a way which alleviates G of blame; karma, not divine judgment, results in moral consequences. However, that also means that G is not to be recognized for the goods that happen as well. This

---

5. Reichenbach, "Karma, Causation, and Divine Intervention," 143.
6. Reichenbach, "Karma, Causation, and Divine Intervention," 145.
7. Reichenbach, "Karma, Causation, and Divine Intervention," 145.

avoids the POE but it also alleviates G being worthy of worship for the goods that do happen.[8] In the second instance, G, who is wielding karma like a lumberjack wields an ax, once again is front and center in the POE discussion as he bears the responsibility for the results of the use of karma. Reichenbach summarizes these fallacies when he states, "If the law of karma is inviolable or necessary, it functions to resolve the problem it was introduced to solved, namely, the problem of evil. But then divinity can play little role in the religious life. If the law of karma is violable or contingent, worship of divinity has its place, but the law of karma no longer solves the problem of evil."[9] If karma is real then it either does all of the work for G, eliminating the POE and G's responsibility for any resultant goods, or G is still completely responsible for all natural evils and the POE is not avoided.

Karma is a concept of causality that takes into consideration intentions in matters of moral agency. Given the rationality of the universe, it is fitting to consider, however briefly, the possibility of karma being a genuine force in the world. Admittedly, there is much more that could be said on the subject, but Reichenbach would seem to correct when he states, "In short, both naturalistic and supernaturalistic accounts [of karma] occasion difficulties, so that much work remains to explain how the law of karma operates for those who want to hold that the law of karma is plausible."[10] Reichenbach takes seriously the existence of causal elements in this world, but in his evaluation of karma as a causal factor in the evils that are observed, he concludes that karma cannot be sustained by naturalistic means, and it does nothing to aid any theistic discussions on the POE. Indeed, there is no easy out for theists in this discussion, but that is to be expected given the complexities of this life.

Natural Law and Divine Humility

As was discussed in the previous chapter, MO is a native aspect of humanity. However, there is more to morality than merely deciphering what is right and wrong like impartial/emotionless referees at a chess match. Emotions are also a part of humanity, and they manifest themselves not only in matters of love

---

8. This consequence of karma bears some resemblance to the discussion on Rowe's argument regarding praiseworthiness discussed in the previous chapter. While it may be possible to show G is praiseworthy for using karma, karma itself is still being evaluated; it is not a necessary characteristic of G. Therefore, such quandaries are not so much obstacles to be overcome as pitfalls to be avoided.

9. Reichenbach, "Karma, Causation, and Divine Intervention," 147.

10. Reichenbach, "Karma, Causation, and Divine Intervention," 148.

and hate but also in matters of morality. Emotions do not merely accompany moral decisions but they flare up in the aftermath of suffering as well. To abandon emotions on the altar of rationality is to turn one's back on what makes one human. Although emotions can lead one toward erroneous judgments, the coexistence of MO, emotions, and the human ability to control both point toward a natural law that in turn points to G.

In *The Abolition of Man*, C. S. Lewis critiques the efforts of those he calls Gaius and Titius to create a means of evaluating literature with rationality devoid of emotion. The appeal of emotionless interpretation is understandable for at least two reasons. First, emotions are notorious for leading to conclusions that are fraught with peril. Each individual human life is rife with examples of where emotion can "get the better of you." For example, two siblings, who otherwise get along well with each other, start arguing and fighting over the last cookie. Why? Emotions of selfishness and potential pleasure rise to the surface and demand immediate action while simultaneously suppressing the rationality that would point out the potential for compromise. Second, this book that Lewis is evaluating was written shortly after World War II. The events leading up to and during WWII were filled with powerful rhetoric that swayed masses of people to either enact or allow many atrocities. In the aftermath of the war, it is not surprising to find people contemplating what could be done to prevent events like this from happening in the future. By creating this work, Gaius and Titius hoped to encourage rational thought by eschewing emotion. One can be sympathetic to their cause, but as Lewis points out the cost of this tact is very high. Lewis states, "By starving the sensibility of our pupils we only make them easier prey to the propagandist when he comes. For famished nature will be avenged and a hard heart is no infallible protection against a soft head."[11] In other words, if students are not taught how to handle emotions they will fill their emotional desires all the more with those who promise emotional fulfillment. This can be likened to placing a starving man in front of a buffet. Food is good, but the imbalance in his life will likely result in harmfully gorging himself on the bounty that has been denied him. Lewis rightly identifies that each person is responsible for the use of their rationality and emotions, and it is this sense of value that points toward the divine.

For Lewis, emotions, rational thought, and the control of both indicate an innate sense of how things ought to be. In other words, each person has a sense that there is a way that things should be and when life does not measure up to those standards something wrong has happened. Lewis sums up these conceptions of good and morality as "Tao," which equates with natural

---

11. Lewis, *Abolition of Man*, 699.

law.[12] In *The Abolition of Man*, Lewis is not concerned with arguing toward a Christian understanding of morality but rather with establishing the existence of fundamental moral standards.[13] Toward that end, Lewis sets about identifying the existence of morality in human life. After summarizing all conceptions of good and morality as Tao, Lewis states, "But what is common to them all is something we cannot neglect. It is the doctrine of objective value, the belief that certain attitudes are really true, and others really false, to the kind of thing the universe is and the kind of things we are."[14] Lewis is asserting that each person naturally has a sense of oughtness, that there is a standard for morality and that this truth is a reality of this universe. Lewis goes on to note that conceptions, such as referring to children as delightful or old men venerable, are no mere factual observations but are qualitative in nature, and this quality "*demands* a certain response from us whether we make it or not."[15] Rationality, and the emotions that accompany it, drive one toward a sense that there is a standard for human conduct.

Lewis spends considerable time establishing that emotion should not rule reason but conform to it.[16] It could also be said that emotions are a flag, an indicator of how things are but not a detailed report. To be clear, Lewis is not arguing that emotions should have a seat of honor at the table of natural law, rather he is observing that natural law, Tao, is only properly considered when all natural factors are given their due course. The danger of embracing a rationality devoid of emotion resides in embracing an ideology that is anemic. Any ideology that does not take human existence at face value (e.g., emotions are an integral part of human life) will only guide humanity away from the truth. Lewis states, "What purport to be new systems or (as they now call them) 'ideologies,' all consist of fragments from the *Tao* itself, arbitrarily wrenched from their context in the whole and then swollen to madness in their isolation, yet still owing to the *Tao* and to it alone such validity as they possess."[17] The best lies have a grain of truth to them, and the same can be said for ideologies. There should be no surprise that various conflicting ideologies exist in this world as all contain at least a small fragment of the truth of reality. Of course, this observation can cause epistemological issues; how is one to

---

12. Lewis, *Abolition of Man*, 713.

13. Lewis, *Abolition of Man*, 714. This is not to say that Lewis does not believe in the truth of Christianity; he views this conversation as being foundational to other potential discussions of Christian truth.

14. Lewis, *Abolition of Man*, 701.

15. Lewis, *Abolition of Man*, 701.

16. Lewis, *Abolition of Man*, 702.

17. Lewis, *Abolition of Man*, 714.

know which ideology is the correct one? For Lewis, the answer to this question is one based in observation of the human condition.

Throughout human history, there have been many ideologies, but a common thread can be seen throughout many of the world's moral systems. For example, Lewis notes that the thoughts of Confucius share much in common with Christianity. Lewis is not arguing for the validity of Confucian thought, rather he is highlighting that the similarity between the two is an indicator of the Tao, natural law. However, this is a great deal different than moving from Christianity to Nietzsche, which Lewis calls innovation. Moral advance is a progression of human understanding of moral/natural law, but the stark difference between Christianity and Nietzsche is an innovation. In other words, it is an invention that may be grounded in an aspect of natural law but it does not consider the whole. In reference to Confucius, Christianity, and Nietzsche, Lewis states, "It is the difference between a man who says to us: 'You like your vegetables moderately fresh; why not grow your own and have them perfectly fresh?' and a man who says, 'Throw away that loaf and try eating bricks and centipedes instead.'"[18] To embrace one aspect of natural law (reason) at the expense of rejecting another (emotion) is to ask oneself to fundamentally change how one is intended to operate in this world. True, emotions are unruly but they do serve a purpose, especially when it comes to suffering.

It would seem that suffering is a constant in this life. However, even though suffering is easy to find it is commonly viewed as abhorrent. How is it that something that seems to be a part of human existence can be understood as an anomaly of that existence? This marks a crossroads in discussions on the POE between theists and non-theists. Indeed, the following chapters will discuss theistic and non-theistic perspectives on the POE, but first Lewis has a viewpoint pertaining to natural law that should be considered. Lewis states, "He [God] thinks that their modest prosperity and the happiness of their children are not enough to make them blessed . . . therefore He troubles them, warning them in advance of an insufficiency that one day they will have to discover. The life to themselves and their families stands between them and the recognition of their need; He makes that life less sweet to them."[19] The assertion that the emotional response that comes with suffering points one toward G is, admittedly, a difficult concept to accept. G, loving creator of the universe, allows suffering to take place for the same reason a referee blows a whistle, to get someone's attention.

---

18. Lewis, *Abolition of Man*, 715.
19. Lewis, *Problem of Pain*, 606.

A potential first reaction to this stance may easily be one of offense. Surely, G could come up with some other means of getting the attention of humanity, why must people suffer? Lewis does not come to this conclusion lightly, and it reflects a strong belief in divine love for humanity. The previous statement by Lewis comes on the tails of a brief discussion on the human inability to desire help from G when all is well. When nothing is wrong help is not sought, but the reality of life is that humanity is imperfect and in need of help. Therefore, G introduces suffering into the world so that it is easier for help to be desired. Lewis states, "The creature's illusion of self-sufficiency must, for the creature's sake, be shattered; and by trouble or fear of trouble on earth, by crude fear of the eternal flames, God shatters it 'unmindful of His glory's diminution.'"[20] Humanity does not deserve consideration by G; he does not need to be active in human existence, for as the omnipotent creator of the universe any wrong actions committed by finite beings are beneath his station. Nevertheless, G humbles himself in providing a means by which attention may be drawn back to him and result in restoration. Lewis calls this Divine Humility.

For Lewis, natural law, or Tao, entails fundamental conceptions of morality and involves the entirety of rational/emotional humanity. To ignore emotions is to have an unbalanced view of human existence and the realities of this life. Ultimately, Lewis understands emotions to play a role in pointing toward the need for help, especially in times of suffering. The very fact that G would interact with humanity is, in and of itself, a humbling choice as there is no requirement that G should concern himself with the affairs of lesser beings. This Divine Humility provides a means by which people, who would otherwise be completely egocentric in their luxury of happiness, are faced with a reality in which they need to call out for help. In short, suffering is a means by which G can call people out of their spiritual complacency.

Spiritual Complacency

In sum of the previous section, it could be said that suffering provokes emotions which demand rational contemplation which should point humanity toward the divine for help. This concept that suffering can be used for good is not meant to be comforting. Lewis states, "I am not arguing that pain is not painful. Pain hurts. That is what the word means. I am only trying to show that the old Christian doctrine of being made 'perfect through suffering' is not incredible. To prove it palatable is beyond my design."[21]

20. Lewis, *Problem of Pain*, 607.
21. Lewis, *Problem of Pain*, 611–12.

Suffering may be unpleasant, and unpopular, but it can have its positive uses. Lewis identifies suffering as the means of overcoming spiritual complacency. This amounts to a soul-making theodicy where suffering is G's means of promoting spiritual growth.

Although suffering creates potential for spiritual gains, Lewis is clear that suffering should not be confused with good. Lewis states, "I answer that suffering is not good in itself. What is good in any painful experience is, for the sufferer, his submission to the will of God, and, for the spectators, the compassion aroused and the acts of mercy to which it leads."[22] Suffering produces a crisis in an individual's life where they should look to G for help. Furthermore, those who observe the suffering are likewise affected in that the suffering gives them opportunity to help the sufferer or, at the very least, observe how G helps in the situation. Lewis is quick to point out that suffering should not be confused with good; producing more suffering does not produce greater amounts of good.[23] This echoes Romans 6:1–2 when Paul exhorts his readers to forsake the idea that continued sinning will result in more grace. Suffering results in opportunity to turn to G for help, resulting in spiritual growth, but suffering is not the only means G has at his disposal. Happiness, rare though it may be, can also point toward G. Lewis states, "The settled happiness and security which we all desire, God withholds from us by the very nature of the world: but joy, pleasure, and merriment, He has scattered broadcast. . . . Our Father refreshes us on the journey with some pleasant inns, but will not encourage us to mistake them for home."[24] However pleasant happiness may be, it is only effective in turning humanity toward G because of the prevalence of suffering. How can it be that a loving being would prefer suffering to happiness as a means of communication? The answer to that question resides in the human condition and will have great significance for further discussion on the POE.

When all is well no change is desired, but when misfortune appears loneliness seems to rule the day. Through contemplations on the loss of his wife to cancer Lewis observed that in happiness G's presence would seem to be an interruption but in despair G seems to hide himself behind a bolted door. Lewis states, "The longer you wait, the more emphatic the silence will become. There are no lights in the windows. It might be an empty house. Was it ever inhabited? It seemed so once. And that seeming was as strong as this. What can this mean? Why is He so present a commander in our time

---

22. Lewis, *Problem of Pain*, 615.
23. Lewis, *Problem of Pain*, 616.
24. Lewis, *Problem of Pain*, 618.

of prosperity and so very absent a help in time of trouble?"[25] Not only does Lewis question G's apparent absence in time of need but he also questions the very nature of G. Continuing on in his struggle through grief, Lewis states, "What reason have we, except our own desperate wishes, to believe that God is, by any standard we can conceive, 'good'? Doesn't all the *prima facie* evidence suggest exactly the opposite? What have we to set against it?"[26] Here, Lewis is beginning to entertain the idea that the evidence shows that G is nothing more than a cosmic sadist, that life is a practical joke. However, Lewis is laying bare the emotions of a person going through suffering, and as time marches on he gains clarity on the situation. In reference to the notion he proposed about G setting up humanity for a torturous life, Lewis states, "I wrote that last night. It was a yell rather than a thought. Let me try it over again. . . . The Cosmic Sadist, the spiteful imbecile? I think it is, if nothing else, too anthropomorphic . . . the picture I was building up last night is simply the picture of a man . . . he'd [the man] never have thought of baits like love, or laughter, or daffodils, or a frosty sunset."[27] After having some time to gain control of his emotions, Lewis notes that he had been making two fundamental errors in his railings against G. First, attributing human motivations for G's actions is shortsighted. Surely, the creator of the universe should not be put into such a box. Second, the anomalies of happiness in this world are not the work of someone who has evil in their heart. There is something qualitatively different about the pleasures of this world and the evils that it contains. They are not from the same source. As for his comment about G being a Cosmic Sadist, Lewis states, "All that stuff about the Cosmic Sadist was not so much the expression of thought as of hatred. I was getting from it the only pleasure a man in anguish can get; the pleasure of hitting back."[28] Here, Lewis strikes upon a profound reality of the human condition: humanity has a great ability to be self-absorbed.

Previously, it was mentioned that Lewis felt as if G had bolted himself behind a door in his hour of need. It should also be remembered that emotions are a powerful factor when suffering occurs. Emotions are an indicator of what is but they are not exact judges of a situation. Lewis's emotions indicated to him that something was not right, and that correctly so. His wife had died, and he had a void in his life. However, emotions can also make it hard to think rationally, and in his anguish over the imbalance that now existed he misunderstood the meaning of the door. Lewis states, "I have

25. Lewis, *Grief Observed*, 58.
26. Lewis, *Grief Observed*, 668.
27. Lewis, *Grief Observed*, 669.
28. Lewis, *Grief Observed*, 673.

gradually been coming to feel that the door is no longer shut and bolted. Was it my own frantic need that slammed it in my face? The time when there is nothing at all in your soul except a cry for help may be just the time when God can't give it. . . . Perhaps your own reiterated cries deafen you to the voice you hoped to hear."[29] Here, Lewis also uses the example of a drowning man who so frantically flails to keep from drowning that his panic prevents the rescuers from helping him. The truth revealed here is that it should not be surprising that G appears absent in times of suffering, for feelings of abandonment are common among humans in despair. The emotional reaction that naturally results from suffering lingers, though its strength does ebb, pointing toward one's own insufficiency to rectify the situation. It is in that moment of recognition of need that one can choose to direct their anger toward G or to look to G for help.

As was discussed in the previous chapter, there is a moral gap, a moral standard, which humanity cannot cross/live up to on its own. Lewis identifies the existence of Divine Humility, that G is willing to help those who are nothing compared to him. Furthermore, suffering highlights the insufficiency of humanity and the need for divine aid in spiritual growth. Lewis states, "God has not been trying an experiment on my faith or love in order to find out their quality. He knew it already. It was I who didn't. . . . He always knew that my temple was a house of cards. His only way of making me realize the fact was to knock it down."[30] Finite humanity is spiritually complacent, and G utilizes suffering to wake humanity out of its slumber.

Much has been said here regarding Lewis's view of natural law and the role of suffering in human development, and there is much more that could be said would time allow. There is no contention here with the idea that suffering can result in spiritual growth. However, soul-making theodicies like that of Lewis's place a particular emphasis on suffering that should be briefly discussed. Lewis states, "The tortures occur. If they are unnecessary, then there is no God or a bad one. If there is a good God, then these tortures are necessary. For no even moderately good Being could possibly inflict or permit them if they weren't."[31] In context, this paper understands this conclusion by Lewis to mean that suffering is a necessary (i.e., required) component of spiritual growth. Suffering is a necessary component of human reality, but not in the sense espoused by Lewis. As will be discussed more in chapter 8, this work holds that suffering is a necessarily potential part of human reality. Being necessarily potential means that the potential for suffering

29. Lewis, *Grief Observed*, 676.
30. Lewis, *Grief Observed*, 678.
31. Lewis, *Grief Observed*, 675.

is a fundamental part of living in a world in which free choices take place. In other words, there are benefits of spiritual growth that come with suffering, but they are more of a by-product, a secondary security measure in the design of creation. To say that G created this world knowing that humanity would be spiritually complacent and that the only way to rouse them from their slumber would be through suffering makes G directly responsible for the suffering that exists. Admittedly, this is an oversimplification, and this in no way is intended to insinuate that soul-making theodicists secretly believe that G is directly responsible for the existence of suffering. Rather, by viewing suffering as a necessary potential for free will agents to exist (which will be discussed more completely in chapter 8), the benefits of suffering for spiritual growth can be maintained/recognized without using language that places G in the position of being a creator who desires suffering so that his children can grow. Of course, there are any number of soul-making theodicists who would wish to challenge this assertion, and hopefully, the discussion in chapter 8 will address many of their concerns. Regardless, the goal of this work is to address the abductive POE. Toward that end, these last two sections have laid a valuable foundation for natural law and how it is that suffering can bring about positive results of spiritual growth.

Conclusion

The subject of natural law has a rich history in theological and philosophical circles. Undoubtedly, there are any number of philosophers and theologians who would have preferred that this chapter focus on other aspects of natural law. However, this chapter accomplishes at least three important tasks toward this present discussion on the abductive POE.

First, discussion on Reichenbach's treatment of karma, brief though it may be, brings qualitative aspects of metaphysics more squarely into focus with causation. Though karma may seem to be a plausible causal explanation for the existence of suffering in this world it has difficulty in accounting for intention. Moral intentions have a qualitative nature which is difficult, if not impossible, to translate into purely causal terms devoid of agency. Furthermore, if karma is nothing more than a tool used by G it bears no responsibility at all; the question of the POE remains focused on G. Therefore, karma highlights the importance of intention (which bears similarity to discussion in chapter 2 regarding MO) but is unable to fully answer the POE. It is the emphasis on intention and morality that is of utmost importance for this present project.

Second, Lewis's treatment of a natural law that accounts for the entirety of the human condition introduces the important role emotions play in suffering and the distinction between humanity and G. Not only is it logically dubious to assume that G would only operate within human motivational constraints, but any action by G, no matter how bizarre, is an act of humility on his part: G has no obligation to rescue humanity from the just consequences of its actions. This difference between G and humanity will be discussed more fully in chapters 7 and 8, but this emotional aspect ties into the third task of this chapter.

Finally, natural law was considered in light of how emotions impact the sufferer and the way in which suffering can be used toward good. Lewis strikes upon the reality that someone in grief becomes deaf and disoriented to the surrounding environment. The sufferer may not see that the door is open because they are unwittingly pulling on the door instead of pushing on it. Lewis understands suffering to be G's way of waking humanity up from its spiritual complacency. Though this author takes small issue with the idea of suffering being necessary (preferring to use the phrase "necessary potential"), what is clear is that there can be a silver lining in the midst of suffering.

These last two chapters have laid a basic foundation for this paper's understanding of moral obligation, the good, and natural law. There exists a standard of morality that is stronger than naturalism can seem to account for, there is good and evil, and the realities of human life point toward a sense that suffering should not be the norm. It is the contention here that theism best accounts for these observations of reality. However, this question remains. "Can theism account for abductive arguments from the POE more fully than non-theism?" Therefore, this discussion now turns toward weighing the effectiveness of theistic defenses in answering the abductive POE.

4

The Free Will Defense

HAVING COMPLETED PRELIMINARY CONSIDERATIONS of the good and natural law, the next four chapters will entail the analysis of specific theistic defenses of the POE. Arguably, there is no defense as significant for the logical consistency of a wholly good and omnipotent God (G) with evil as the Free Will Defense (FWD) of Alvin Plantinga. Although Plantinga has dialogued with many non-theists throughout his career, J. L. Mackie stands out for his emphasis on the causal rationality of the universe. Analyzing the philosophies of Mackie and Plantinga not only brings more understanding to the history of discussion on the POE but it will also provide valuable information for how abductive arguments for the POE can be more thoroughly addressed by theists.

J. L. Mackie

Causation and Teleological Reality

Coming off of chapter 3's emphasis on theistic understanding of natural law, it is fitting that Mackie should be the focus of consideration now. Mackie not only proposes some challenges to Plantinga's FWD but he also offers a naturalistic (i.e., non-spiritual) accounting of the causal operation of the universe. Foundational to his thoughts on the POE are his considerations of causation. Therefore, understanding causation and perceptions of intended ends is instrumental in properly elucidating Mackie's interpretations of the existence of morality, pain, and suffering in the world, which will be the subject of the following section.

Mackie devoted a significant portion of his publications toward questions of causality in terms of the plausibility of knowing. Two concepts that play an important role in his considerations of the mechanisms of the universe are the Inverse Principle and the INUS condition. In simple terms, the Inverse Principle states that an observation combines with background knowledge to prove a hypothesis iff that hypothesis is more plausible in light of the observation and background knowledge.[1] For example, Bob sees a raven. All the ravens that Bob has observed are black. Furthermore, Bob does not know of anyone who has seen a raven that was not black. Therefore, Bob hypothesizes that all ravens are black. The hypothesis that all ravens are black is nothing more than words in and of itself. However, when Bob's observations and background knowledge conjoin with the hypothesis the assertion bears more weight. "All ravens are black" becomes more than words; it manifests as a plausible explanation for the observations and background knowledge.

The Inverse Principle, like a braided cord, is stronger in its claims because of the synergy of observation, background knowledge, and hypothesis than any of these three parts would be on their own. Elsewhere, Mackie refers to this same concept as the relevance criterion of confirmation. Mackie states, "An hypothesis (h) is confirmed by an observation (b) in relation to a body of background knowledge or belief (k) if and only if what is observed would have been more likely to occur, given the hypothesis together with the background knowledge or belief, than it would have been given that background knowledge or belief alone."[2] Like multiple witnesses in a court room, hypothesis, observation, and background knowledge (or belief) are stronger when in harmony together than they are apart. Perhaps the most notable difference between Mackie's two different accounts of the same concept is the inclusion of belief with background knowledge. Here can be seen the underpinnings of how Mackie will bridge is understanding of the causal world to that of moral concepts/beliefs. Before that discussion is had, however, there is at least one other perspective on causation that should be considered. For Mackie, an often-overlooked aspect of causation in the INUS condition.

INUS stands for the Insufficient but Necessary part of a condition which is itself Unnecessary but Sufficient for the result.[3] To illustrate the INUS condition, Mackie uses the example of a house fire "caused" by an electrical short. "Cause," here, is encased in quotes because there are prior questions of causation for the short. Was the short due to negligence, faulty wiring, deliberate sabotage? Though there are more links in this causal chain to be explored, it will suffice to say that the electric short "caused" the fire. INUS applies here because house fires are not necessarily (i.e., always)

---

1. Mackie, "Paradox of Confirmation," 267.
2. Mackie, "Relevance Criterion of Confirmation," 27.
3. Mackie, "Causes and Conditions," 245.

dependent upon electric shorts for their cause. An unattended candle knocked over by the wind, a live cigarette butt left on a couch, and many other events can cause a house fire. However, in the case of this particular house fire, the electrical short was necessary (otherwise there would not have been a fire), though not in all cases, and therefore, it becomes sufficient for the result of the house fire. In other words, INUS highlights an aspect of causal reality: an event may have many potential causes but only one actual causal scenario. In relation to the INUS condition, Mackie states, "I suggest that when we speak of the cause of some particular event, it is often a condition of this sort that we have in mind."[4] In essence, people have a tendency to follow the Inverse Principle without considering INUS.

Consider the above house fire. Suppose that the only times the smoke detector went off in that house were due to the owner leaving a live cigarette butt on the couch. Now there is a house fire. The hypothesis of the neighbor is that the fire was caused by a wayward cigarette butt. This becomes plausible when considered alongside observations of poor smoking habits and background knowledge of many near misses of the couch catching fire. It can become easy to affix a necessary quality that any fire at this residence will be caused by cigarette butts, but to do so invites misunderstanding. What is needed is adherence to the Inverse Principle but with a dose of humility so as to be aware of the possibility of the INUS condition. A relationship exists between observation, background knowledge, and hypothesis, which needs to be wary of the existence of causes that may not be necessary but sufficient. Toward that end, Mackie identifies a phenomenon of reality that can mislead the observer to have mistaken beliefs which affect perception of background knowledge and, therefore, one's understanding of causal events.

Consider the solar system. Planets, a star, moons, orbits, and gravitational pulls all work together and the result is a habitable planet quaintly known as Earth. Earth has optimal temperatures, due to its precise proximity to the sun, tides which aerate the oceans (due to gravitational pulls), and many other features that are present thanks to the formation of this grouping of celestial bodies. Upon observation of this solar system, it can appear that there was/is a goal in its formation, the goal of sustaining human life. However, Mackie understands this sort of goal setting as a misunderstanding of causal and teleological reality. After some discussion on how teleology does not necessarily explain causality in the solar system, Mackie states, "That each response when triggered by the appropriate situation should lead to the same goal G is, on the face of it, an extraordinary coincidence which demands some further explanation. . . . This is

---

4. Mackie, "Causes and Conditions," 245.

the element of truth in the theological Argument from Design: there are kinds of things, notably the behaviour of various organisms, which exhibit 'marks of design.'"[5] Since it can be observed that there are beneficial consequences to causation it is understandable that teleological intent could be misidentified. Mackie views these teleological conclusions as indicators of something requiring further explanation. The appearance of design in the universe should not be taken to be actual but rather evaluated for its authenticity. For Mackie, that means analyzing the information from a causal perspective. Mackie states, "We thus have the slightly paradoxical but not, I hope, really obscure consequence that although the evolutionary explanation of what, taken on its own, invites a teleological description . . . that evolutionary story is not itself a teleological one. The steps it narrates both are and are described as processes of efficient causation only."[6] For Mackie, one should not be surprised to find that the effects of causation have use, but error comes when use is construed as goal.

The issue here is one of perspective. There is great challenge in being in a defining moment in reality and attempting to look back. Challenges come in the form of perceptual obstructions, events and environmental conditions in this present time that obscure reality. Having the Earth as a place to live is, all things considered, fortunate, but it is one thing to recognize fortune and quite another to attribute to it goal-fulfilling properties. For Mackie, theism presents a potentially sufficient cause for reality but not a necessary one. Furthermore, background knowledge and observations of causality become more probable when conjoined with a hypothesis born of causation rather than theism. The tendency to attribute teleological meaning to a universe of causation is a by-product of a concept which Mackie calls Metaphysical Double Vision.

Metaphysical Double Vision

As beings within a causal world, humans have the opportunity, and the challenge, of coming to terms with events that are influenced by causes beyond the perceptual capacities of individuals. As was previously seen with perceptions of teleology in relation to causation, it can be deceptively simple to identify goals when there are merely causes. Humans have the amazing ability to fit ontological reality into epistemological boxes. In opening these boxes and examining the contents, Mackie seeks to correct misconceptions

---

5. Mackie, *Cement of the Universe*, 280.
6. Mackie, *Cement of the Universe*, 283.

of reality by bringing Metaphysical Double Vision (MDV) out of the shadows and into the light of reason.

As a means of explaining MDV, Mackie considers the properties of glass and copper. Mackie states, "If for any causal process we need to postulate a preexisting power or powers, latent in each of the things that enters relevantly into the process, we shall have to do the same for all. . . . As a set of serious ontological claims, this is gratuitous multiplication."[7] What Mackie here refers to as "gratuitous multiplication" is the categorizing of abilities for conducting electricity and heat, the inability to conduct electricity and heat, the way electrons move through materials, etc. In other words, the idea that glass has the property of being an insulator, or copper a conductor, is a misconception of reality. Glass and copper are what they are independent of the existence of rampant electrons, for they would remain glass and copper even if stray electrons were nowhere to be found. Mackie states, "It is far more reasonable to suppose that electrons and the like have, intrinsically, merely whatever categorical features they do have, and that these, in interaction with the categorical features of other things, generate the causal behavior of which 'dispositions' or 'powers' are a shadow."[8] To associate the interactions of copper and electricity with the identity of copper is to add a layer of perception that is not fundamental to copper. In so doing one is making the ontological claim that conducting electrons is essential to copper, but this claim is mistaken; it is an epistemological perception layered upon ontological reality. Copper is what it is in and of itself. Conductivity can only be observed when another outside entity is placed into contact with it. Mackie states, "By mixing up ontology and epistemology we may inadvertently take what might seem to be a modest step, but is really a pretentious one, of making our ontology directly match our knowledge, of taking what belongs only to the way in which we know certain important properties as constitutive of the objective properties as they are in themselves."[9] This is MDV. When perceptions of properties are allowed to dictate the essence of a thing the observer begins to see two things at once while mistaking them to be the same. Granted, in much of the day-to-day operation of the world, MDV is harmless. Identifying copper by its conductive properties, rather that its physical molecular structure, is not likely to cause one to misidentify it, and it may actually assist in the efficient operations of some occupations. After all, an electrician would not be harming himself if he thought of copper ontologically as a conductor. However, there does exist a

---

7. Mackie, "Dispositions, Grounds, and Causes," 366.
8. Mackie, "Dispositions, Grounds, and Causes," 366.
9. Mackie, "Dispositions, Grounds, and Causes," 369.

theater in which an awareness of MDV can be most valuable, an arena of life experienced by all: morality.

The significance of recognizing MDV in morality can be seen in how one recognizes the authority of moral obligation. Mackie, for his part, believes he has found a lens by which to view morality so as to avoid MDV: the biological conclusions of Richard Dawkins. In applying Dawkins's selfish gene theory to morality, Mackie concludes that much thought of morality is little more than the effect of natural causation. Specifically, the selfish reproductive tendencies of genes and memes help to explain why certain moral behaviors/concepts have traditionally been passed down. For Mackie, the ontological truth of morality, that morality is not preordained, should not be confused with the epistemological perception of the strength of morality, that moral obligation is absolute. In other words, to understand morality as having an eternal truth for human life is to be viewing the world through MDV. Mackie states, "What implications for human morality have such biological facts about selfishness and altruism? One is that the possibility that morality is itself a product of natural selection is not ruled out, but care would be needed in formulating a plausible speculative account of how it might have been favoured."[10] In other words, Mackie holds that evolutionary causes have shaped morality but there is difficulty in parsing it out so that naturalistic causes can adequately explain moral obligation. The fluidity of morality then becomes a direct implication of this belief, and this is something to which Mackie and Dawkins are aware. Mackie states, "[Dawkins] suggests that conscious foresight may enable us to develop radically new kinds of behavior. 'We are built as gene machines and cultured as meme machines, but we have the power to turn against our creators. We, alone on earth, can rebel against the tyranny of the selfish replicators.'"[11] Mackie, and Dawkins, assert that morality is something that can be changed. Indeed, this conclusion is consistent with a naturalistic perspective of reality, one in which cause and effect reign supreme and the spiritual is nonexistent. However, in the telling of his account of morality, Mackie raises an important question.

In addition to the comment above calling for a deliberate shaping of morality, elsewhere Mackie even more bluntly expresses that morality should be made, not discovered.[12] Again, Mackie states, "The best explanatory hypothesis to account for the phenomenon of moral thinking does not include

---

10. Mackie, "Law of the Jungle," 463.

11. Mackie, "Law of the Jungle," 463.

12. Mackie, "Genes and Egoism," 555. This is a summation of some thoughts on morality he had in *Ethics*, pp. 106 and 123.

the postulate that there are any such objectively moral truths . . . belief in such truths results from moral emotions . . . [which yield] the misleading appearance of objective reality."[13] For Mackie, all of the moral obligations that are felt by individuals are the result of physical and social evolutionary causes. Therefore, morality is what humanity makes it; there are no objective moral truths. However, consider his agreement with Dawkins that humanity alone has the ability to rise up and rebel against the morality that evolution has given. If there is no such thing as objective moral truth what cause does one have for rebelling against the morality naturalism has provided? From whence comes the solid foundation upon which can stand upon and rail against how things are in an effort to make things better? In other words, if morality does not matter, from an ontological perspective, why even bother with trying to change it? However, theism does provide at least two explanations for this perspective of Mackie's. First, it could be that one recognizes how others have disobeyed natural law and desires to make things right. Second, it could be that one finds natural law restrictive and desires to break free from obligation. In either account, theism can explain these conclusions of non-theists such as Mackie, but what remains is for naturalism to give a proper account of the import that moral obligation has in human life if it is indeed little more than happenstance. Regardless, in the end, Mackie holds a view of morality that is relativistic in that morality has no foundation other than whatever naturalistic causes have affected it. For Mackie, morality is something that can be changed in a fundamental way, and this view of morality has a profound effect on his perspective of the POE.

Mackie does not have an issue with the existence of evil in the world, for evil would be little else than events occurring that run contrary to the standards of normality that he has been conditioned to since birth. However, he does see evil as a problem for theists. Mackie states, "The problem of evil, in the sense in which I shall be using the phrase, is a problem only for someone who believes that there is a God who is both omnipotent and wholly good."[14] For Mackie, complete and utter goodness will eventually run afoul of omnipotence resulting in a contradiction that cannot be overcome. Two concepts are foundational for Mackie's expedition for these contradictions: good always eliminates evil as far as it can and there are no limits to what an omnipotent thing can do.[15] Mackie is aware of there being logical limits to omnipotence, that omnipotence does

---

13. Mackie, "Morality and the Retributive Emotions," 7.
14. Mackie, "Omnipotence and Evil," 25.
15. Mackie, "Omnipotence and Evil," 26.

not entail doing what is logically impossible.[16] However, he does not think that eliminating evil is something that is logically limiting. Mackie states, "The rule that good cannot exist without evil would not state a logical necessity of a sort that God would just have to put up with."[17] In other words, a wholly good and omnipotent God (G) would be in no logical contradiction to eliminate evil in the world.

Mackie postulates that a redesign of humanity could have resulted in the absence of evil. Mackie states, "There was open to him the obviously better possibility of making beings who would act freely but always go right."[18] Herein resides the elements of paradox, in Mackie's view. If good eliminates evil as far as it can, and if G is omnipotent, then evil should be eliminated. Either G is not good, because evil exists and he does not want to eliminate it completely, or G is not omnipotent due to an inability to make humanity so that it does no evil. Mackie states, "Quite apart from the problem of evil, the paradox of omnipotence has shown that God's omnipotence must in any case be restricted in one way or another, that unqualified omnipotence cannot be ascribed to any being that continues through time."[19] It is in this statement that Mackie's moral relativism can be seen to obscure his vision of omnipotence. Above, it was shown that Mackie recognizes that there can be logical limits to omnipotence. Indeed, this will be discussed more fully in the next section with Plantinga. However, Mackie sees no logical limits in terms of eliminating evil. Therefore, for Mackie, G has no limitations as to what he can do with his omnipotence in terms of evil. His epistemological beliefs about morality, and his view that free will is an incoherent notion,[20] are shaping his view of the ontological nature of G. If free will is an illusion and morals are contrived, then there is no potential conflict between overriding free will toward a given moral end. In other words, because Mackie has a prior belief in the non-absolute nature of morals he views G to not have any morals which would present a logical limitation on his omnipotence. At this point, it could be asked if Mackie is suffering from MDV.

Mackie's observations on causation and morality are helpful in that they help one to remember to be aware of the complexities of reality and to seek out things for what they really are. Although, his accounting of morals is devoid of any universal morality, and his bias in this regard carries over into his critique of theism in relation to the POE. As a result of his view of

---

16. Mackie, "Omnipotence and Evil," 28.
17. Mackie, "Omnipotence and Evil," 29–30.
18. Mackie, "Omnipotence and Evil," 33.
19. Mackie, "Omnipotence and Evil," 37.
20. Mackie, "Omnipotence and Evil," 33.

morality, G's omnipotence is not held logically accountable to moral restrictions. However, it is the contention of Alvin Plantinga that there are such logical limits on G's omnipotence, and therefore, G's omnipotence is not in contradiction with his goodness.

Alvin Plantinga

Properly Basic Belief & Rationality

Alvin Plantinga makes the argument that belief in G is a warranted properly basic true belief. Warrant is used by Plantinga as "that quantity (whatever precisely it is) *enough* of which is what distinguishes knowledge from mere true belief.... A belief constitutes knowledge only if it has a certain degree of the quantity in question; a true belief that enjoyed at least some warrant could still fail to be knowledge if it didn't have sufficient degree of warrant."[21] In other words, there is a difference between believing in what is true and having warrant, or justification for that belief. For example, an ancient human may have had the true belief that the sun was a ball of gas many times larger than the earth. However, a modern human has a warranted true belief in the sun being made of gas because of the evidence that humanity now possesses for that belief. More than just needing to be correct in their belief in G, the theist must show that belief in G is warranted in such a way as to be knowledge rather than blind luck combined with faith. Toward this end, Plantinga makes use of the concept of proper basicality to show that there is foundational proof for warranted true belief in G.

In his discussion of basicality, Plantinga makes a distinction between properly basic beliefs and propositions. Propositions are those beliefs that are based upon other more basic beliefs. Plantinga states, "Some of my beliefs, however, I accept but don't accept on the basis of any other beliefs. Call these beliefs *basic*."[22] Here, Plantinga uses mathematics as an example. $72 \times 71 = 5112$. While belief in this equation is proper it is not basic, for it is based upon more fundamental principles that are properly (i.e., irreducibly) basic, such as $2 + 1 = 3$. Simple addition, regardless of one's language or physical location in the universe, retains its truthfulness. The underlying principle that Plantinga flushes out here entails the idea that basic beliefs are not groundless beliefs.[23] Of course, this concept carries much weight for the theist. If the theist is correct in asserting that G is the creator of all then

---

21. Plantinga, "Warrant and Accidentally True Belief," 140.
22. Plantinga, "Is Belief in God Properly Basic?," 41.
23. Plantinga, "Is Belief in God Properly Basic?," 46.

belief in G would need to be properly basic. If, on the other hand, it cannot be shown that such belief is properly basic then theistic arguments become cut off at the knees, for others, such as Mackie, could claim that causal effects are more basic than G and therefore are more capable of explaining the states of goods and evils in the world.

For Plantinga, there are many conditions and circumstances that call for a belief in G, such as guilt, gratitude, a sense that G exists and communicates, and more.[24] These elements of Natural Law point toward a properly basic belief in G. However, and objection can be raised here that if conditions such as these are enough to warrant a properly basic belief in G then any human inclination could potentially be used to declare any belief properly basic inviting irrationalism and superstition to the table of truth. Plantinga is well aware of this critique and asserts that there are rational limiters which affirm properly basic belief in G without succumbing to such a slippery slope argument. For example, Plantinga states, "God has implanted in us a natural tendency to see his hand in the world around us; the same cannot be said for the Great Pumpkin, there being no Great Pumpkin and no natural tendency to accept beliefs about the Great Pumpkin."[25] As was mentioned previously in this chapter, Mackie views the appearance of teleology to be a result of metaphysical double vision, but Plantinga sees no need to contort one's mental abilities so as to explain away that which is obvious to all of humanity (at least until one attempts to rationalize it away): the elements of nature draw humanity toward the thought that G exists. However, the recognition of a naturally basic tendency to search for G does not commit oneself to belief in anything. Not all beliefs, whether it be the Great Pumpkin or the Flying Spaghetti Monster, are properly basic in that they are not natural inclinations but rather deliberate fabrications. Plantinga sums this up when he states, "One who holds that belief in God *is* properly basic is not thereby committed to the idea that belief in God is groundless or gratuitous or without justifying circumstances. . . . Like everyone should, he begins with examples; and he may take belief in the Great Pumpkin as a paradigm of irrational basic belief."[26] For Plantinga, the idea that G exists is so foundational to human reality that belief in G is properly basic, but what does belief in G entail? Is he so powerful that anything is possible? Are there any restraints that an omnipotent being can logically be held accountable to? Plantinga affirms that there can be and are logical constraints on G, and his explanation for these are crucial for his Free Will Defense of the POE.

24. Plantinga, "Is Belief in God Properly Basic?," 46.
25. Plantinga, "Is Belief in God Properly Basic?," 51.
26. Plantinga, "Is Belief in God Properly Basic?," 51.

For the purposes of this present discussion, there are two rational limits on G's omnipotence: propositions and free will. Plantinga states, "What God has created are the heavens and the earth and all that they contain; he has not created himself, or numbers, propositions, prosperities, or states of affairs: these have no beginnings."[27] Take, for example, numbers. Numbers exist, at least theoretically, regardless of the universe that is being conceived. Material items, language, and written word may change, but the concept that $1 + 1 = 2$ will not change. G can actualize a world in which counting takes on a certain form (such as being able to count ducks in one world but there being no ducks to count in another world) but there is no creating of the concept $1 + 1 = 2$; it is properly basic. Therefore, to expect an omnipotent being to be able to make $1 + 1 \neq 2$ is to irrationally hold that being to a capability that is not logically consistent with reality. There is no limitation of power in G not being able to make $1 + 1 \neq 2$. G can actualize a state of affairs such that a pair of ducks can be understood to be $1 + 1 = 2$, but the existence of this mathematical truth has no beginning, just as G has none. Furthermore, the conclusion can be reached that it is rational to understand an omnipotent being as having the "limitation" of not being able to be logically inconsistent/contradictory with basic truths. This concept of logical constraint is perhaps most provoking when applied to free will.

As has been established previously, it is the contention of this paper that the existence of free will is a fundamental aspect of reality and not merely an illusion. That is not to say that free will is properly basic in and of itself. There is no necessity of free will for a created world. In other words, had G chosen to do so, he could have created this world without free will. However, since G has created humans with free will there now exists a logical constraint upon G's omnipotence. While this constraint may not be of the same caliber as that of numbers it still retains the property of being a standard of reality that G must adhere to if free will is to have any real meaning in life. It is this "real meaning in life" that sheds light onto what the restraint of free will looks like for G. Plantinga states, "Although of course God may cause it to be the case that I *am* free with respect to A, he cannot cause it to be the case either that I freely take or that I freely refrain from this action—and this though he is omnipotent."[28] In other words, G creates the world, including free agents, and the circumstances free agents will interact with, but G cannot determine for those agents what action they will take, for to do so would be to nullify free will, a characteristic of reality that this world was created with. What this freedom, and divine limitation, means

---

27. Plantinga, "Which Worlds Could God Have Created?," 540.
28. Plantinga, "Which Worlds Could God Have Created?," 452.

for the individual is responsibility for actions. Where *t* represents the time an action took place, Plantinga states, "A person is *significantly free* at *t* if at *t* he is free with respect to an action that is morally significant for him."[29] The implication here is that although a person may enjoy free will not every action/event in a person's life is something to which free will is a necessity, but it is also the implication here that there are times where free will is vitally important.[30] Of course, as has been discussed previously, the ability to make moral choices entails the existence of moral and immoral actions in a given event and this factors in with free will as well.

Plantinga posits that it is possible that when G created the world, he created free creatures who would at some point in time go wrong. As an example, Plantinga discusses Curley, a fictional person who has taken a bribe. Curly is significantly free, but there is the possibility that there exists a state of affairs in which he will choose the wrong action. Of particular import here is the use of the term "possible." Plantinga states, "And the present claim is not, of course, that Curley or anyone else is *in fact* like this, but only that this story about Curley is *possibly* true."[31] Here, Plantinga is proposing the possibility that free creatures will do at least one wrong thing in their free will existence. He calls this possible condition Transworld Depravity (TWD), a possible condition inherent in free will creatures.[32] Not only is G bound by the rational constraint of allowing free will agents to live out their morally significant events according to their own choices, but it is possible that these creatures are themselves incapable of doing what is right in every instance. This concept of TWD is essential to Plantinga's Free Will Defense to the POE.

The Free Will Defense

The Free Will Defense (FWD), as its name suggests, is a theistic explanation for the POE that makes use of the human quality known as free will. As its goal, the FWD seeks to show the existence of a God that is omnipotent, omniscient, wholly good, and that the existence of evil is not inconsistent with the existence of God (G).[33] Toward that end, Plantinga understands free will to entail the ability to perform or refrain from a given action.[34] The

29. Plantinga, "Which Worlds Could God Have Created?," 548–49.
30. A further implication is potential ability for G to interact in this world without violating free will, but this concept will be discussed more in chapter 8.
31. Plantinga, "Which Worlds Could God Have Created?," 549.
32. Plantinga, "Which Worlds Could God Have Created?," 551.
33. Plantinga, *Nature of Necessity*, 165.
34. Plantinga, *Nature of Necessity*, 165–66.

existence of free will and how it relates to G following logical constraints runs through the core of the FWD.

Plantinga defines the FWD as follows, "A world containing creatures who are sometimes significantly free (and freely perform more good than evil actions) is more valuable, all else being equal, than a world containing no free creatures at all . . . but he [God] cannot *cause* or *determine* them to do only what is right. For if he does so, then they are not significantly free after all; they do not do what is right *freely*."[35] For Plantinga, free will does not preclude the possibility of there being circumstances in one's life that have causal influence; the existence of free will simply means that causation does not rule every aspect of the life of a free agent and that there are times when that person retains the ability to free make moral choices. Furthermore, free will entails the logical constraint of freedom. G cannot override a person's free will without encroaching upon that person's identity as a free will being. Of course, the existence of free will implies the ability to make moral choices, and this is not insignificant to the FWD. Plantinga states, "The heart of the Free Will Defense is the claim that it is *possible* that God could not have created a universe containing moral good (or as much moral good as this one contains) without creating one containing moral evil."[36] Here, Plantinga is referring to the idea that the identity of goodness is tied to moral correctness, and by implication evil is tied to moral wrongness. Without there being at least the possibility of evil there can be no good action, for something is good by virtue of it being more valuable than the alternative. Is it then logically possible for G to create a world with moral goodness but no evil? Plantinga states, "What is really characteristic and central to the Free Will Defense is the claim that God, though omnipotent, could not have created just any possible world he pleased."[37] The existence of moral goodness and free will pose a logical constraint upon G's creative acts.

Plantinga asserts that TWD is possible, and if actual, a world cannot be created with the potential for significant moral goodness without the presence of TWD. In other words, humans have free will and it appears that every person goes wrong in regard to morality at least once, therefore it is possible that anyone who lives in a world with free will suffers from TWD. Plantinga states, "What is important about the idea of transworld depravity is that if a person suffers from it, then it was not within God's power to actualize any world in which that person is significantly free but does no wrong—that is, a world in which he produces moral good but not

---

35. Plantinga, *Nature of Necessity*, 166–67.
36. Plantinga, *Nature of Necessity*, 167.
37. Plantinga, "Nature of Necessity," 87.

moral evil. But clearly it is possible that everybody suffers from transworld depravity."[38] TWD is an essential element of free will. If G had made a world in which there were no free will agents TWD would still exist but there would be no evidence of it; it would be dormant. However, as soon as free will (which allows for moral choices to be made) is actualized TWD awakens and runs parallel with free will. It is then possible that TWD can be observed in any free agent regarding moral decisions. Plantinga states, "If an essence E *does* suffer from transworld depravity, then it was not within God's power to actualize a possible world W such that E contains the properties *is significantly free in W* and *always does what is right in W*. Hence it was not within God's power to create a world in which E's instantiation is significantly free but always does what is right."[39] In other words, it is possible that G could not create a world in which people are free to make good moral choices without allowing for TWD.

TWD and the FWD provide an accounting of why/how it is that G would allow moral evils to take place. In short, if good is to take place there is a logical need for the potential of evil, for any negation of evil in its entirety would render those very same acts not morally praiseworthy, and therefore not morally significant. However, what of natural evils? How is it that the condition of TWD and the application of the FWD (which is concerned with free agents) can address such things? The answer resides in the possibility of unknown free agents.

As a description of the condition(s) of this world, Plantinga's defense is not a specific telling of why things are the way that they are. It is descriptive rather than prescriptive. When it comes to accounting for natural evils, Plantinga chooses to adapt a theodicy employed by St. Augustine into a defense. Plantinga states, "So the natural evil we find is due to free actions of non-human spirits. . . . St. Augustine believes that natural evil . . . is *in fact* to be ascribed to the activity of beings that are free and rational but non-human. The Free Will Defender, on the other hand, need not assert that this is *true*; he says only that it is *possible*."[40] If G is real the possibility exists that he could create nonhuman agents bearing free will. Therefore, it is possible that these agents are responsible for occurrences of natural evil. Admittedly, this is a fantastic notion in that it depends upon beings who cannot be directly observed (if they can be observed at all beyond instances of natural evil). However, the key here is the concept of *possibility*. Plantinga, unlike St. Augustine, does not make the assertion that spiritual free will beings

---

38. Plantinga, *Nature of Necessity*, 186.
39. Plantinga, *Necessity of Evil*, 188.
40. Plantinga, *Necessity of Evil*, 192.

are responsible for natural evil, rather his claim is more modest, though no less potent for its demeanor. The existence of spiritual beings with free will is logically consistent with the concept of G. Therefore, it is *possible* that they exist and are responsible for natural evil. Plantinga's goal here is not to argue for the probability of this claim, but in arguing for its possibility he is successfully showing that natural evil, as well as moral evil, are logically consistent with the existence of G. Although he may not be arguing in probabilistic terms, he does make the observation that this explanation should not be dismissed out of hand. In reference to the above defense of natural evil, Plantinga states, "The mere fact that belief is unpopular at present (or at some other time) is interesting from a sociological point of view but evidentially irrelevant."[41] In other words, the popularity of a concept in the minds of the populace has no direct bearing on its logical viability. While Plantinga is correct in his assessment of logic versus popular belief, his accounting of natural evil is difficult to accept from an abductive perspective.

Although Plantinga's FWD is logically sound, and possible, it lacks in its explanatory power for specific instances of natural evil. As was discussed in chapter 1, current arguments in the POE are abductive in nature; they plead to an inference to the best explanation for a given event. To be fair, it does not appear that Plantinga had the abductive POE (APOE) in his crosshairs when developing the FWD; he was primarily concerned with the logical consistency of G and evil. However, later in his development of the FWD Plantinga does address evidential/abductive arguments. In reference to a child dying from leukemia and the idea that there is no apparent reason for why G would allow such a thing, Plantinga states, "But . . . can we just *see* that he [God] doesn't have a reason? Perhaps his reason lies in some transaction involving free creatures of sorts we have little conception of."[42] Here, Plantinga is reasserting the possibility of nonhuman free agents as the source of natural evil. There are some hints here of skeptical theism (which will be discussed in chapter 7), but Plantinga seems to be satisfied with the logical consistency and the possibility of his FWD in terms of natural evil.

Scientific advances in physical science and biology continue to show the natural causes at work in earthquakes, diseases, etc., and this advancement makes spiritual causes of natural evil less probable. Yes, it is still possible that spiritual forces are at work in natural evil, for scientific advancement could, possibly, just be showing the initial steps that such a being would need to take to cause natural evil, but, in the end, possible does not necessarily equate to probable. But, is pleading to spiritual beings the

---

41. Plantinga, "God, Freedom and Evil," 62.
42. Plantinga, "Epistemic Probability and Evil," 73.

only logical recourse the free will defender has? It is logically possible and consistent, but would not the theistic case be made stronger if it could be shown that there is a theistic perspective on natural evil that has abductive fortitude? There does exist a means by which theistic defenses can present an abductive defense in specific instances of intense natural evil, as will be shown in chapters 8 and 9.

Conclusions

As has been seen, Mackie views this world through a causal lens which views beliefs in G to be little more than evolutionary happenstance. For Mackie, one's temporal and geographical perspective can cause one to misunderstand the makings of the universe. Mackie refers to this tendency as metaphysical double vision (MDV). Although Mackie applies MDV toward theism, what is good for the goose is good for the gander. In his discussions of morality, Mackie calls for a rebellion against the moral imperatives evolution has dealt humanity. However, if morals have no absolute grounding, being the by-products of evolution, it lends one to wonder if Mackie may himself be experiencing MDV when it comes to morals, for what is the point of rebellion if morals are groundless? Nevertheless, Mackie provides much for theists to ponder, and his emphasis on understanding the entirety of a causal event, and to not just assume a cause, is a valuable lesson.

Plantinga, being a theist, naturally disagrees with Mackie's non-theistic position, and in his endeavor to provide a theistic defense of the existence of G and evil he pursues the logical limits that coexist with G's omnipotence. Transworld depravity (TWD) is put forth as a possible condition which all free will agents possess. Therefore, if G were to make people with free will (which is necessary for there to be significantly good moral actions) then it is possible that those people will go wrong with regards to moral actions at least once. Plantinga's Free Will Defense (FWD) makes use of TWD, and G's logical constraint of not overriding free will, to explain the logical coexistence of G and moral evil. Once again, Plantinga utilizes the language of possibility to explain natural evil when he affirms the possibility that natural evil can be caused by spiritual free will beings. It is the contention here that though Plantinga's explanation for natural evil is possible and logically consistent it lacks in its explanatory power from an abductive perspective.

Having laid a foundation for free will defenses, this discussion now turns toward further developments in discussions of the POE. Specifically, Bruce Russell's claim that G could stop just one more instance of evil and Peter van Inwagen's expansion upon the FWD will be the subjects of the next chapter.

5

The Expanded Free Will Defense

UNLIKE NON-THEISTS WHO ARGUE for the logical incompatibility of a wholly good, omniscient, omnipotent God (G), Bruce Russell takes a different approach. For Russell, the great question of the Problem of Evil (POE) relates to why it is that G cannot stop just one more instance of intense evil. Surely, Russell argues, there are instances of such evil where it is possible that G could have prevented it without lessening the sum total of goods in the world. Peter van Inwagen is more than willing to address non-theistic claims such as this, and what is more, he proposes an Expanded Free Will Defense (EFWD) to more fully account for the amounts and kinds of evils that are present in this world.

Bruce Russell

Experience as the Foundation of Justification

Fundamental to Russell's claim that if G exists he could prevent at least one more instance of intense evil from occurring is his understanding of the relationship between experience and justification for belief. For Russell, background knowledge and experience provide all the information required to be accurate in one's estimation of why there are intense evils of the amounts and kinds seen in this world.

Russell uses crows as the subject of a thought experiment designed to show how it is that experience and background knowledge work together toward justified belief. Consider a person, who will here be called Jane. Jane has observed crows her entire life, and all of the crows that have been observed are black. As far as Jane knows, no one has ever been reported to have seen a crow that had a color other than black. The experience and the background knowledge that Jane possesses lead her to the conclusion that all crows are black. However, just because Jane's experience and background knowledge have only observed one color does not necessarily preclude the possibility of there being a blue crow. After all, perhaps the blue crows are more skittish and are therefore harder to find. Nevertheless, the possibility of a different color of crow does not require Jane to believe that such a crow is likely or real. Russell states, "But when considering whether the sample is representative we need to take account of goods beyond our ken only if there is reason to believe there are any."[1] Does there exist any evidence or any phenomenon that could be better explained by the existence of blue crows? Since such unanswered questions do not exist Jane is within her epistemic rights to conclude that her sampling of black crows is representative of the nature of crows. There are no circumstances which would benefit Jane to seriously entertain the possibility of blue crows. In response to the idea that blue crows may be hiding themselves, Russell states, "Similarly, the defender of the evidential argument from evil can object that we have every reason to believe the sample is representative unless there is reason to believe that there are goods beyond our ken."[2] Here is the crux of the matter for Russell in regards to evidential/abductive arguments from evil: Russell believes that there exists no evidence to support the existence of hidden goods that would make sense of evil in the face of certain cases of intense evil, and since there is no evidence of these goods it is epistemically responsible to conclude that no such goods exist. For Russell, background knowledge provides the foundation for justified belief in the non/existence of G.

While arguing for a relationship between background knowledge and justified belief, Russell maintains an imperative to examine the evidence. Russell states, "Justification (and so knowledge) requires the ability to discriminate between evidence for X and evidence for Y, and in that sense requires sensitivity to the evidence. . . . But while sensitivity to the evidence is required for justification, and hence for knowledge, sensitivity to the truth is not."[3] In other words, evidence will eventually lead to a true belief; having that true belief prior to examining the evidence is not required. Application of Russell's relationship between background knowledge and evidence can perhaps be most poignantly seen in his creation thought experiment. Russell posits the possibility of the world being only one hundred years old. If the world were only a century old, its young age, coupled with modern knowledge of ancient history, would necessitate that when the world was created so too were false memories of times beyond one hundred years. Of course, when faced with such a claim there is also the possibility that the

---

1. Russell, "Defenseless," 194.
2. Russell, "Defenseless," 194.
3. Russell, "How to Be an Anti-Skeptic," 251.

world is as old as it seems, at least certainly more than one hundred years, based upon the background knowledge of the populace. In reference to this thought experiment Russell states, "The naturalistic theory which says that the causes have always been of the same sort seems simpler and so more reasonable to accept."[4] Not only does background knowledge and the physical evidence support the idea of an earth that is more than one hundred years old, the explanations for why everyone is so thoroughly deceived are much more convoluted. Since the world has operated the same way for the last hundred years it is reasonable to assume that it has done so for all of the time of history which has been preserved.

Russell establishes not only the relationship between background knowledge and justification for belief but also the idea that naturalistic explanations are more convincing than supernatural ones (which is what would have been needed for this one-hundred-year-old earth). One other factor in Russell's consideration is the worth of the claim being evaluated. Russell states, "The evidence a person needs before she has knowledge is directly proportional to what is at stake if her belief is false."[5] Belief in a finite one hundred-year-old earth is one thing, but belief in G is another as it potentially has eternal consequences. Therefore, the evidence required for belief in G should equal the severity of the claim,[6] and Russell believes that he has found evidence that is a defeater for the claim that G exists in this world full of intense evil.

The evidence in consideration as proof for the nonexistence of G is the rape/murder of a five-year-old girl in Flint, Michigan.[7] Truly, it is challenging to find any good that could possibly come out of allowing any young child to be abused and murdered. If G exists, why did he not stop this from happening? The evidence, as Russell sees it, points toward an utter absence of good in this situation. Furthermore, what kind of moral behavior would be expected of a bystander in this event? Russell states, "I am arguing that if we are not justified in believing that no reason would justify god in allowing the brutal rape and murder, then we are not justified in believing

---

4. Russell, "Defenseless," 197.

5. Russell, "Contextualism," 35.

6. From Russell's perspective, it is belief in G that needs to be proven since the natural world is evident to all. However, this reflects an *a priori* naturalistic leaning. Given the eternal stakes involved with belief in G, the existence and the nonexistence of G *both* require evidence directly proportional to their severity.

7. This tragic incident is commonly used by non-theists as proof that G does not exist. Therefore, this paper will be specifically addressing this case in chapter 9. As the specific details of the incident are not as important here as they are in chapter 9, further details as to the specifics of the case will be given then. For the purposes of this discussion, the victim in this case will be referred to as Sally.

that no reason would justify the onlooker in allowing the same act."[8] In other words, those who would say that G could have his just reasons for allowing Sally to suffer have no ground to stand on if they were to chastise an onlooker who could have done something but did not. Since it is clear that any such onlooker carries blame if they do nothing when they could do something to save Sally, G, who is omnipotent and omniscient, carries blame for not intervening on Sally's behalf. As is implied in the summation of this position, Russell does believe in there being moral demands,[9] and, for Russell, having the ability and knowledge to save Sally would constitute just such a moral demand.

G, having ability and knowledge in abundance, is, in Russell's estimation, a candidate for being a blameworthy onlooker who does nothing to help the innocent when it was within his power to do so. The inference to the best explanation is that a good, omnipotent, omniscient God would have prevented this tragedy, and there is no evidence perceptible to human observation that could possible justify inaction. Russell's criterion on background knowledge and evidence conjoin and give birth to the conclusion that one is justified in viewing Sally's case as evidence against the existence of G.[10] But what of free will? Could not an argument be made against Russell that G's intervention would have required an overriding of free will and that such a violation of basic human identity would, on the balance, lessen the amount of good in the world in a detrimental way? Russell is aware of this objection and he counters by asserting that goodness is not such a fragile thing as free will defenders would make it seem.

The Flexibility of Greater Amounts of Good

In evaluating the claim that G exists, Russell highlights an important question that deserves attention: What are the bounds of free will upon G in relation to greater amounts of good? In other words, does free will impose a restriction upon G that could justifiably prevent acts of goodness? Russell challenges theists by proposing that the good of free will is flexible, that there exist instances of intense evil (e.g., Sally's murder) in which G's violation of free will would not significantly disrupt the amount of good present in this world.

Russell identifies free will as being the primary reason theists have for believing that G would allow someone like Sally to be a victim of intense evil.

---

8. Russell, "Defenseless," 198.
9. Russell, "Moral Relativism," 448.
10. Russell, "Rock Bottom," 98.

In short, free will possesses such a high caliber of goodness that its violation would be worse than allowing the evil to happen. So, either Sally is saved by G, which would violate free will, or she is condemned, which is unconscionable. Russell states, "Even if our world is better than a world without significant freedom, I do not believe those are the only two alternatives. That is because it does not follow that God should intervene to prevent all very bad things from happening if he should intervene to prevent some."[11] Here, Russell contends that the overriding of someone's free will in one case would only significantly harm free will as a whole if it required that free will should be dominated in all, or most, cases. For Russell, the worth and dignity of people are important moral concepts,[12] so a good God could not allow evil, such as Sally's, to occur, even if that meant that the only way to prevent such things from happening would be to override free will. Therefore, Russell finds himself in the position of needing to defend the argument that violating free will is not a slippery slope to a significant loss of free will.

Before delineating Russell's anti-slippery slope (i.e., flexibility of free will) argument, it is helpful to consider Russell's estimation of duties as he is asserting that G, should he exist, had a duty to help Sally. In defining duty in terms of wrongness, Russell states, "A person has a duty to something if it is not wrong of him to do it and wrong of him to fail to do it."[13] Of course, for Sally the doing would involve the overriding of free will of at least one person involved in the incident. For Russell, the good of helping an innocent like Sally creates a duty for someone, like G, who has it in their power to help her. Therefore, G had a duty to help Sally, and, from Russell's perspective, Sally was not helped which means G failed in his duties. After all, as Russell states, "a world with one less instance of a brutal beating, rape and murder of a little girl is morally better than one with such an instance."[14] The need of the innocent combined with duty borne from ability and opportunity conjoin to form Russell's belief that it would have been better, on the whole, if free will should have been violated so that Sally could have been spared her fate. It is with this sense of moral fortitude that Russell embarks upon his quest to show that if this had happened the good of free will would not have been endangered.

Russell succinctly gives his position on intense evils, such as Sally's, when he states, "Neither the violation of the laws of nature nor the interference with people's freedom that would be required would be so great as to

---

11. Russell, "Persistent Problem of Evil," 128.
12. Russell, "On the Relative Strictness," 96.
13. Russell, "Epistemic and Moral Duty," 34.
14. Russell, "Defenseless," 201.

justify God's failing to intervene."[15] Interestingly, in context, Russell does not prove this assertion of the greater good of violating natural laws and free will; he assumes it as common sense. Perhaps the greatest question that arises from Russell's stance is the slippery slope argument Russell assumes is not an issue. Where does the buck stop? At what point does interfering with natural laws and free will result in a significant disruption of the good? The reason that this statement appears to be assumed rather than "proven" resides in Russell's contention that the line of demarcation for justified violations of free will can be known intuitively. In order to demonstrate this claim, Russell puts forth a thought experiment involving actions driven toward the good but which have no empirically clear boundaries.

Consider a town that has a concern for drunk drivers. As is common in the United States, police officers are on high alert for drunk drivers around holiday times and on weekend evenings. Due to their concerns, the police set up checkpoints where they stop drivers to see if they are intoxicated. Taking action to make sure that irresponsible drivers are not a mortal danger to others qualifies as a good deed. However, a balance needs to be maintained. Stop too few drivers and the chances of a drunk driver continuing on the road increase; stop too many drivers and there could be riots from angry law-abiding citizens trying to carry on with their lives. At what point does this police activity infringe upon the populous in a negative way? Russell contends that the answer to this question cannot be clearly known, although there can be a sense of it. Russell says the example of the police checks are similar to how G should act in cases of intense evil. Russell states, "Similarly, we can be justified in believing that if God exists, he would reduce by at least one instance the terrible suffering there is, since there is no reason to think that doing that would have awful results and good reason to think it would have a very good effect."[16] The police officers may not have an exact number in mind for how many people to pull over, but they can have a sense of the need, or lack thereof, for more traffic stops. Russell's contention that G's intervening in human affairs likewise bears a sense of not/enough is a natural extension of his views on evidence and background knowledge informing justification. Surely, if one has the sense that there would be no significant loss of good resulting from the impeding of free will (and how could one little girl break the balance) then based on the evidence of the crime and the observer's background knowledge, Russell concludes that G is not justified in allowing the intense evil to take place. But, at what point will the non-theist stop saying "just one more" instance could be stopped?

15. Russell, "Defenseless," 201.
16. Russell, "Defenseless," 202.

In answer to that question, Russell states, "We would think that until we came to a point where it was doubtful whether important goods would be lost, or significant evils produced, if more evils were prevented, that is, until it seemed a relevant threshold were being approached."[17] Here again is seen evidence with background being used to justify a belief. For Russell, the evidence of Sally's murder combines with the vastness of the world (i.e., how could G's intervention in this one instance impact the whole of reality) and the duty one has to do good points to an abductive case against theism. Russell does admit that there is a threshold, a "freedom threshold," that if breached G would be significantly harming the greater amount of good by overriding free will.[18] However, as is clear from the traffic example, Russell believes that such a threshold would be intuitively known, and in the absence of evidence to the contrary it should be assumed that the threshold has not yet been reached.

The abductive nature of Russell's argument can be seen in his conclusions regarding G's moral obligation to stop one more instance of evil, such as Sally's. Russell states, "Hence, any hypothesis that implied that this was not nearly certain would be improbable on what we know. And if an hypothesis is improbable on what we know, it cannot serve as an adequate defense of theism."[19] Given moral duties, G's abilities, the tragedy of Sally's murder, and the seemingly small impact on the greater good that intervening would entail, Russell concludes that Sally's murder constitutes as evidence that abductively argues against the existence of G. However, there is at least one more argument against this conclusion that Russell anticipates the theist to make. For Russell, the next best argument theists have in justifying G's inactivity in Sally's murder is that of soul making.

Soul-making theodicies attempt to explain instances of instance evil by highlighting fallen humanity's need for spiritual growth. Growth can be a painful process, and in the midst of suffering one comes face-to-face with one's inadequacies. This results in the opportunity to turn to G for spiritual healing/growth. Therefore, G could be justified in allowing intense evil to happen if the victim, or perhaps those otherwise involved with or observing the incident, is presented an opportunity for making a spiritual investment toward eternity. In response to soul-making theodicies, Russell states, "No one would give up striving to perfect himself just because someone like the little girl in Flint was saved. People are not encouraged to make themselves better because they have observed what seems to be a case of gratuitous

---

17. Russell, "Defenseless," 202.
18. Russell and Wykstra, "'Inductive' Argument from Evil: A Dialogue," 141.
19. Russell, "Defenseless," 203.

suffering, nor discouraged form perfecting themselves if some such suffering is prevented."[20] Russell makes a big assumption in claiming that no good could come out of Sally's murder, but he does have a point. Contra Russell, there does seem to be a possibility for someone to have gained a valuable spiritual lesson here for people's actions can always serve as inspiration/motivation toward right thought (even if that inspiration is borne out of repulsion at someone else's behavior). However, possibility does not equate to probability. Though possibility for spiritual growth is present difficultly arises in seeing how that possibility is greater than the suffering endured by Sally. Admittedly, answers to the soul-making presence in Sally's case may require information beyond human ken, therefore the possibility exists that soul-making is the reason G allowed Sally's murder, but aside from an *a priori* belief in the primacy of soul-making theodicies it is difficult to see how the good of soul-making could outweigh the evil experienced by Sally.

While the potential spiritual benefits outlined in soul-making theodicies do exist, there is an issue with its emphasis. The existence of spiritual growth in the midst of trials does not necessitate accepting that benefit as a primary intension of the design of the universe. Fail-safes are built into designs on a regular basis, and there is no good reason to assume that G is incapable of designing this world with a fail-safe as well. Soul-making could be just such a fail-safe; when humans go wrong there still exists opportunity for spiritual growth. However, to identify soul-making as a primary design feature is to needlessly attribute a necessity of intense evil to G's designs, especially if there are other explanations that can account for suffering in a manner that does not place G in a position of requiring such evils for spiritual growth. It is the contention here that free will defenses, such as the Free System Corollary, provide just such an explanation. Although this author does not agree with Russell's conclusions that there can be no justifiable spiritual growth in Sally's death, there is agreement that soul-making is not an abductively powerful argument.

It is Russell's position that evidence and background knowledge give justification to the belief in the nonexistence of G. G, should he exist, would have had the means and opportunity to aid Sally. Therefore, Russell believes he is justified in asserting that G must not exist. So confident is Russell in his conclusions that G could have intervene in this one instance without significantly harming good that he states, "Van Inwagen has no adequate response to someone who says that, if God exists, he would be obligated to reduce *to some extent* the level of terrible suffering that exists

---

20. Russell, "Persistent Problem of Evil," 128–29.

in the actual world."[21] Van Inwagen, a theist, not only hears Russell's charge he is prepared to answer it as well. Central to van Inwagen's response is the concept of the good of regularity and how this defeats the call for just one more intervention by G.

Peter van Inwagen

Moral Lines in the Sand

Peter van Inwagen, despite Russell's aforementioned charge that he does not possess an adequate response to the levels of intense evil in this world, is prepared to take on Russell's argument that G could/should have reduced the intense evil in this world by at least one more instance. Of course, having a response qualitatively is not the same as having an "adequate" response, but van Inwagen offers some thought experiments which emphasize the good of regularity which, at the very least, are thought provoking and may even be adequate. Van Inwagen responds to these sorts of charges by pushing the concept of "just one more" to its logical ends.

In responding to non-theistic arguments that highlight the long agonizing death of a fawn in forest fire (which is a common example that will be discussed more thoroughly in chapter 9), van Inwagen offers a thought experiment involving refugees from Atlantis. As the experiment goes, only one boat remains that can take the last citizens of Atlantis to safety. Time only allows for one more trip. One thousand men remain (women and children having already been evacuated) and the boat is capable of holding many people. However, for every person who boards the boat the odds of the boat reaching safety decreases by .1%. Clearly, decreasing the odds by .1% is not a significant impediment to safety in and of itself. However, if 999 people board the boat the odds of a safe journey decrease by 99.9%. Surely, .1% odds of survival are not good. The question, then, is at what point does the level of acceptable risk lower to a point of endangerment? Van Inwagen argues that G is in a similar situation when he states, "If He [G] is to preserve the lawlike regularity of the world there must come a point at which He will refrain from saving a fawn (or whatever) even though performing this act of mercy would not significantly decrease the lawlike regularity of the world. The 'must' is the must of logical necessity, which constrains even an omnipotent being."[22] An action taken alone may amount to little in the events of the world. Saving one person with a .1% chance of failure seems like such a low risk that any

21. Russell, "Defenseless," 201.
22. Van Inwagen, "Reflections," 235.

morally responsible person should be willing to help. However, actions do not exist in a vacuum. To take a single action and attempt to compare it to the entirety of existence, without considering how that action relates to the other actions that make up that world, is to distort reality. Taken as a whole, the great number of evils that exist constitute a situation similar to that of the Atlantis refugees. There is a point at which helping will harm the whole. However, there is difficulty in identifying the point of no return, but it would seem clear that such a point must exist.

Another thought experiment by van Inwagen reinforces the notion that insignificant alterations can eventually have significant results. Van Inwagen describes an inmate known as Blodgett. Blodgett, who is to be in prison for a long time, appeals for a one-day early release. After all, what is one day compared to the rest of his sentence? However, if the appeal is granted what is to stop Blodgett from repeating the argument and getting off another day early? While a single day reduction in sentence may not seem like much if there is no line, no limit, no set boundary of acceptability, Blodgett could reduce his sentence to a point of absurdity. In reference to this, van Inwagen states, "This result is, I take it, a *reductio ad absurdum* of the moral principle. As the practical wisdom has it (but this is no compromise between practical considerations and strict morality; this *is* strict morality), 'You have to draw a line somewhere.' And this mean an *arbitrary* line. The principle fails precisely *because* it forbids the drawing of morally arbitrary lines."[23] The "principle" referred to here is the idea that G would be morally required to cause at least one more instance of intense evil from occurring. In arguing against this principle with the example of Blodgett, and the Atlantis refugees, van Inwagen asserts that arbitrary moral lines are needed. Admittedly, there exists some similarity between van Inwagen's thought experiments here and Russell's example of traffic stops. Both take into consideration the idea that there are goods that could be done and that no one refugee, day off, or stopped car is a significant impediment to greater amounts of good. However, they both also recognize that there is a point where the boat will capsize, an inmate will serve no time, and riots could ensue. Additionally, both van Inwagen and Russell admit that there is a cutoff point, a line in the sand, where just one more will violate the good being done. What then is the difference between van Inwagen (theist) and Russell (non-theist)? The answer resides in background knowledge.

Central to a distinction between Russell and van Inwagen in terms of moral lines in the sand is their perspectives on background knowledge. Russell maintains a very egocentric perspective of background knowledge.

---

23. Van Inwagen, "Local Argument from Evil," 102.

The truth of a situation remains accountable to his own understanding of how things are. This reflects Russell's *a priori* rejection of G. If there is no being possessing a greater background knowledge than his own, Russell feels justified in relying upon his own perceptions. Van Inwagen, on the other hand, attempts to show a defense for how evil can exist with G. Therefore, van Inwagen recognizes that there does exist a being with greater amounts of background knowledge. If G does exist then it is logical to conclude that evils happen because G knows where the arbitrary moral lines are; he knows when acting to stop an instance of intense evil will disrupt the amounts of good in the world. For van Inwagen, regularity constitutes a good of vital importance to human existence and one which should be duly considered when evaluating instances of intense evil.

Regularity and the Expanded Free Will Defense

In order to fully appreciate Peter van Inwagen's response to claims that G is responsible for not interrupting a case of intense suffering one more time than he has, it will be helpful to understand the Expanded Free Will Defense (EFWD) and how it addresses the existence of evil in the world. Specifically, van Inwagen is concerned with what he calls the problem of radical evil,[24] which is what has been referring to in this book as intense evil, evils of a sort that entail suffering that have an initial appearance of having no goodly benefit, and how those evils can coexist with G. It is van Inwagen's understanding of the interaction/relationship between radical/intense evils and the good of regularity that are foundational to his EFWD.

Van Inwagen understands evidential arguments to rely heavily upon the Hypothesis of Indifference (HI) which he defines as: "Neither the nature nor the condition of sentient beings on earth is the result of benevolent or malevolent actions performed by nonhuman persons."[25] HI is a possible explanation for the existence of the amounts and kinds of evils that are in this world, and while it does not assert that G does not exist it does claim that G is not needed for a proper explanation to be had for the existence of intense evils.[26] Therefore, if theism is true it will be able to provide a more convincing explanation for the coexistence of intense evils with G. Van Inwagen notes that non-theists taking this line of argument find that HI is much more convincing than theism due to the belief that there cannot exist a theodicy which fully takes seriously G and the amounts and kinds of

24. Van Inwagen, "Problem of Evil and the Argument from Evil," 14.
25. Van Inwagen, "Problem of Evil, the Problem of Air," 153.
26. A more detailed description/analysis of HI will be given in the next chapter.

evils that exist.[27] The non-theist embracing this argument then concludes that theism is irrational given human ken.[28]

Van Inwagen chooses to counter HI through a defense which asserts that the assumption of theism yields no prima facie grounds for expecting a pattern of suffering different from that which is observed in this world.[29] Against the temptation to hold a defense in too high a regard van Inwagen states, "The theist should not assume that there is a single reason or a tightly interrelated set of reasons for the suffering of all sentient creatures." Here, van Inwagen is simultaneously asserting that there is a defense, a possible explanation for the state of the world, and that the defense is not intended to be the final answer for why the world operates as it does. Van Inwagen is showing humility in recognizing that his EFWD, which he believes answers non-theistic arguments from evil, is not necessarily a completely accurate picture of reality. Rather, it is a possible explanation that reasserts the compatibility of G with evil in this world. Toward that end, van Inwagen looks to what he sees to be a fundamental principle of the universe: regularity as a good.

In setting up his EFWD, van Inwagen notes that this present world is the result of a very tightly structured process;[30] there exists a regular set of laws and conditions which has allowed for life and the universe to take the shape that it has. Van Inwagen, being a theistic evolutionist, emphasizes the good of regularity as it helps to explain the pain and suffering involved with the evolutionary process. Van Inwagen notes, "A *massively irregular world* is a world in which the laws of nature fail in some massive way."[31] Evolution, as a process requiring the physical laws of the universe to be regular, involves pain and suffering as a means of growth. Part one of the EFWD emphasizes the good of regularity in relation to evolutionary processes. Since pain and suffering are a requirement for evolutionary growth, if this world were highly irregular there would be no growth through evolution, and this relationship between regularity and evolution validates the existence of suffering throughout the course of evolutionary history.[32] Van Inwagen states, "Pain

---

27. Van Inwagen, "Problem of Evil, the Problem of Air," 154.
28. Van Inwagen, "Problem of Evil, the Problem of Air," 155.
29. Van Inwagen, "Problem of Evil, the Problem of Air," 155–56.
30. Van Inwagen, "Problem of Evil, the Problem of Air," 160.
31. Van Inwagen, "Problem of Evil, the Problem of Air," 158. Here, van Inwagen also notes that the miracles of the New Testament would not count as being massively irregular as they are a small anomaly in a large history of regularity.
32. Van Inwagen, "Problem of Evil, the Problem of Air," 159–60. Van Inwagen takes the truth of evolution as a given along with the good of regularity. However, even if one does not subscribe to theistic evolution van Inwagen's observations about regularity as a good are still of great value.

is an indispensable component of the evolutionary process after organisms have reached a certain stage of complexity. And, for all we know, the amount of pain that organisms have experienced in the actual world, or some amount morally equivalent to that amount, is necessary to the natural evolution of conscious animals."[33] Given evolution, there exists every reason to suspect that sentient creatures could not exist without first having a history of pain and suffering, and this leads to the second part of the EFWD.

As has been discussed in chapter 2, free will of humanity allows for moral choices to be made. Without the ability for such choice there would be no choosing toward right action. Therefore, without the ability to choose there would be a decreased likelihood of good in the world. Van Inwagen echoes this concept in the second part of his EFWD when he states, "Some important intrinsic or extrinsic good depends on the existence of higher-level sentient creatures; this good is of sufficient magnitude that it outweighs the patterns of suffering."[34] The potential for the existence of good in the world is only possible as a result of the existence of higher reasoning which results in the ability to make moral choices. Since a human evolving directly from a worm is impossible the regular pattern of pain and suffering in the evolutionary process must be continued if higher-level sentient creatures are to become a reality.[35] Once again, this process of evolution, resulting in free will creatures able to make moral choices, can only happen if this world is highly regular. This makes regularity a good since it allows for consistent development. Herein lies the third part of the EFWD. Van Inwagen states, "Being massively irregular is a defect in a world."[36] Van Inwagen contends that a world that is massively irregular would be as bad as all of the suffering recorded in this world.[37]

Whereas Alvin Plantinga argued for the logical coexistence of G and evil in his Free Will Defense, but merely ascribed natural evils to nonhuman entities, van Inwagen argues in his Expanded Free Will Defense that the natural evils that exist are a result of the good of regularity. The pain and suffering of evolution is needed for the development of high-level sentient creatures, whose existence is needed for the goods that can come from choice. Therefore, a world that is massively irregular is not good as sentient creatures would not exist and neither would the greater amounts of good. The world is regular, and regularity allows for consistency of moral actions.

---

33. Van Inwagen, "Problem of Evil, the Problem of Air," 160.
34. Van Inwagen, "Problem of Evil, the Problem of Air," 160.
35. Van Inwagen, "Problem of Evil, the Problem of Air," 161.
36. Van Inwagen, "Problem of Evil, the Problem of Air," 161.
37. Van Inwagen, "Problem of Evil, the Problem of Air," 161.

Part and parcel with moral actions and regularity, van Inwagen explains the pain and suffering in this world as being a result of the Fall of Man. He argues that before the fall G protected Adam and Eve from natural disasters, but after the fall that protection was removed. This is a consequence of moral actions. Therefore, G would be deceiving humanity if he were to always come to the rescue. Van Inwagen states, "If He [G] always saved people about to be destroyed by a chance encounter with a violent phenomenon of nature, He would engender an illusion with the following propositional content: It is possible for human beings to live apart from God and not be subject to destruction by chance."[38] Therefore, if G intervened in every case of natural evil he would become a deceiver. This applies to cases of moral evil as well since humanity now lives with the consequences of a damaged relationship with G. The reference to the fall is part of van Inwagen's narrative which shows how the EFWD can be consistent with theistic belief. Being a defense, the EFWD does not claim to give an account for every instance of intense evil, but it does claim to be able to tell a story which helps to explain the existence of the amounts and kinds of evils in this world. Van Inwagen is not unaware of the potential for criticisms of his EFWD, and one which he gives particular attention to is "difficulty."

Despite the eloquence of the FWD and the EFWD, theists can still find themselves in the position of having to account for difficult evidence regarding G and evil. The existence of such difficulties, such as the case of Sally, occur despite sound defenses to theistically account for the POE. However, van Inwagen acknowledges that theists are capable of acknowledging such difficulties even when they are not sure what to say as a response, but even still this is not evidence against theism. Van Inwagen states, "[Saying that difficulties are a defeater for theism] is really a recipe for rejecting just about any interesting theory. Just about any interesting theory is faced with phenomenon that make the advocates of the theory a bit uncomfortable."[39] Be that as it may, the existence of difficulties with theories does not necessarily help the theist's case against HI. Van Inwagen concedes that patterns of suffering do not pose a difficulty for HI like they do for theism, but the good of regularity tempers the objection of difficulty rendering it unusable as evidence against theism in favor of HI.[40] Van Inwagen concludes, "It follows that the evidential argument from evil fails, for it is essential to the evidential argument that those patterns of suffering be evidence that favors HI over

---

38. Van Inwagen, "Magnitude, Duration, and Distribution of Evil," 181.
39. Van Inwagen, "Problem of Evil, the Problem of Air," 169.
40. Van Inwagen, "Problem of Evil, the Problem of Air," 170–71.

theism."⁴¹ The EFWD, with its emphasis on the good of regularity, makes a striking defense against evidentialist arguments. Indeed, van Inwagen seems to be successful in his attempt to give a defense that upholds theism in the face of evidentialist arguments that rely upon HI. However, does the EFWD speak to the entirety of evidentialist arguments?

There is an abductive element to evidential arguments from evil. The EFWD logically shows how the good of regularity can account for the amounts and kinds of evils that are in this world, but does it also account for the abductive aspect of such arguments? Defenses that show a logical compatibility between G and intense evil are valuable, for the logical aspect of evidential arguments need to be addressed. However, in the end non-theists are still able to say, "Yes, regularity can account for G and evil, but based on what I *know* the existence of G in the face of this evil still does not seem likely." It would seem that ample room still exists for non-theists to stake an abductive claim to the POE. While it is true that it is possible for anyone to continue to claim "this seems right" regardless of the information/argumentation provided, the difficulties that still exist with theistic defenses provide a comfortable amount room for non-theistic abductions to be made. The Free System Corollary, as will be discussed in chapter 8, will discuss how the good of regularity can be used in an abductive sense, regardless of one's evolutionary beliefs. Admittedly, addressing the abductive aspect of evidential arguments was not the focus of van Inwagen's work. His work offers a helpful foundation for developing a defense that can speak to the abductive aspect of evidential arguments from evil.

In summarizing the intent behind the EFWD, van Inwagen states, "Theist does not put forward the expanded free-will defense as a theodicy, as a statement of the real truth of the matter concerning the co-presence of God and evil in the world. Nor would I, if I told it. Theist contends only, *I* contend only, that the story is—given that God exists—true for all anyone knows."⁴² Van Inwagen's EFWD highlights the good of regularity in relation to the development of humanity. In short, the regularity of the universe is needed in order for higher-level sentient creatures to evolve and bring about acts of goodness. The intent of van Inwagen was to create a defense against evidential arguments from evil that would assert the nonexistence of G based on the background knowledge of evil in this world. As a result, the EFWD offers a more robust accounting of natural evil than the FWD. What is more, van Inwagen's work with regularity provides and answer to Bruce Russell's claim that G, should he exist, would be

41. Van Inwagen, "Problem of Evil, the Problem of Air," 171.
42. Van Inwagen, "Global Argument Continued," 92.

morally obligated to reduce the amount of intense evil in this world by at least one more instance.

Conclusions

Following a discussion on the logical coexistence of G and evil with Plantinga's FWD, this chapter has focused on the non-theistic claim by Bruce Russell that logical compatibility does not equate to reality. Russell asserts that instances of intense evil, such as the death of Sally, constitute as evidence that conjoins with background knowledge to form an argument against the existence of G. Since humanity has a sense of the good of a situation, and since Russell can see no good in allowing Sally's death, Russell concludes that G should have stopped this intense evil from happening. The power of G makes G morally responsible as an onlooker for Sally's fate. Therefore, Russell concludes that G must not exist, for surely G could have stopped at least one more instance of intense evil without significantly decreasing the amount of good in the world.

Van Inwagen counters Russell's claims by showing that arbitrary lines of morality must exist otherwise G would be obligated to intervene in all cases which would override free will. Russell too agrees that such lines exist, but he asserts that the location of those lines can be known by humanity. Van Inwagen, having no *a priori* belief in the nonexistence of G, argues for the logical existence of arbitrary moral lines and that while G would know where those lines are humanity may not. Central to van Inwagen's Expanded Free Will Defense is the concept of regularity as a good. Regularity allows for evolutionary development (which is required for higher level beings who can choose good actions), and a significantly irregular world would be an evil world. Since the world is regular it is logical that G would not stop all instances of intense/radical evil.

Van Inwagen's purpose was to counteract arguments such as Russell's "just one more" intervention by G and the Hypothesis of Indifference (the claim that nonhuman entities are not required to explain the amount and kinds of evils in this world). The EFWD levels the playing field in that it takes the teeth out of HI. In light of the EFWD, HI no longer is logically more probable, but it is the contention here that van Inwagen's work does not address the entirety of non-theistic arguments such as Russell's and HI. For, while van Inwagen, and Plantinga as seen in the previous chapter, addresses the logical existence of G and evil there still exists an abductive quality to non-theistic arguments that remains unchecked. The claim that just one more instance of evil being thwarted would not significantly diminish the good and the claim that nonhuman forces are not needed for an explanation of evils retain a sense of probability. As was mentioned in the previous section, van Inwagen does not claim that the EFWD proves theism over HI; it only claims to remove HI from a stronger position to one which is more or less on the level with theism. Therefore, the seeming of abductive thought still retains strength, for all else being equal people will believe what seems most probable based on what they know. This book will build upon the theistic work being discussed here to make an abductive case for theism in light of intense evil. First, however, a more detailed discussion of HI and alternative theistic responses to it will be discussed.

6

Inculpable Nonbelief

Following discussions on the Free Will Defense, Expanded Free Will Defense, and the non-theistic arguments from evil that they address, this discussion now turns toward a non-theistic account of intense evils with agnostic, rather than atheistic, origins. Agnostic philosopher Paul Draper proposes an accounting for the reality of evils through a Hypothesis of Indifference (HI) which neither affirms or denies the existence of God. Furthermore, Draper contends that such a "neutral"[1] position is supported by the coexistence of pain and pleasure in this world. In considering Draper's arguments, it is fitting to also examine those of theist Daniel Howard-Snyder. Like Draper, Howard-Snyder attempts to take seriously the differences between inscrutable and pointless evils and in so doing he offers a defense of inculpable non-belief. This idea of inculpable non-belief comes as a result of the kinds of observations, which both Draper and Howard-Snyder make, of the seeming absence of God in times of crisis.

Paul Draper

The Hypothesis of Indifference

Although popular criticisms of agnostic positions view agnostics as being unable to make up their minds, Paul Draper does not arrive at his "neutral" position lightly. Indeed, for Draper, his position of indifference has little to do with indecisiveness and much to do with attempting to weigh all evidences for theism and naturalism as fairly as possible. Draper's argumentation focuses on one concept: what should be expected. By making observations about reality and evaluating those observations in light

---

1. Agnosticism is, of course, antithetical to theistic belief and is therefore not neutral. However, "neutral" here refers to the intent of neutrality, even if the position is not neutral in actuality.

of theism/naturalism, Draper highlights strengths and weaknesses of both worldviews. It is this evaluation of theism/naturalism that leads Draper to a position of indifference regarding the existence of a deity.

In considering a position of indifference, and one's justification for such belief, Draper notes that the agnostic is confident that either naturalism or theism is true but lacks confidence in determining which position is the correct answer for reality. Draper states, "One possible basis for such agnosticism is that naturalism and theism each faces at least one serious evidential problem when compared to the other: a problem of moral agency in the case of naturalism and a problem of evil in the case of theism."[2] Moral agency and the POE, both of which are realities of this world, coexist but, as far as Draper is concerned, naturalism and theism (Draper's use of the terms "naturalism" and "theism" align with their use in this book)[3] are ill equipped to explain the existence of both in an equally plausible manner. Draper states, "There are reasons on theism that are not available on naturalism to expect the existence of moral agents. For example, the fact that such beings have a distinctive sort of dignity or worth does not raise the probability of their existing on the assumption that naturalism is true, but it does raise the probability of their existing on theism."[4] Altruistic behavior, sanctity of life, the ideal that all should live with dignity are concepts that can be explained by naturalism, but the value of Draper's observation entails the recognition that theism provides a more probable accounting for these traits in human life than does naturalism. Draper states, "Moral agency requires moral responsibility. If such responsibility is incompatible with determinism . . . then moral agency is much more likely on theism than on naturalism because mental substances are needed to make sense of agent causation and the existence of such substances is much more likely on theism than on naturalism."[5] Draper's conclusions regarding the need of moral agency for a mental capability that is more probable on theism than naturalism would seem to be a boon for theism. Indeed, Draper's comments here will be of value in chapter 8, but the manner in which moral agency manifests in this world gives Draper evidence for naturalism. Specifically, the reality of embodiment (e.g., physicality) is argued to be evidence for naturalism. Draper states, "Of course, given that there are moral agents, the fact that they are embodied is more probable on naturalism than on theism,

---

2. Draper, "Cosmic Fine-Tuning," 311.
3. Draper, "Cosmic Fine-Tuning," 313.
4. Draper, "Cosmic Fine-Tuning," 313.
5. Draper, "Cosmic Fine-Tuning," 313.

but not much more probable."[6] Thus far, it would seem that Draper is making a case for theism over naturalism, and from the perspective of moral agency and physical reality Draper does admit that the probability for truth resides with theism.[7] However, moral agency points not only toward good action but evil as well, and Draper contends that considerations of the POE show a higher probability for the truth of naturalism.

Given theism, one would expect there to be a moral order and the being living in that world to have the ability to make moral choices. Given naturalism, one would expect there to be a cause and effect relationship between the physical being and objects in that world. Both naturalism and theism can account for moral agency and physicality, but on the whole theism explains the existence of both more satisfactorily than naturalism. However, the existence of intense evil in this world causes problems for theism and gives hope to naturalism. Draper states, "It is a known fact that many sentient beings never flourish, many others flourish only briefly, and many languish for extended periods of time. . . . Theism is not intrinsically more probable than naturalism."[8] Here, Draper is arguing that the probability of the amounts and kinds of evils in this world (E^*) is more probable on naturalism than on theism: $Pr(E^*/N) > Pr(E^*/T)$.[9] Though this would appear to be a victory for naturalism in Draper's estimation this "victory" equates to a leveling of the odds of truth: naturalism is now as likely as theism all things considered. However, Draper issues a warning to not take this argument for the probability of naturalism beyond its reasonable limits.

Despite the great number of instances of intense evil in this world, Draper cautions naturalists to refrain from over estimating their observations. In offering a critique of Rowe's use of instances of evil, Draper states, "It is one thing to infer from the fact that the pit bulls I have encountered are vicious that the next pit bull I see will be vicious, but quite another to infer that ALL pit bulls are vicious. The latter conclusion is much more likely to turn out to be false. . . . So it requires much stronger evidence than the former conclusion to render it probable."[10] In the case of pit bulls, if one pit bull in the world is calm the verdict regarding pit bulls crumbles. Keep in mind, Draper is not concerned with proving the absolute truth of theism nor of naturalism. As was discussed above, he makes strong arguments for both. As a result of the evidence for theism and naturalism, Draper is in tension

6. Draper, "Cosmic Fine-Tuning," 313–14.
7. Draper, "Cosmic Fine-Tuning," 314.
8. Draper, "Cosmic Fine-Tuning," 315.
9. Draper, "Cosmic Fine-Tuning," 315.
10. Draper, "Probabilistic Arguments from Evil," 313.

between evidences for naturalism (the most compelling of which belong to the POE) and the evidences for theism (the most compelling of which belong to moral agency). In order to resolve this tension, Draper proposes a hypothesis that, on his view, is more probable than both theism and naturalism: the Hypothesis of Indifference (HI).

Draper's HI comes as a result of his study and admiration for David Hume's Indifference Hypothesis. Because of the strong ontological commitments that come with theism, Draper views theism as requiring much more evidence to prove its truth. Herein resides the appeal of Hume's Indifference Hypothesis. Draper states, "The Indifference Hypothesis is clearly an alternative hypothesis to G ... G is a very specific supernaturalist hypothesis with strong ontological commitments ... the Indifference Hypothesis is consistent with naturalism as well as with many supernaturalist hypotheses and its ontological commitments are much weaker than G's."[11] As with the case of the vicious pit bulls, Draper finds the concept of indifference to be more probable than a definitive stance, one way or another, in regards to theism and naturalism. He insists that this conclusion is obviously not ad hoc as the evidence for and against theism/naturalism is inconclusive.[12]

Draper refers to his revision/refinement of Hume's Indifference Hypothesis as the Hypothesis of Indifference (HI). He defines HI as follows: "HI: neither the nature nor the condition of sentient beings on earth is the result of benevolent or malevolent actions performed by nonhuman persons."[13] As was discussed above, Draper recognizes that moral agency is more probable on theism, naturalism barely accounts for the embodiment of moral agents more than theism, and he views the POE to be more probable on naturalism, which brings theism and naturalism to an equal probability. Coinciding with the POE is the existence of pain and pleasure which Draper views as causing trouble for theism, for pain and pleasure have moral value.[14] Perhaps Draper pays special attention to theism in this regard for the same reason he is unwilling to say that all pit bulls are vicious: naturalism in and of itself demands too much by way of its rejection of the possibility of theism. HI, on the other hand, does not seek to denounce theism but rather to show that HI is more probable. Specifically, it is in Draper's discussions of pain and pleasure that HI attempts to gain ground for naturalism on theism's explanatory power of moral agency thereby bringing balance to naturalism and theism and resulting in a justified agnosticism.

11. Draper, "Probabilistic Arguments from Evil," 316.
12. Draper, "Probabilistic Arguments from Evil," 316.
13. Draper, "Pain and Pleasure" (1996), 13.
14. Draper, "Probabilistic Arguments from Evil," 317.

Biologically Gratuitous Pain

Draper summarizes the intent behind his evaluation of the POE when he states, "One cannot determine what facts about evil theism needs to explain or how well it needs to explain them without considering alternatives to theism."[15] The POE is only truly a problem for theism if there exists an alternative hypothesis of reality that can more probably account for the amounts and kinds of evils and pleasures in this world. Where "O" represents observations of pleasure and pain (any kind of physical or mental suffering) in humans and animals,[16] Draper sets out to show that HI presents a more compelling explanation for the state of O as opposed to its theistic rivals.

Draper takes no issue with the logical coexistence of G and evil, for he recognizes that G could not truly create beings with free will and make it so that they will never perform morally wrong actions.[17] What vexes Draper is the necessity of pain and suffering in routine life. Draper notes that free will explains why morally wrong actions occur in theism, but that does not explain why pain exists as it does. In reference to this observation of free will, Draper states, "Notice that, so far, we have no explanation of the existence of pain. For there are morally right actions and morally wrong actions that do not entail the existence of pain. Wrong actions of this sort include some instances of breaking promises, killing, attempting to cause pain, and depriving someone of pleasure. So, God could have given humans freedom* without permitting pain."[18] Here, Draper begins laying the foundation for an argument that takes aim at theistic free will defenses that argue pain and suffering exist because of the potential for morally wrong choices. If the free will theistic arguments are correct, the good of free will allows for and justifies O. However, Draper notes that there are amounts and kinds of morally wrong actions that do not necessarily entail pain.

Consider Draper's assertion that depriving someone of pleasure is a morally wrong act that does not necessitate pain. Jane knows that Janet desires a promotion at work. Jane also knows that Janet is content with her current position but thinks that the promotion might improve the quality of her life even more than it currently is. In an act of selfishness, Jane removes Janet's application from the applicant folder and shreds it. No one except Jane knows this has occurred. Jane has committed a morally wrong act (selfishness, vandalism, and betrayal of trust, to name a few moral offences). She

---

15. Draper, "Pain and Pleasure" (1989), 332.
16. Draper, "Pain and Pleasure" (1989), 333–34.
17. Draper, "Pain and Pleasure" (1989), 341.
18. Draper, "Pain and Pleasure" (1989), 341.

has deprived Janet of pleasure, but due to her current position and her ignorance, Janet suffers no pain as a result of this immoral act. With his claim that morally wrong actions do not necessarily entail pain Draper opens the door for questioning the usefulness of pain reported by O.

It is Draper's contention that HI explains O better than theism,[19] and his reasoning for this conclusion is what he calls "biologically gratuitous" pain, a concept that takes root in the unnecessary relationship between pain and morally wrong actions. If pain is not a necessary component of free will, and if it can be shown that there exists pain that serves no moral good, then theism will need to account for why it is that G would allow such gratuitous pain to exist. Draper states, "There is also much pain and pleasure in our world that is not biologically useful: for instance ... pain resulting from burns that ultimately prove fatal. (I will sometimes call this kind of pain and pleasure 'biologically gratuitous.')"[20] Draper is not arguing that sensations of pain have no use. Indeed, if one is starting to burn, pain can alert one to step away from a fire, thereby saving someone's life. What Draper does argue is that any pain beyond usefulness becomes gratuitous. Not only does Draper assert that biologically gratuitous pain is incompatible with G, he concludes that since pain does not necessarily follow from moral wrongness G has no morally justifiable reasons for allowing the balance of pain and pleasure observed in O.[21]

Theism has the task of explaining O in terms that explain why it is that G would allow O to happen, all while maintaining the goodness of G; HI has comparatively less to defend. If there are no supernatural beings that need to be accounted for, no need arises for defending O. O becomes a recognized state of reality that happens to make theism less probable. This does not harm theism to the point of favoring naturalism, however. Rather, Draper argues that O, conjoined with all other evidences (including the existence of free will), results in a reality better explained by HI than by theism or naturalism. Draper states, "Ambiguous evidence provides justification for agnosticism rather than for theistic leaping or atheistic tipping."[22] For Draper, theism equates to wishful thinking and naturalism to pessimism. Perhaps it would be fair to summarize his views on theism as being a glass half full and naturalism as being half empty. HI, on the other hand, would simply be a glass containing water. Although Draper does make a compelling argument

---

19. Draper, "Pain and Pleasure," (1996), 14.
20. Draper, "Pain and Pleasure," (1996), 16.
21. Draper, "Pain and Pleasure," (1996), 17.
22. Draper, "Seeking but not Believing," 198.

for agnosticism, it assumes to much in its evaluation of the relationship between pain and morality.

To sum Draper's argument on pain and morality: since immoral actions can exist without pain any pain that exists without use is gratuitous and serves as evidence against theism. Someone burning alive in a fire experiences pain, but the pain they experience no longer serves its biological usefulness. The pain becomes gratuitous, which Draper asserts is less likely on theism since G should be able to make a world without gratuitous pain. Two questions come to mind regarding Draper's conclusions on pain. First, is the nonexistence of gratuitous pain compatible with free will? Second, what counts as gratuitous? Toward the first question, Draper is essentially asking for a world in which biologically useful pain exists (get your hand out of the fire) but the mechanisms in place for that pain become altered when they no longer serve a purpose. How is the human body to make such a decision? A body does not possess the capability of determining the moral quality of a situation (e.g., is the pain still useful), so G would need to disrupt the nervous systems of a great many creatures on a regular basis. To ask for G to turn on/off human and animal pain receptors when pain becomes gratuitous is to ask G to constantly manipulate his created world in a way that countermands the systems that allow it to function: G created the world with moral agents, and he created those same moral agents (and other creatures) with the ability to know when something has gone wrong on a physical level. However, perhaps he could have given said creatures the ability to turn off their pain receptors. How might people act differently if they could turn off their ability to feel pain on a whim? It is not hard to imagine that with a decreased accountability for self-interest that the behavior of people would be negatively affected by this kind of responsibility. To eliminate the potential for gratuitous pain is to either fundamentally change how the human body operates or to ask G to act in a manner inconsistent with how this world was created. Here, an objection could be raised that it was still within G's power to create a world with less pain than this one, and if G did create such a world then the arguments presented here no longer carry any weight, for G would no longer be acting contrary or humanity would have been created with a suitable demeanor for handling such responsibility. This objection leads to the second question, "What counts as gratuitous?"

The relevance of the question of gratuitousness to Draper's argument resides in a human ability that can be readily observed. People around the world have a great tendency to have a relativistic view of problems. Living in the United States, a middle-class family may feel the burden of the world because they are unable to purchase pizza for their child's dinner tonight. Payday is Monday, maybe next week will be better. Living in Manila, the average family may be wondering where the next meal will come from, let alone if they get to order pizza. The point of the illustration is this: how does one know if pain is gratuitous? Yes, there can be an appearance of uselessness to some pain, but considering that pain does have useful functions how is one to know that the regularity of the operation of this world is a good that justifies seemly gratuitous pain? To take the question one step further, how is it to be known when a balance between pain/pleasure is to be had for the welfare of persons? The possibility exists that for there to be a maximal amount of utility born from pain and a maximal amount of pleasure there needs to be a balance of acceptable pain and how it is that pain receptors work. Living in this world it may appear that gratuitous pain exists, but it is possible that G could have created this world with even more pain being perceived. When someone stands the molecules on the bottom of their feet are feeling the weight of an astronomically large number of molecules baring down on them. Under normal conditions no pain registers in the mind. However, if that same person were sat upon by a number of people equal to the number of molecules pressing on the bottom of the foot that person would definitely feel pain. It is possible that G has created this world with a balance of pain. Furthermore, suppose for a moment that Draper's call for no gratuitous pain were honored by G and G recreated the world with new parameters. Pain still has biological usefulness, but gratuitous pain does not exist, or rather, current understandings of gratuitous pain no longer exists. For, the beings of that world could easily lament the existence of pain and "misidentify" the existence of the pain of a hangnail to be gratuitous once the owner of the hangnail is aware of its existence. In short, Draper's argument assumes a state of human ken that can accurately account for all pain (potential or actual) and determine its worth, and the argument presented here is skeptical of human ken to account for pain fully. Indeed, it is the argument here that skepticism conjoined with the law like regularity of the world finds O to not be troubling for theism. Regardless, Skeptical Theism will be the subject of the next chapter, but there is one more charge by Draper that should be discussed here.

In considering O, Draper concludes that in addition to gratuitous pain there exists an aspect of pain that causes problem for theism. Despite the existence of undue amounts of pain, it follows that G, being perfectly good, would, in the very least, comfort those experiencing gratuitous pain, but experience does not seem to show the presence of G in such situations. Draper states, "Many people do not seem to feel God's comforting presence when tragedy strikes. This fact is much more probable on naturalism than on theism."[23] This

---

23. Draper, "Seeking but Not Believing," 205.

charge that G's absence in times of need is troubling for theism is not unique to Draper. Theist Daniel Howard-Snyder has also observed this phenomenon, and his considerations and conclusions in the matter will prove useful as this discussion moves forward with its answer to the abductive POE.

Daniel Howard-Snyder

Inscrutable Evil

Daniel Howard-Snyder challenges HI on two basic fronts: seeming and inscrutability. Although seeming and inscrutability are not without their similarities, each work together to addresses an important aspect of arguments that make use of HI. Specifically, they refer to assumptions that are made by the proponents of HI regarding one's belief about one's capability to know.

Recently, Howard-Snyder has offered a critique of HI that speaks to seemingness. Though this particular argument is levied at Trent Dougherty, Howard-Snyder explains HI in light of Draper, since he feels that Dougherty does not provide a sufficient explanation of HI. Through his critique, Howard-Snyder emphasizes the inability for seeming to account for knowledge in an absolute sense. For, seeming does not appear to be a property that something can intrinsically have. Howard-Snyder states, "There's a world of difference between saying something of the form 'p seems *to* me to be true' or 'it seems *to me* that p' and saying something of the form 'p seems to be true' or 'it seems that p.' . . . The proposition that the universe is indifferent seems . . . to be true [to me]. But it hardly follows that the proposition has the property of seeming to be true."[24] Here, Howard-Snyder highlights if not the assumption of seeming then the overutilization of seeming in HI. Seeming is subjective. If one person claims that something seems to be true it does not necessarily follow that another person will concur. Now, seemingness is not without weight, and it will play an important role in Howard-Snyder's views on Inculpable Non-Belief, but in this present conversation it is worth noting that seemingness does not necessarily equate to an accurate assessment of a given state of affairs. Elsewhere, Howard-Snyder delineates Draper's understanding of the types of pain that exist (i.e., how pain seems to operate for Draper).

Howard-Snyder summarizes Draper's categorizing of gratuitous pain as being either biological pathological (pain resulting from the failure of an organic system, like with cancer), biologically appropriate (such as when someone burns to death), or biologically useful (pain as a warning of

---

24. Howard-Snyder, "How Not to Render," 3.

harm).[25] As was mentioned in the previous section, Draper believes this is evidence for HI since it works against theism, for surely G could have made a world in which biologically pathological and appropriate pain would not exist. While a brief critique of Draper's position has already been given, Howard-Snyder explores an alternate evaluation of such pain in relation to HI. He notes that Draper reasons that HI best explains the existence of biologically pathological, appropriate, and useful pain, barring any reason to not expect it. What is good for the goose is good for the gander, and Howard-Snyder observes that, barring any reason to not expect it, theism can likewise account for these categories of pain.[26] Howard-Snyder states, "If we are allowed to consider HI-istic stories to assess . . . then we ought to be permitted to consider theistic stories for the same purpose. Otherwise, we stand the chance of judging unfairly, or what's worse, inaccurately [the probability of HI over theism]."[27] Howard-Snyder is asserting that HI seems to be more probable than theism given the story/narrative that explains how one should expect the world to operate if there is no need for the intervention of spiritual beings to account for pain and pleasure in temporal life. However, he also asserts that, given the chance, theism can similarly tell a story/narrative that accounts for the amounts and kinds of evils that are in the world. In short, HI seems to be true because it assumes that there is sufficient knowledge to accurately determine the value/worth of pain. It is Howard-Snyder's contention that such pain only appears to be inscrutable because of a lack of knowledge.

In describing arguments from inscrutable evil, Howard-Snyder defines inscrutability as, "I: We cannot see how any good we know of justifies God in permitting so much horrific evil rather than a lot less."[28] Howard-Snyder takes no issue with the concept that there are evils which appear to have no overriding good behind them,[29] and he likewise believes the truth that if God exists there are reasons that would justify the allowance of such evil/pain.[30] Where Howard-Snyder differs with the argument from inscrutable evil is the move from I to Q, where Q states, "No good justifies God in permitting so much horrific evil rather than a lot less."[31] The move from I to Q is one of seemingness: since it seems that there are inscrutable evils it

---

25. Howard-Snyder, "Theism, the Hypothesis of Indifference," 455.
26. Howard-Snyder, "Theism, the Hypothesis of Indifference," 457.
27. Howard-Snyder, "Theism, the Hypothesis of Indifference," 459.
28. Howard-Snyder, "Argument from Inscrutable Evil," 289.
29. Howard-Snyder, "Argument from Inscrutable Evil," 290.
30. Howard-Snyder, "Argument from Inscrutable Evil," 289.
31. Howard-Snyder, "Argument from Inscrutable Evil," 289.

also seems likely that G would have no justification for allowing said evils. Howard-Snyder recognizes that though a seeming may resonate strongly in the mind of the observer it is a leap in logic to assume the observer possesses all relevant information.

Howard-Snyder illustrates the move from I to Q by utilizing the blue crow thought experiment. He describes looking for blue crows in Washington state, but upon the absence of seeing any blue crows one concludes that blue crows do not exist. In making the non-theists case Howard-Snyder states, "Similarly, we have conducted an appropriate search for goods that would justify god in permitting so much horrific evil rather than a lot less but we have found none."[32] Howard-Snyder's critique of this thought experiment at once recognizes the claim of the non-theist and finds fault in its assumptions. In reply to the blue crow thought experiment he states, "Now, while we have good reason to believe that blue crows are the sorts of things we will see by looking around (without this assumption the analogy is a nonstarter), what reason is given to think that by thinking, talking, and reading about the matter, we will very likely comprehend God-justifying goods, if there were any? None."[33] To compare observations about the amounts and kinds of birds in this world to the amounts and kinds of pains in this world is akin to claiming that because Molly can count to ten on her fingers that she is capable of performing calculous. However, even this comparison fails to account for the vast amounts of knowledge that would be needed to accurately determine the comparative states of good and evil in this world. Howard-Snyder finds fault with arguments such as HI which presume to know enough about the overall state of good and evil in this world to assert that the existence of G is less likely to account for this state of affairs than theism.

Howard-Snyder efficiently calls into question the ability of seeming to account for inscrutable evil. While observations of inscrutable evils are common and can seem to be unanswerable, to conclude that human knowledge possesses the scope and range to move from seeming to the conclusion that G does not exist, or that his existence is less probable than HI, invites error as there are limits to human knowledge. However, though Howard-Snyder finds HI to be unconvincing in its ability to counter theism, he does believe that seeming and inscrutable evil have import for theistic conceptions about G's relationship with humanity.

---

32. Howard-Snyder, "Argument from Inscrutable Evil," 291.
33. Howard-Snyder, "Argument from Inscrutable Evil," 292.

Inculpable Non-Belief

Though Howard-Snyder finds HI to be an insufficient defeater for theism, he does recognize that HI highlights a troubling aspect of reality for theists: the apparent absence of G in times of crisis. Howard-Snyder states, "Jewish and Christian theists believe that their flourishing as persons depends on their being in a personal and social relationship with God. For many such theists, however, there is no such discernible relationship. God is hidden, if not in fact at least in their experience."[34] This absence of G in time of need is referred to by Howard-Snyder as Divine Hiddenness (DH). DH, born out of theist belief conjoined with O, takes Draper's observations of inscrutable evil and applies them to what it means to be a theist. If G is omnipresent, omnipotent, loving, and good, why would he abandon those devoted to him when they need him the most? In answering this question, Howard-Snyder critiques an argument of the Skeptical Theism variety and posits the possibility of there being no fault for some in not believing in G, which he calls inculpable non-belief.

In an article he coauthored with John O'Leary-Hawthorne, Howard-Snyder critiques a style of argument espoused by Stephen Wykstra, William Alston, and Alvin Plantinga. The line of reasoning follows Skeptical Theism (which will be discussed more thoroughly in the next chapter) and makes use of a simile between a baby in distress an inscrutable evil. A baby has very little knowledge compared to the parents. The parents may allow a doctor to poke and prod the baby, and even though the baby screams and agonizes over its ordeal the parents know that there is a greater good to come out of the experience. Furthermore, although the baby is unaware that the parents are close by the fact of their closeness is not negated. Like the baby, someone undergoing an agonizing ordeal may believe that they are alone in their anguish but it is possible that G is nearby and knows more about what good exists in this situation than the person living it out. Howard-Snyder finds this line of reasoning insufficient as it does not take seriously enough the knowledge of the "baby." In response to this sort of argument Howard-Snyder states, "That an omniscient being would know lots more than us in general shows nothing about whether we are ignorant of items in some particular domain.... The scope of God's knowledge does not, by itself, show that we would be unable to tell there was a morally sufficient reason for some horror were there one.[35] Howard-Snyder's critique is significant for at least two reasons. First, it takes some of the teeth out

---

34. Howard-Snyder and Moser, "Hiddenness of God," 1–2.
35. O'Leary-Hawthorne and Howard-Snyder, "God, Schmod," 864.

of a skeptical theist response to inscrutable evil which in turn affords HI more ground to stand on. Second, it attempts to take seriously the human capability for epistemic discernment.

Although Howard-Snyder's critique does have the effect of weakening a particular theistic defense of inscrutable evil, his goal is not to defeat theism but rather to make theistic arguments stronger by grounding them more fully in truth. To be clear, he does not believe that his observation justifies HI to the point of validating it as truth. Howard-Snyder states, "We can't help but conclude that many atheists writing on the problem of evil have been overly optimistic about the evidential power of facts about evil."[36] Although the critique of a skeptical theist response to DH would seem to be in favor of a non-theistic position, Howard-Snyder in fact maintains his theism. His reasoning for such a position can be seen when his understanding of human epistemic discernment is more fully considered in terms of culpability.

As was mentioned above, Howard-Snyder maintains that humanity does possess the capability of making accurate observations about the surrounding world. While it does not appear that he would say people are capable of knowing everything in a given situation, Howard-Snyder does maintain that enough information is available to a given individual to render them inculpable or culpable for their un/belief. Howard-Snyder rightly observes that the love of G requires that he not force his creation to love him as that would be coercion that overrides free will.[37] With this observation comes three conclusions. First, there are acceptable grounds for believing in G. Second, there are situations in which a person may culpably (i.e., knowingly/unjustifiably) reject G, and in such cases one could not rightly expect G to render aid.[38] Third, there may be situation in which a person may inculpably (i.e., unknowingly or justifiably) not believe in G.[39] This inculpable nonbelief is of special import here as it is a product of Howard-Snyder's admittance to there being inscrutable evil and his belief that humans contain enough epistemic capability to render justifying conclusions regarding DH.

The idea of inculpable nonbelief arises from DH which in turn has roots in inscrutable evil. If G is loving where is he in times of crisis? Since there appears to be good reason to believe that there are inscrutable evils, Draper concludes that HI is more probable than theism. This puts DH, which is a subset of the POE, front and center for theists to consider. As

---

36. O'Leary-Hawthorne and Howard-Snyder, "God, Schmod," 874.
37. Howard-Snyder, "Argument from Divine Hiddenness," 434.
38. Howard-Snyder, "Argument from Divine Hiddenness," 434.
39. Howard-Snyder, "Argument from Divine Hiddenness," 438.

was mentioned above, Howard-Snyder finds DH lacking in its ability to denounce theism; it is too strong in its claim. Howard-Snyder states, "*The hiddenness of God* is an inapt term to use in an argument for the conclusion that there is no God since God is hidden only if there is a God; the term *inculpable nonbelief* is better."[40] So, how can G be truly hidden if it is possible for someone to even have the ability to question his apparent absence? This amounts to an inherent contradiction in need of correction, which for Howard-Snyder inculpable nonbelief provides. However, as has been already mentioned, Howard-Snyder does recognize the appearance of inscrutable evil. Inculpable nonbelief, being a conclusion based on O and subsequent nonbelief in G, holds that there are people who are justified in their nonbelief of G. To those who would say that no reason exists which would justify G in allowing inculpable nonbelief, Howard-Snyder argues to the contrary when he states, "So far as I can see, nothing we reasonably believe rules out there being a prima facie reason for God to permit inculpable nonbelief."[41] His claim that G can allow inculpable nonbelief is rooted in his understanding of G's love.

For Howard-Snyder, the love of G equates to a governor on inculpable nonbelief. He states, "Nothing I have said implies that God would have a reason to refrain forever from personally relating to those capable of such a relationship. I have only argued that there is a prima facie reason for God to permit inculpable nonbelief for a time."[42] So, though one may be justified in having nonbelief in G (due to experiences with inscrutable evil), the love of G will ultimately result in a restoration of relationship. This understanding of G's love extends not only to inculpable nonbelievers but culpable nonbelievers as well. Howard-Snyder states, "Nothing I have said rules out the possibility that nonbelievers will someday not only come to see that God exists but be coerced to love Him if they are not so inclined of their own accord."[43] The conclusion to be drawn here identifies G's love as an ultimate recompense for the evils of this world, whether moral or natural. It would appear that G's love is the final answer for Howard-Snyder in his response to non-theistic arguments. He states, "I conclude that a properly qualified expectation that God will bring it about that we reasonably believe that He exists does not warrant an argument for atheism on the basis of divine hiddenness."[44] In attempting to take seriously instances of inscrutable evil,

---

40. Howard-Snyder, "Hiddenness of God," 352.
41. Howard-Snyder, "Argument from Divine Hiddenness," 448.
42. Howard-Snyder, "Argument from Divine Hiddenness," 452.
43. Howard-Snyder, "Argument from Divine Hiddenness," 452.
44. Howard-Snyder, "Argument from Divine Hiddenness," 453.

Howard-Snyder proposes a possible version of theism in which nonbelief in G may be justified and the love of G will ultimately rule create/restore relationship between humanity and G for all peoples. However, the cost of this theistic approach is very high.

Howard-Snyder's conclusions, though born of a desire to take seriously DH, are ultimately not in line with orthodoxy. While this paper is not concerned with realities of heaven and hell and the eternal consequences for temporal actions, it is worth noting that Howard-Snyder's position is antithetical to traditional theistic beliefs (of the kind prefaced in chapter 1). Rather than reject this position outright, it is worth asking, "Does Howard-Snyder's position provide the most cogent accounting of O in relation to G?" It would be a leap in logic to conclude that Howard-Snyder's solution is a necessary response to DH and/or the POE. For example, as to the aforementioned critique Howard-Snyder made of Skeptical Theism's baby analogy, it is perhaps accurate to say that he was not entirely fair in his accounting of human ken. The baby analogy is not meant to convey that a suffering person possesses no faculties by which to make conclusions regarding life. Rather, it was an attempt to show the inadequacies of human reasoning to account for the knowledge possessed by G. Furthermore, previous experiences and the experiences of others are within human ken. These experiences can serve as a reminder to the person in grief that they are not alone. But, it could be objected, this does not negate the possibility of a person suffering while unaware of these evidences, and they still would have inculpable nonbelief. C. S. Lewis offers some insight into DH when he makes this observation about grief: "The time when there is nothing at all in your soul except a cry for help may be just the time when God can't give it. . . . Perhaps your own reiterated cries deafen you to the voice you hoped to hear."[45] In other words, an appearance of DH does not necessarily mean that G is in fact hidden. It is entirely possible that G's voice, whether literal or figurative, is being drowned out because it is easier to scream in despair than to assert control over one's faculties and look for the comfort of G that is waiting to be accepted.

Of course, it is entirely possible that some will find this brief counterargument unconvincing, but the question of inculpable nonbelief being the most cogent explanation for DH/POE remains. The cost of Howard-Snyder's conclusions are very high for theism. Given who G is, it is fitting that the best theistic defenses will be those which maintain the holiness of G and humanity's inability to attain to holiness without G. This paper asserts that there does exist a theistic defense which can account for the

---

45. Lewis, *Grief Observed*, 676.

amounts and kinds of evils that are in this world, in a more probable way than non-theism, without the need for cheapening soteriology and softening hamartiology, as is done with Howard-Snyder's defense. That defense will be considered in chapters 8 and 9.

Conclusions

Discussions of the POE can easily be considered in light of theistic and atheistic perspectives, but the agnosticism of Paul Draper provides another viewpoint in need of consideration. HI, with its plea to conflicting evidence for and against theism, calls into question the need for making a/theistic claims regarding reality. Particularly, Draper's accounting of inscrutable evil gives theism pause to explain why it is that G would allow people to experience gratuitous pain. As was briefly considered, HI and inscrutable evil are open to the critique of the logical limits of G's intervention in creation and where the line of gratuitousness is located. Draper's work is thought provoking, and the emphasis on inscrutable evil can also be found in the works of theist Daniel Howard-Snyder.

Howard-Snyder, recognizing the existence of inscrutable evil, finds HI insufficient to countermand theism. In short, he asserts that theism can provide stories accounting for O that are just as compelling as those found in HI. For Howard-Snyder, inscrutable evil and DH conjoin to give rise to inculpable nonbelief, and the assertion that G's love will eventually draw all peoples to a redeemed relationship with G. However, Howard-Snyder's inculpable nonbelief contains a high cost in compromising on orthodox views of G and his relationship with creation. Furthermore, theism possesses the capabilities of accounting for DH without resorting to such tactics, as was briefly discussed with C. S. Lewis's drowning man analogy. One's own uncontrolled cries for help may drown out G's voice, but it does not mean that G is not there.

Throughout this chapter the concept of limits of human knowledge have been periodically touched upon. Chapters 8 and 9 will discuss the Free System Corollary as a theistic defense to the abductive POE, but before that discussion it is fitting that there be a brief overview of the limits of human ken and its significant for the POE. This next chapter will address Skeptical Theism as a response to evidential arguments from evil and the non-theistic charge that Skeptical Theism is little more than a run-away trolley that questions the basis of any and all human knowledge.

7

Skeptical Theism

THE ABILITY/LIMITS OF HUMAN ken is a recurring theme. At times implicit and explicit, from moral obligation to the existence of free will to the logical constraints of a given argument, the question of what can be known lurks behind every corner. As this austere review of theistic and non-theistic thoughts on the POE draws to a close, it is fitting that there be at least a brief discussion on Skeptical Theism. Borne out of a response to evidential arguments from the POE, Stephen Wykstra proposed Skeptical Theism as a counterargument which calls into question the human ability to doubt the wisdom of G's goodness in cases of intense evils. Counter to Wykstra, Rowe responds with what this author views as the most strident critique of Skeptical Theism: the danger of moral relativism. Since the Free System Corollary also makes use of questions of epistemic limitations, understanding Skeptical Theism and Rowe's critique will be of immense value in the following chapters.

Stephen Wykstra

CORNEA

Skeptical Theism, being the idea that there exists just cause for doubting the ability of humanity to comprehend divine levels of knowledge, is a potent tool for theists in countering evidential type arguments from evil. For his part, Stephen Wykstra introduced the concept of CORNEA as a critical response to the inductive arguments of William Rowe which claim that evidences of intense evils give probability to a non-theistic reality. CORNEA stands for "Condition of Reasonable Epistemic Access" from which Wykstra states, "In brief, CORNEA says that we can argue from 'we see no X' to 'there is no X' only when X has 'reasonable seeability'—that is, is the sort of thing which, if it exists, we *can reasonably expect* to see in the situation."[1] In other words, one is justified in proclaiming the non/existence of a thing if it is reasonable to expect to have the resources needed to formulate such a position. For example, Wykstra uses the imagery of a doctor inspecting a needle for germs. To the naked eye, it appears that there are no germs on the needle, but the doctor is not warranted in assuming the cleanliness. It is one thing for the doctor to say, "It appears that there are no germs," and another for that statement to be true. Then, in reference to Rowe's inference that there appears no good for which God would allow certain evils, Wykstra states, "Similarly, I contend, Rowe's inference must be questioned at its first step. To grant [Rowe's inference] lets Rowe not just in the game but ninety-nine yards down the field."[2] Unlike Howard-Snyder, Wykstra does not admit to the existence of (to use Howard-Snyder and Draper's terminology) inscrutable evil.

Acknowledging inscrutable evil is tantamount to saying human ken is sufficient to know the mind of G, for the claim of inscrutable evil, while it might not claim to know all that G knows, entails the proclamation that human ken, though not perfect, is fully capable of knowing enough about a given situation to accurately determine divine culpability. Therefore, theistic acknowledgment of inscrutable evil gives non-theists an advantage in making truth claims about the balance of good and evil in the world. It is one thing to say "this appears to be inscrutable evil" and another to say "this is an example of inscrutable evil." Wykstra states, "By CORNEA, one is entitled to claim 'this suffering does not appears (i.e., appears not) to serve any Divinely-purposed outweighing good' only if it is reasonable to believe that if such a Divinely-purposed good exists, it would be within our ken."[3] CORNEA not only challenges presumptuous claims of knowing divine motive/thought it also expects there to be divine knowledge beyond human ken. Given the magnitude of G's knowledge it would be reasonable to expect there to be classes of knowledge that humanity can only guess as to their content. Indeed, in reference to Rowe mentioning that knowledge of Divine motive is beyond human ken, Wykstra states, "If we think carefully about the sort of being theism proposes for our belief, it is entirely expectable . . . that the goods by virtue of which this Being allows known suffering should very often be beyond our ken."[4] Rather than being a defeater for theism, the observation that the existence of G would entail an inability for humanity

---

1. Wykstra, "Rowe's Noseeum Arguments from Evil," 126.
2. Wykstra, "Rowe's Noseeum Arguments from Evil," 127–28.
3. Wykstra, "Humean Obstacle," 157.
4. Wykstra, "Humean Obstacle," 159.

to know all divine motives is not only logical but is anticipated as well. Therefore, Wykstra states, "If we have realized the magnitude of the theistic proposal, cognizance of suffering thus should not in the least reduce our confidence that it is true." The existence of apparent inscrutable evils is only troubling for the theistic believer who lacks understanding and is unwilling to accept that reality. However, apparent inscrutable evil naturally flows from a theistic belief in G that accepts the cognitive disparity between G and humanity, and while apparent inscrutable evil may be puzzling it does not pose a defeater for theism. Although, Wykstra does wish to show that Skeptical Theism, driving by CORNEA, is capable of addressing abductive arguments as well as logical inductive type arguments.

When Wykstra speaks of an abductive argument he refers to an argument that is an "inference to the best explanation . . . it is explanatory in that it moves from judgments about the degree of explanatory fit with data to conclusions about the probable truth or falsity of a hypothesis."[5] Being an inference to the best explanation, abductive arguments do not need to claim to know all information, rather they come to conclusions about the truth of a situation based upon available information. Wykstra refers to Drapers arguments (which were discussed in the previous chapter) as "abductive atheology,"[6] and he finds them to be unique for their lack of dependence upon encyclopedia type knowledge one could expect from observations of pain and pleasure (O). In reference to Draper and his Spartan use of O, Wykstra states, "We find nothing very specific about the distribution of tragedy or triumph among the plant, animal, and human population . . . what data Draper offers seems to us very thin data—a modest assortment of armchair science generalizations that would perhaps take up but a paragraph or two in the *Encyclopedia of Good and Evil (EGE)*."[7] The strength of Draper's HI is its ability to argue for the truth of a situation based upon available data in a probabilistic sense. In short, HI speaks to experiences that people know to be true: pain and suffering exist. Based upon the ubiquitous testimonies of pain and suffering throughout human experience, Draper makes a strong abductive inference toward agnosticism.[8] However, there is more that can be known from these experiences than a befuddled conclusion toward indifference.

Not only are there consistent examples of pain and suffering throughout human history but concepts of the divine are also known. When

---

5. Wykstra and Perrine, "Skeptical Theism, Abductive Atheology," 144.
6. Wykstra and Perrine, "Skeptical Theism, Abductive Atheology," 155.
7. Wykstra and Perrine, "Skeptical Theism, Abductive Atheology," 156–57.
8. See the previous chapter for more on the Hypothesis of Indifference (HI).

the *Encyclopedia of Good and Evil* is read in light of the possibility of G something interesting happens. The data that a moment before seemed to support HI no longer seems to do so. Once one fully considers the ramifications of G, one begins to see the very real possibility of there being divine knowledge that humanity is incapable of knowing. HI, being an abductive inference based upon O, becomes less probable once one examines theism in light of the limitations of human ken. In reference to this observation of the inadequacies of O to account for HI, Wykstra states, "A judgment based on data too thin to partition theism into theoretically fruitful disjuncts will have little evidential weight."[9] In other words, HI and O do not account for the logic of there being divine reasons for allowing pain and suffering that are beyond human ken (i.e., it places too much trust in human epistemic capability). As a result, HI and O do not have the strength to be able to push theism to its logical limits. Therefore, HI and O pose no real problem for Skeptical Theism's defense of G. That is not to say, however, that there does not exist a more potent argument against Skeptical Theism.

Skeptical Theism, informed by CORNEA, challenges appearance claims and argues for the logical consequence of G possessing information beyond human ken that speaks to the existence of the amounts and kinds of pleasure, pain, and suffering that exists in this world. Of course, an objection could be raised that this is a sort of God-of-the-Gaps types argument, where anything that is inconvenient for theism can be subsumed under the auspices of divine knowledge, and hence divine justification for any observed evil. How does one argue against Skeptical Theism when the Skeptical Theist will undoubtedly claim that there is a reason for a given instance of apparent inscrutable evil, but it is unknown to all but G? Non-theistic arguments may not be able to discount Skeptical Theism for its possible truth, but they can push Skeptical Theism to its logical limits (claiming "G does not exist" is harder to defend then "it seems G does not exist"). Arguments such as these pose the greatest threat to Skeptical Theism. This next section will discuss what is quite possibly the most potent argument against Skeptical Theism: the charge of runaway morality.

William Rowe

A Trolley Ride to Obscurity

In countering Skeptical Theism, Rowe does not take issue with CORNEA but rather with Wykstra's conclusions regarding what amounts to

---

9. Wykstra and Perrine, "Skeptical Theism, Abductive Atheology," 157.

reasonable knowledge. In examining the limits of CORNEA, Rowe pushes Skeptical Theism toward its logical limits and arrives at a conclusion that is dubious of Wykstra's claims.

Part of his examination of Wykstra entails a strict definition of the god under scrutiny. Specifically, Rowe wants to discuss god in terms of what he calls Restricted Standard Theism (a powerful god exists, but no religious trappings aside from power are considered).[10] A significant aspect of Rowe's argument against Wykstra entails what is meant by references to the divine, and Rowe accuses Wykstra of exceeding the bounds of Restricted Standard Theism in his arguments. In reference to this, Rowe states, "But the mere assumption that *[g]* exists gives us no reason whatever to suppose *either* that the greater goods in virtue of which he permits most sufferings are goods that come into existence far in the future of the suffering we are aware of, *or* that once they do obtain we continue to be ignorant of them and their relation to the sufferings."[11] In other words, the existence of *[g]* does not necessarily entail human ignorance in matters of good and evil. Of course, this does not mean that the goods and evils of a situation will be within human ken either. At this point, it could be said that Rowe is taking a position of indifference in relation to human ken. Rowe states, "Restricted standard theism gives us *no* reason to think that these goods, once they occur, remain beyond our ken."[12] By calling into question the guarantee of there being knowledge of goods and evils beyond human ken Rowe is setting the stage for what is, in this author's opinion, his most compelling argument against Skeptical Theism. However, Rowe has not yet finished highlighting the difference between *[g]* and G.

The foundation for Rowe's critique of Wykstra is the charge that Wykstra has moved beyond *[g]* (Restricted Standard Theism) and on to Expanded Standard Theism. In essence, the claim exists that Wykstra has added to a basic understanding of who the divine is (should he exist) into areas that are informed by religious conjecture rather than what could be considered properly basic. Rowe states, "My own best judgment is that the

---

10. Rowe, "Evil and the Theistic Hypothesis," 161. Here, Rowe refers to the god of Restricted Standard Theism as O. To avoid confusion with the use of "O," since this term has been used in Draper's context thus far in this paper, any use of "O" by Rowe will be referred to/replaced with "*[g]*" in any referenced quotes and/or discussion. The difference between "*[g]*" and "G" is the difference between Rowe's understanding of Restricted Standard Theism and Expanded Standard Theism (which, from Rowe's perspective, reflects the use of "G" in this paper). The former entails power claims, and nothing more, while the later can also entail relational/moral claims (e.g., G is necessarily loving, *[g]* may or may not be loving).

11. Rowe, "Evil and the Theistic Hypothesis," 164–65.

12. Rowe, "Evil and the Theistic Hypothesis," 165.

crucial proposition Wykstra claims to be implicit in theism is in fact an added postulate that produces a version of expanded theism."[13] Of course, Wykstra asserts that he has successfully brought clarity to Rowe's *[g]* (which would equate to G), but Rowe insists that Wykstra has expanded upon *[g]*.[14] The import of this claim resides within a vital component of theistic arguments from Skeptical Theism: it is the character of G that gives one the impetus to claim that knowledge beyond human ken entails unknown goods. However, if Rowe is correct that the goodness/lovingness of G results from trappings that gild the lily of Restricted Standard Theism, Skeptical Theism becomes vulnerable.

Non-theistic arguments from the POE are willing to allow for the existence of G because they believe they can use the goodness of G as proof that he does not exist. Rowe, on the other hand, allows for an omnipotent, omniscient being but is unwilling to grant goodness as part of the equation. The reason for this restriction (as built upon the observations above) can perhaps be best seen when considering justification for good (J). Where E_1 and E_2 refer to instances of intense evil, Rowe states, "What is much more difficult, I believe, is to determine of some good *that it has J*. For suppose we do know of some good that far outweighs in value either E_1 or E_2 . . . [an] omniscient being could not obtain that good without permitting E_1 or E_2 . . . for all we know, that there is some good state of affairs [better than the first] . . . [that could obtain only] by *preventing* E_1 and E_2."[15] Here, Rowe is calling into question the human ability to determine if a good result is the best possible result. If the goodness of the divine is understood as being a basic quality then there exists a basis for assuming the best. However, if goodness results from religious trappings, and the divine cannot be assumed to be good, what basis is there for thinking that any possible good that results from intense evil is the best that could happen? In other words, not only do people have the right to be skeptical about their amounts of knowledge in relation to the divine but they also have grounds for doubting whether or not any good state of affairs is the best state of affairs. For Rowe, this amounts to a defeater for the claim that Skeptical Theism makes theism more likely than non-theism. Where P represents the idea that no known good justifies *[g]* in permitting intense evil,[16] Rowe states, "Wykstra can rest content that my argument is insufficient to justify a move from square agnosticism to square atheism. But . . . the argument would still show that P *significantly lowers* the

---

13. Rowe, "Evil and the Theistic Hypothesis," 166.
14. Rowe, "Evil and the Theistic Hypothesis," 167.
15. Rowe, "Ruminations about Evil," 77.
16. Rowe, "Evidential Argument from Evil: A Second Look," 263.

probability of G and makes belief in atheism more reasonable than belief in theism."[17] In other words, Rowe's critique of the knowability of goodness may not be an iron clad argument for atheism but it does make atheism more probable than theism. This line of Rowe's argumentation is perhaps best highlighted by his trolley analogy.

After summarizing arguments against Skeptical Theism[18] that he had made over the years, Rowe culminates his critique of Wykstra by comparing the logical weaknesses of Skeptical Theism to that of a malfunctioning trolley. Rowe states, "Skeptical theists choose to ride the trolley car of skepticism concerning the goods that God would know.... But once on that trolley car it may not be easy to prevent that skepticism from also undercutting any reasons they may suppose they have for thinking that God will provide them and the worshipful faithful with life everlasting in his presence."[19] In short, when questioning one's ability to know of goods that exist one also calls into question evils that may exist. Presupposing the goodness of G adds to what can be assumed about a divine being, should he exist. Therefore, arguing from Skeptical Theism for theism is akin to stepping onto a trolley, but the trolley has no brakes, no means of stopping. Once on that ride skepticism will continue until it calls into question not only the possibility of goods beyond human ken but the evils as well.

For Rowe, any properly constructed argument for the divine entails only that which can be basically known/assumed. Divine power is one of those things, divine goodness is not. William Hasker echoes these concerns for Skeptical Theism when he states, "If he [the Skeptical Theist] is to remain consistent with his skeptical principles he must *abandon the aim of maximizing the good and minimizing the bad*. He must do this because, in his judgment, *no information is available* concerning the all-things-considered goodness or badness of any state of affairs whatsoever."[20] Skeptical Theism, for all of its well-founded conclusions regarding the limits of human ken, finds itself in a pit with a pendulum swinging overhead. The very quality that gives Skeptical Theism recourse to challenge non-theistic arguments from the POE has the potential to be its undoing. Therefore,

---

17. Rowe, "Evidential Argument from Evil: A Second Look," 274.

18. Although space does not allow for a full treatise of Rowe's arguments against Wykstra, the core of his argumentation mentioned here has been summarized in this section. The largest argument that is missing is Rowe's take on Divine Hiddenness, but while his thoughts in this regard are thought provoking it is his observations regarding goodness in relation to the divine (which have already been discussed) that are the main supports of his trolley analogy.

19. Rowe, "Friendly Atheism," 91.

20. Hasker, "All Too Skeptical Theism," 29.

any successful theistic theodicy/defense that makes use of Skeptical Theism will need to be capable of pulling the cord and stopping the trolley before it crashes into an ocean of relativism.

Conclusions

Stephen Wykstra presents a compelling argument for the inability of humanity to comprehend all the knowledge of G, which includes divine reasons for allowing intense evils to occur. CORNEA (Condition of Reasonable Epistemic Access) serves as a foundational principle for Skeptical Theism which urges one to think in terms of what can be expected in a given situation. In relation to the POE, an application of CORNEA results in skepticism regarding the capability of human ken to know divine levels of knowledge in instances of intense evil. In other words, given G one should expect to be ignorant of potential goods that can result from cases of evil. Skeptical Theism, being built upon what is expected, provides a probable theistic explanation for the POE. However, there exists a critique of Skeptical Theism that questions its ability to argue so successfully for theism.

William Rowe engages Skeptical Theism in two stages. In stage one, Rowe defines the diving being whom he is willing to entertain the possibility of in terms of Restricted Standard Theism, which allows for divine power but not goodness/love. For Rowe, concepts of goodness and love result in Expanded Standard Theism which guilds the lily with religious faith/opinion. In other words, goodness/love are assumptions that are not necessarily a basic quality of the divine. By removing goodness/love from the equation, Rowe pushes Skeptical Theism to its logical limits. His conclusion (stage two): Skeptical Theism gives one cause to be doubtful of one's ability to know all potential/actual evils as well as goods. Rowe contends that siding with Skeptical Theism is akin to boarding a trolley car that does not stop. For all that can be known, there are a greater amount of evils than goods, and the goods that are seen may not be the best possible goods. This amounts to a mortally challenging critique of Skeptical Theism.

Thus far, this discussion has surveyed conceptions of morality, natural law, free will defenses, and challenges to theism based upon the POE. This brief overview has shown that non-theistic criticisms of theistic defenses ultimately consist of abductions. These arguments have been modified over time, but that is to be expected. Wykstra states, "We theists should view our theism, while grounded in the past, as also *dynamic*, and as needing better specification as we learn more and more, individually and communally, about ourselves and the world we live in, so as to refine theism into its best and truest versions."[21] Indeed, discussions on the POE are ever changing, constantly reacting to developing and refined argumentation. Not only is this true for theism but it is also true of non-theistic arguments as well. The tendency of non-theistic arguments to make implicit/explicit abductions from the POE (APOE) equates to a challenge for theists to provide argumentation that has more abductive weight than non-theistic arguments. This next chapter is an effort to live up to Wykstra's charge of the dynamic nature of theism, and to show the abductive probability of theism over non-theism.

---

21. Wykstra, "Skeptical Theism, Abductive Atheology," 163.

8

The Free System Corollary

HAVING NOW COMPLETED a brief overview of developments in the POE, this discussion now turns toward providing a defense that can abductively answer non-theistic challenges more completely than the FWD and the EFWD without falling into the quagmire of moral relativism that seems to tug at skeptical theism. This is not to say that these defenses are problematic or irrelevant. Rather, the goal of this chapter, and indeed this entire project, is to provide a more complete telling of the POE that builds upon these defenses and can be used to make abductive arguments in favor of theism. In offering a theistic account of the POE, this chapter will face at least two primary challenges: individual abduction and apologetic bias.

Every functioning member of society lives out their lives in an abductive sense. Whether it be trusting the car to work (just as it has every other day) or believing that the next step taken will be sound and not result in a fall, people operate under an assumption which infers that what worked before will be the best explanation for how to proceed with their lives. In short, people live abductively. However, this outlook on life also poses a problem for discussions on the POE. William Hasker states, "Human beings, when considering what to believe about important matters, simply do not behave, epistemically, as probability theory says they ought to. On the contrary: when we have reached a conclusion that is convincing to us, we *commit ourselves* to that conclusion, and take it as a basis for our further reflection."[1] In other words, when someone thinks they have a good understanding of an issue it can be difficult to get them to see otherwise. A significant portion of the reason for the continued debate about the POE can be found in Hasker's observation. People trust what they know, and personal experience, or an argument that resonates with personal experience, can establish itself as being incontrovertible even when it is not. Therefore, a defense that speaks to the abductive aspect of human reasoning/experience

---

1. Hasker, "Is Christianity Probable," 262.

has the potential to give theism a probabilistic advantage over non-theism. The basis for this defense will reside in a basic aspect of human reality that can be experienced by all: free will. However, this very proposal leads to the second challenge of apologetic bias.

The charge of apologetic bias comes from non-theist Paul Draper. Draper's agnosticism informs his opinion of arguments that try to prove theism. Draper states, "Genuine philosophy today is superior to apologetics precisely because it does not face the 'paradox of apologetics.' Briefly, this paradox arises because apologists, unlike philosophers engaged in genuine inquiry, seek to justify their religious beliefs (as opposed to seeking to have beliefs that are justified)."[2] Much like the person who looks for a face in the clouds and finds it, Draper views apologetic endeavors as being doomed to fail since they are more interested in finding their thesis than they are in finding the truth. For Draper, truth should be the object of philosophical inquiry. Draper states, "Paradoxically, one cannot obtain justification for one's religious beliefs by seeking it directly. To obtain justification, one must directly seek, not justification, but truth."[3] In short, Draper is arguing for an agnostic philosophy that will eventually arrive at a non/theistic conclusion. However, given that Draper himself remains agnostic one does wonder if an agnostic perspective can truly separate oneself from bias sufficiently to address Draper's own concerns. Nevertheless, Draper's caution against allowing bias to cloud one's judgment is well taken. Whereas this book has been written from a theistic perspective, that perspective was born out of a line of reasoning that made use of basic observations of the human condition (e.g., humans are fallible and have free will) and sought to put non/theism to the test with the question, "What should be expected?" The defense provided in this chapter will reflect this and endeavor to refrain from looking at intense evil through rose-colored glasses.

Of course, any form of communication has and will be open to scrutiny. This is true for theistic as well as non-theistic arguments from the POE. As such, it is unlikely that any one paper will be capable of addressing all concerns that may exist for the abductive nature of the POE (APOE). However, this book, and this chapter specifically, proposes the foundation for a theistic defense that can speak to abductive sensibilities in its search for truth.

---

2. Draper and Nichols, "Diagnosing Bias in Philosophy of Religion," 439.
3. Draper and Nichols, "Diagnosing Bias in Philosophy of Religion," 439.

The Free System Corollary Defined

As has been mentioned previously, the FWD and the EFWD are important theistic defenses to the POE, but they both have limitations that give abductive non-theistic arguments resilience. Both address logical issues levied at theism, but they are incomplete from an APOE perspective. Similarly, skeptical theism highlights epistemic difficulties with non-theistic arguments but it runs the risk of falling prey to moral relativism. Each of these will be discussed later in this chapter to show how the proposal in this paper can augment their case for theism. Since this proposal is an extension, an augmentation, of the FWD, EFWD, and skeptical theism, it will be referred to as a corollary. Specifically, it correlates free will, the systems required for free will to be actualized (free systems), and theodical suggestions with free will based defenses. Thus, the Free System Corollary to Free Will Defenses is defined as follows:

> Free System Corollary (FSC)$_{df}$ = Theodical suggestions, born from the conjunction of free will and the systems needed for free will to be actualized, provide plausible explanations, that could be true for all we know, in response to specific instances of intense evil.

There are three main components to the FSC: free will, systems which enable free will, and theodical suggestions.

It is the contention here that once the roles of free will and free will systems are identified in a given situation that theodical suggestions arise which present a case for theism that is abductively more attractive than non-theism. Of course, given the work done by Alvin Plantinga, Peter van Inwagen, and Stephen Wykstra this is a bold claim, and there exists the additional task of showing that the FSC is more than merely an application of these defenses. However, while the FSC works alongside these defenses it has as its goal the application of the implications of free will toward abductive, and not solely logical, aspects of intense evils. Toward that end, the elucidation of the relationship between free will and the systems needed for free will to exist are critical for the FSC. However, before a discussion on free systems can be had, a proper understanding of theodical suggestions and how they will be used in this present project is foundational for any application/use of the FSC.

William Alston and Theodical Suggestions

The term "theodical suggestion" comes from the work of William Alston. Since this phrase finds use here it should be made clear how Alston makes use of theodical suggestions and how it will be used here (the latter of which will be the subject of the next section). He makes use of theodical suggestions as a means of addressing what he calls the agnostic thesis, which is the basis for William Rowe's arguments from the POE. Alston summarizes this agnosticism when he states, "An omnipotent, omniscient being could have prevented it [evil] without thereby losing some greater good or permitting some evil equally bad or worse."[4] The sort of evil that Alston refers to here is gratuitous suffering,[5] which aligns with this discussion's understanding of intense evil but with an element of pointlessness. It is to this claim, that humanity has the capability of knowing that there are evils which G could have eliminated/prevented without diminishing some greater good or allowing a worse evil, that Alston employs the use of theodical suggestions.

Alston refers to the above argument of gratuitous suffering as agnostic because humanity lacks the natural ability to confirm or deny its claim. However, he does see a way to break through this stalemate when he states, "For particular cases of suffering we might conceivably be able to establish nongratuitousness in this way, but what I shall argue in this paper is that no one can justifiably assert gratuitousness for any case."[6] In other words, Alston is proposing a means by which evidence can be found which supports the possibility of an instance of evil not being gratuitous while he simultaneously argues that gratuitousness can never be proven. What Alston is referring to here are theodical suggestions which, when considered, give cause to doubt the existence of gratuitous evil.

Alston describes theodical suggestions as being a partial list of reasons (gleaned from various theodicies) which may explain why G might conceivably be permitted in allowing gratuitous evil/suffering. This list of theodical suggestions would then constitute a set of parameters which would need to be addressed by non-theists if they are to be rational in accepting the agnostic thesis.[7] By drawing upon theodicies for their possible correctness one can identify potential answers (i.e., suggestions) for why it is that G allows the observations of pain, pleasure, and suffering in this world (O). In short, theodical suggestions are possibilities that G may have for allowing intense evil

---

4. Alston, "Inductive Argument from Evil," 98.
5. Alston, "Inductive Argument from Evil," 98.
6. Alston, "Inductive Argument from Evil," 99.
7. Alston, "Inductive Argument from Evil," 103.

that are within human ken, or at least within the human ability to anticipate if it is not known with certainty. Although humanity cannot account for all possibilities it is possible to formulate potential answers which, if nothing else, give cause to conclude that if these possibilities can be known there very well may be more that exist beyond human ken.

Alston uses theodical suggestions to cast doubt upon inductive arguments such as the aforementioned agnostic thesis. While theodical suggestions do not necessarily prove theism over non-theism they do provide a type of evidence that equates to a positive claim (contra the negative claims of the agnostic thesis) which finds possible reasons for why G would allow O. With this basic understanding of theodical suggestions it is now relevant to establish how theodical suggestions are to be used/understood in the FSC.

Theodical Suggestions as Applied in the FSC

For many theists, defenses are preferable to theodicies. Theodicies have the daunting task of providing answers for why the world is the way that it is, and this includes all instances of O. Given the limits of human ken and ability, it could be said that theodicies are behind the eight ball since it would be an extremely difficult task to account for O in every instance. Defenses, on the other hand, also tell a story, but theirs is a story of parameters/guidelines. Rather than trying to explain why every instance of O occurs, defenses have the more modest task of explaining the logical consistency of how the world operates and how this is consistent with conceptions of G. Theodical suggestions then become a sort of bridge between defenses and theodicies. Indeed, Alston makes no claims of theodical suggestions being capable of providing a theodicy, rather he draws upon theodicies for inspiration to explain O. Alston states, "Note that it is no part of my purpose here to develop or defend a theodicy. I am using theodicies only as a source of *possibilities* for divine reasons for evil."[8] Theodicies, rather than looked upon as gospel truth, become tools by which non-theistic claims can be challenged. This book takes no issue with this passive[9] understanding/use of theodical suggestions, but it does seek to employ this concept in a more active sense.

As will be seen in the following sections, the FSC builds upon the FWD, EFWD, and skeptical theism. In so doing, the FSC makes use of theodical suggestions that arise from applications of free will and the systems needed

---

8. Alston, "Inductive Argument from Evil," 103.

9. "Passive" here is meant to convey the harvesting of concepts from theodicies, as opposed to the more "active" condition of formulating theodicies. It is not mean to imply that employing theodical suggestions is a passive act.

for free will to be actualized. Rather than taking concepts from theodicies and applying them to a given situation, an understanding of free will and free systems will be applied to that same situation. This will give rise to possible theodical suggestions which can account for why G allowed a specific instance of evil to occur. In other words, in the FSC, theodical suggestions are born out of the application of a theistic defense which is based upon free will and free systems. The resulting theodical suggestion will provide an abductively strong argument for theism by nature of its close relationship to the instance of evil it attempts to account for.

Although the process at arriving at theodical suggestions may be slightly different here than with Alston, the goal of identifying aspects of a theodicy that can support a theistic defense remains the same. As such, it is fitting to remember Alston's caution in regards to evaluating examples from the POE: "We are often in a poor position to assess the degree and kind of a certain person's sinfulness, or to compare people in this regard."[10] Here, Alston cautions against presuming to know the entire spiritual/moral condition of an individual. This point is well taken. By examining the role of free will and its environment in instances of intense evil, it may be possible to know more regarding a particular state of affairs than appears at first.

The Necessity of a Free System for Free Will

The Nature of Free Will

Free Will, and its implications, are an integral part of the FSC. Admittedly, this does leave the FSC vulnerable to critiques which attack the very existence of free will. This potential limitation of the FSC will be addressed later in this chapter, but before that discussion it is fitting and proper to explore what is meant with the use of "free will" here. Chapter 2 provided the following definition of free will:

> Free Will$_{df}$ = the ability to intentionally perform, or refrain from performing, an act without that intention being fully determined by prior causes.

Of import to this present section is the limited impact that certain causes can have upon free will. As was mentioned in chapter 2, this definition strives to be mindful of two competing realities that seem to vie for supremacy in human endeavors: causation and free will. The world is replete with examples of how a chain reaction can lead to consequences, but also

---

10. Alston, "Inductive Argument from Evil," 104.

ubiquitous in the world are people who live out their lives as if free will is an indelible aspect of human identity. Understanding the nature of free will, how it can operate within causal circumstances, how there can be freedom within limits, becomes invaluable in discussing the FSC.

In discussing the limits that can be found on free will, Robert Merrihew Adams argues for an economy of freedom. There may be restrictions but the value of an act can ultimately be found in the choices that existed prior to that act. Adams states, "The greatest values in human life depend on people being able, and allowed, to make their own decisions in these matters, so that an interference with *freedom* to make such choices is apt to be a violation of something sacred, whether the actual choice will be a good one or not."[11] The freedom to choose not only brings value to an act but it also reflects a valuable aspect of human identity. Adams should not be misconstrued to be advocating an understanding of free will that required free will to be completely unfettered/without influences. Adams is not arguing that there cannot be restrictions on freedom but that such restrictions do not debilitate free will. For example, a stop light and the limits of a car's abilities represent restrictions of driver freedom. However, these "restrictions" guide motorist behavior. The motorist can still act contrary to the restriction, and can control when they stop, which lane they are in, how fast they go, etc. This kind of restriction is categorically different from, say, a computer controlling the vehicle and the motorist having no control at all over the vehicle and/or its destination. In the case of the later, one could argue that the vehicle's occupant is not a motorist but merely a passenger. Just as control over a vehicle identifies someone as a motorist (and traffic laws and vehicle capabilities do not impinge on that identity) so too is free will an identity of humanity which can coexist with restrictions, so long as the freedom to act/choose remains intact. For, it is not necessarily a lack of restrictions that gives one free will but it is the ability/capacity for choice wherein its identity is found.

Potential restrictions on free will can be generally categorizes into two groups: mental and physical. Although overlap does exist between mental and physical causation, such as a fallen tree causing a traveler to reevaluate a route being taken, there remains a mental and a physical component to human considerations of in/action. For example, the mental thought of an action can result in a corresponding physical reaction in the body. Philosopher Richard Swinburne observes, "Humans (as pure mental substances) cause brain events which cause bodily movements which they intend to cause, and that when they make difficult moral decisions we will never have

---

11. Adams, *Finite and Infinite Goods*, 328.

enough evidence to predict in advance what they will decide."[12] Swinburne highlights not only the mental and physical aspects of humanity but he also brings the predictability of action to the forefront. Here, Swinburne does not take up an argument for the unpredictability of human behavior in an absolute sense. As has been argued previously, humanity operates abductively in day-to-day life, and this inference to the best explanation for how the world operates involves a degree of predictability (this chair did not break with use the past thirty days so it should not break now). However, there does remain a degree of unpredictability in human life. It has often been said, "To err is human." To err is to make a mistake; the implication being that a better action was readily available but instead of performing the better option someone chose the lesser action. Human behavior contains a degree of unpredictability, and it is to this that Swinburne speaks. Specifically, Swinburne draws out that there are causal chains which exist in human thought, guided by desires, but the existence of causation does not necessarily eliminate the opportunity for free will. Swinburne states, "I have urged that the natural probability of a sequence of brain events leading to some movement may correspond to the relative strength of a desire to bring about that sequence. It is hardly news that it is harder for humans to do some free acts than to do other free acts; but that doesn't mean that we don't have free will. It means only that our free will is a limited one."[13] Causation exists, as is evident to anyone who has ever played with a row of dominos, but the existence of causation, and the strong desires it can create, can only account for the entirety of human behavior iff there exists no other evidence that can account, at least in some way, for the actions performed by humans. Free will offers just such an accounting. Swinburne proposes that within the restrictions of causation that the opportunity/ability for choice remains; free will may have to work within certain parameters but it can/does still operate in human life. Evidence for the existence of free will resides not only in the ubiquitous belief that individuals possess the capacity for choice[14] but also within that other sense that exists in humanity: obligation.

As was discussed in chapter 2, a sense of moral obligation can be consistently found throughout humanity. Related to moral obligation is the

---

12. Swinburne, *Mind, Brain, and Free Will*, 201.
13. Swinburne, *Mind, Brain, and Free Will*, 208.
14. Yes, there are those, such as J. L. Mackie, who believe free will is merely an illusion, but even in the belief that free will is an illusion the seeming is so strong that they need to go to great lengths to make their case. Furthermore, the world operates as if people do have free will (take criminal law, for example). Therefore, a recognition of free will (even if one does not believe it to be actual) can be seen in a universal sense in humanity.

sense of obligation that one should cling to truth and avoid falsehood. Bruce Reichenbach states, "As we have obligations to realize the right or the good, so we have obligations to believe what is significantly true contextually and avoid what is false."[15] Here, Reichenbach is making an argument toward the existence of moral obligations; their strong seemingness warrants an epistemic belief in their validity/authority. But, not only does Reichenbach make an argument for the truth of moral obligation, he also identifies moral obligation as having implications for free will. In reference to philosopher Sharon Ryan (who says that she cannot run over a mother and child with her car), Reichenbach states, "The 'cannot' here is controlled not by physical conditions but by normative conditions: she cannot bring herself to act contrary to moral norms."[16] Contra the assertion that causal patterns dictate an inability to run over a mother and child, Reichenbach observes that it is the call of moral obligation, not an unavoidable dictum of causation, that strongly influences Ryan to not kill the mother and child. In other words, moral obligation presents a strong desire, but it does not cause an action. Reichenbach correctly concludes that even if there are so many influences upon a person that a free will act is rare this does not eliminate the truth of free will, for "it confuses what is the case (we typically yield control) with what is possible (we could exercise control)."[17] In short, influences exist which can be causally or intrinsically born, but the existence of influences does not necessitate the abolition of free will. Free will may have restrictions, but restrictions do not inherently nullify the existence of free will.

Free will is at once a defining attribute of humanity and a great cause of concern for the POE. Free will gives people the opportunity to choose good actions, thereby bringing about good into the world. However, it also presents the potential for evil. This section has discussed free will in terms of being a universal aspect of humanity and one whose seeming is so strong that it should not be dismissed out of hand due to the existence of causation. Indeed, it has been argued that causation does offer a restriction upon free will but not one that eliminates its nature. However, a common critique of theism is that G could have prevented evil by enacting further restrictions upon free will without losing any significant good.[18] Alston replies to this charge when he states, "Human agents would no longer have a real choice between good and evil, and the surpassing worth that attaches to having such

---

15. Reichenbach, *Epistemic Obligations*, 124.
16. Reichenbach, *Epistemic Obligations*, 137.
17. Reichenbach, *Epistemic Obligations*, 140.
18. Alston, "Inductive Argument from Evil," 113.

a choice would be lost."[19] Restrictions on free will exist, but any increase on such restrictions would result in a loss of free will. Not only does this observation have great import for human identity and the potential for oppression by G should free will be altered, but this also raises an important question that should be answered prior to a discussion of divine oppression: What are the restrictions on free will? Regularity and consistency in the operation of this world not only present a set of constraints upon the operation of free will but they also make it possible for free will to be fully actualized.

Regularity/Consistency as Part of a Free System

The regularly consistent laws which govern nature are a good even when pain and suffering are a result. This, essentially, is the underlying principle behind Peter van Inwagen's EFWD. As was discussed in chapter 5, van Inwagen expands upon Alvin Plantinga's FWD so as to offer a more complete telling of natural evil. Regularity provides for consistent application of natural laws. While this may at times seem to be arbitrary, for surely G would compromise regularity to help a single person, van Inwagen argues arbitrary lines must be drawn otherwise the just-one-more thesis will compromise the integrity of this world. Specifically, of concern for van Inwagen is a theistic understanding of why G would allow the pain and suffering present in evolution. As was shown, van Inwagen argues that the seemingly gratuitous/intense suffering of the evolutionary process resulted in a greater good: sentient beings capable of making significant moral choices. The FSC has no interest in defending or defeating evolutionary claims, but it does recognize a vital connection between regularity and the application of free will in this world.

The relationship between the divine and free will has long been a talking point in the POE. William Hasker sums up this relationship when he considers what possible good could be lost if G were to prevent a certain evil: "The only plausible candidate for this 'lost good', is, I submit, the exercise of free will on the part of the human agent who has the opportunity to prevent the evil but decides not to do so."[20] Even within a case of gratuitous/intense evil, there remains a component of free will that is preserved. Of course, this then becomes a question of the value of free will: "Does the protection of free will outweigh the evil?" The non-theistic position asserts that it does not and that this constitutes evidence for the nonexistence of G. Surely, the argument goes, a scant bit of freedom has less value that a

---

19. Alston, "Inductive Argument from Evil," 113.
20. Hasker, "Defining 'Gratuitous Evil,'" 306.

great amount of evil. This position should not be surprising to theists. History books are replete with examples of people surrendering freedoms in the name of safety.[21] Non-theists have the emotional "high ground," as it were, for the desire to spare an innocent fawn or child from severe pain and suffering. This strikes a chord that resonates with the sense of moral obligation within humanity that such things are not to be desired. Indeed, Hasker seems to echo this sentiment when he makes this observation about the value of free will: "It would hardly do, for example, to say that the evil of a murder is compensated for by the intrinsic good of the free choice made by the one who committed the murder!"[22] Here, Hasker argues that though there is value in an individual's ability to exercise free will it would be an error, or a stretch of logic, to ascribe so much value as to compensate for a particular act of gratuitous evil. Indeed, it does appear difficult to show that the preservation of a single person's free will has more value than the life of an innocent fawn or girl. However, the reality of human existence is not necessarily weighed by the value of free will for one person.

Take, for instance, a grain of sand. An individual grain of sand weighs so little as to be imperceptible to human senses and to most readily available scales. The most value that can be found in an individual grain is a negative one, if it should find its way into someone's shoe. The single grain of sand is insignificant. Now, consider a great many numbers of grains of sand. Sand now has value for art, electronics, cookware, entertainment, etc. It can be formed into glass, circuit boards, castles, and a seemingly endless array of possibilities. No difference can be found in the intrinsic properties of the pile of sand or the individual grain except that of quantity. What would happen if the individual grain lost the property which allows it to be turned into glass? At best, it would cease to be sand and at worst it would cause a chain reaction that would affect all grains of sand. An individual's free will may not weigh much in the balance of goods and evils, but the reality of that person's free will does not exist in a vacuum. That which affects an individual's free will has implications for the exercise of free will for all people.

For anyone to exercise their free will regularity is needed. To be able to attempt to lift a box one day and then no longer have the ability to attempt to lift a box (with nothing changing but the ability to choose) would constitute an irregular environment. Consider what would happen if such irregularity were the norm. Someone wishing to donate to a charity could do so one day but not another. The restriction here is not one of changes

---

21. For example, consider the willingness of Germany and Austria to give up their arms to the Nazi government in the name of security and peace.
22. Hasker, "Defining 'Gratuitous Evil,'" 307.

in financial or physical ability but is one of a loss of free will. Regular laws of nature are a good, as was discussed in chapter 5, but this good extends beyond evolutionary processes. The network of regular laws which govern this world create an environment in which free will agents have the consistent opportunity to act out their free will. There are restrictions upon free will (someone may wish to fly with only a thought, but the laws of physics prevent this), but it is within these restrictions that free will finds its fulfillment. Indeed, the regular laws which govern this world create a system of guidelines within which free agents can consistently enact free will choices. In other words, without systems of regularity one would not know if the same action performed will have different results from hour to hour, day to day. Therefore, free systems are those systems of regularity which allow the fruition of free will acts.

The Potential for Oppression

The implications of free systems (which as far as can be reasonably adduced are consistent throughout the universe) are profound for the claim that an individual's free will is a greater good than the evil that results from a poor choice. A person's free will can only be compromised at the expense of the good that is inherent in free systems. Any truth claim that speaks to fundamental attributes of human identity bears serious implications for understanding the good and/or evil in a situation. Therefore, the assertion that an individual's free will should be compromised for the greater good should be examined to determine the cost of that belief.

There are at least two primary areas that are affected by the claim that individual free will is not as important as a negation of intense evil (call this FW1). The first area entails the relationship between free will and free systems. Suppose that a person, Dave, does not have a right to free will in all cases. Furthermore, suppose, in the interest of preserving free will as much as possible, that the overriding of Dave's free will occurs only when Dave performs, or is about to perform, an act of intense evil. If he were to burn down a building full of children for his own amusement Dave would be guilty of exercising his free will in such a manner as to warrant the overriding of his free will. Surely, a world in which children are not burned alive for amusement retains more good than a world in which the good of a single person's free will is preserved. However, while such an example compels one to consider the primacy of free will as a good it would be an error to end the discussion there. For, there is more at stake in this scenario than a balance of goods between human lives and one person's free will. The systems of regularity that govern the universe encompasses not only laws of motion and energy, the whole of regular systems conjoin to create an environment where free will can be exercised with regularity. These free systems are an integral part of the physical universe which allow free agents to act freely. So, the question then becomes, what is the cost of overriding Dave's free will?

Altering Dave's free will involves more than a 1:1 of goods versus evils. Saving the lives of those children (say there were thirteen of them) does not, on the balance of things, equate to a net gain of twelve if Dave's free will becomes altered. The reality of free will is more weighted than that. Just as turning a key to start a car causes a chain reaction much greater than the simple motion performed by the driver so too does altering free will entail much more than a simple inconvenience to one person. Dave's free will can only be overridden by directly oppressing his free will or indirectly by altering the free systems which allow him to make a moral choice. These free systems can include, but are not limited to, his physical abilities and those laws of physics and chemistry which allow combustion to take place with regularity. Upholding FW1 requires a commitment to compromising free systems (which impact every person's life) for the sake of avoiding intense evil. As heart-wrenching as it is to consider the suffering those children endure at the hands of Dave, to assert that Dave's free will should be overridden is to assert that it is acceptable/appropriate that, for the sake of a few, the regularity of fundamental laws which govern the universe should be compromised. Furthermore, to argue that Dave's free will should be directly overridden establishes a precedent that anyone's free will should be violated should their moral choices be deemed unworthy. What then, should someone be judged for actions they have not committed? To live in such a world would be to live in a state of irregularity.

Undoubtedly, this conclusion seems harsh; how dare someone attempt to quantify the good of a situation when children's lives are at risk? While this does sound harsh it should be remembered that it is the proponent of FW1 that has first begun quantifying the situation. FW1 says that Dave's free will is less important than the lives of thirteen children. However, once the implications of free will and free systems are considered the quantity of people involved with Dave's intense evil are found to be much greater. Indeed, not only are there over six billion people in the world but there are countless animals and other living organisms who, though they do not have free will to the same extent as humans, live within the bounds of those same free systems which allow for free will to be actualized. Though no one wishes to tell the families of those children that a greater good was preserved when G did not override Dave's free will, it does appear that, overall, the preservation of free will has a greater benefit for humanity in general than what it costs to override free will.

Of course, the claim could still be made that G could isolate the environment locally and suspend the free systems involved in order to preserve the lives of the children without compromising the greater good. This is a valid observation, and perhaps it is one that is potentially within G's power to execute. However, this then becomes an instance of just-one-more argumentation, such as was discussed in chapter 5.

For G to interfere with free will and/or free systems in Dave's case involves the complexities briefly delineated above, and it entails all instances that may be warranted in the world. If G is justified in interfering with Dave's free will, directly or indirectly, then he may also be justified in interfering with a great many more instances of potential intense evil. There is a line in the sand, a point at which interference causes more harm than good to the regularity of free systems. Knowledge is required to determine this line, knowledge that is beyond human ken. Furthermore, this leads to the second area affected by FW1: the identity of G.

As has been understood throughout this paper, G represents a wholly good, loving, omnipotent, and omniscient God consistent with the God of Christianity. When non-theists address the POE, quite often G's attributes are at the forefront. For surely, they say, a good, loving, etc. God would prevent at least the example of intense evil that is a fawn dying in a fire or the abuse and murder of a little girl. Indeed, these are evidences that should be addressed, and will be addressed in the next chapter, but the essence of their claim is that G cannot be both good and omnipotent otherwise intense evils would not happen. However, this is a false dichotomy. Not only does there not need to be a conflict between goodness and omnipotence but the cost of G overturning free will, for even one person, is extremely high.

The issues of goodness/power and dis/honoring free will are not entirely separate from each other. Unrestrained power does not equate to goodness. Goodness is, if nothing else, a bridle on power. If G were omnipotent but not good there would be no predicting how or when G would exercise his power. G's goodness, however, works together with his omnipotence, and this benefits humanity, and the world, for there remains an assurance that G will not abuse his power. Of course, the charge of the non-theist in FW1 is that G either neglects his power or is not completely good and powerful. As to power, the existence of G's goodness explains why he may not exercise his power in a given situation, but what of his goodness? Surely, the goodness of G would require him to stop Dave and save the children. Truly, the theist's position is that G does desire good action on the part of humanity, and that is the crux of the situation: choice. The world G created has been equipped with free systems which allow free will beings to actualize their free will (i.e., live it out consistently). As was discussed above, free systems entail regularity which fosters free will choices. What would it mean if G were to override free will? It would mean that G is exerting his power to countermand an act of free will, the ability for which is part of human identity.[23] In short, G would become an oppressor, which is inconsistent with being good. Unbridled power is not good, goodness provides assurances as to the use of power, and goodness being incompatible with oppression requires that G respect the choices of free will agents, even if those choices run counter to the nature of G.

On the surface, claims such as FW1 appear to be completely reasonable. If G entails goodness and omnipotence, surely G would prevent intense evil even at the expense of one person's free will. Since intense evil exists anyway, G either doesn't exist or is not wholly good, loving, omnipotent, and omniscient. However, once FW1 undergoes an examination for the cost of its belief a different picture emerges. Free will, and its dependence upon free systems, require that there be a respect for regularity. Furthermore, the relationship between these two is such that the violation of one negatively impacts the other. To override free will would require an alteration of free systems which could impact all of humanity, not just those isolated to a particular situation. Additionally, to assert that G, should he exist, would be required (by nature of his attributes) to override free will is to claim that G should act as an oppressor. Since being an oppressor is inconsistent with being wholly good, it would be an error to claim that G would act in an oppressive manner. The relationship between free will and free systems paints a picture of a world in which it is reasonable for theists to expect there to be intense evil in the world, for G could only prevent it by altering the systems of regularity that govern this world and/or by becoming an oppressor, which is contrary to his nature.

At this point one can hear the non-theist saying, "Even if the above claims are granted theism still faces immense difficulties because theism is replete with accounts of divine interaction with humanity!" Indeed, the above portrays a world in which G faces severe logical limitations in his interaction with free will beings. However, the relationship between free will beings and free systems (which is essential to the FSC) is capable of accounting for divine interaction. While miracles will be specifically addressed later

---

23. It could be objected here that there are persons who have no free will, such as those in a persistent vegetative state. It is worth noting that a lack of ability toward free will does not defeat the idea that free will is part of human identity. For, it is a lack of free will (in part) that signals to doctors and loved ones that something unfavorable exists with the person in such a condition. Therefore, rather than being a defeater for this free will thesis, medical conditions such as these affirm the importance of free will to human identity.

in this chapter, the role of free will in a free system will be considered next for its implications regarding individual responsibility in moral actions and the important role of prayer in G's interaction with humanity.

Free Will in a Free System

Individual Responsibility for Moral Actions

As has just been discussed, the FW1 thesis claims that it would be acceptable for G to override an individual's free will so that some intense evil may be avoided. However, when this concept is taken to its logical end it results in a divine being who willfully undermines a defining attribute of humanity, thus becoming an oppressor. Since being an oppressor is incompatible with being wholly good and loving it would be oxymoronic to conclude that G could be an oppressor. There are then two possibilities regarding moral evil: (ME1) G does not exist or (ME*) there exists a valid reason for why G would allow intense moral evil. Just as ME1 is a natural extension of FW1, ME* is a natural extension of FW* (free will is a fundamental good for all of humanity). If ME* attains its justification will likely be found within the implications of FW*.

Simply put, free will is the capacity for choice. As has already been discussed in this chapter, the ability to make a choice does not negate the possibility of there being restrictions. Indeed, restrictions (e.g., gravity) define the parameters by which choices can be made. There are two natural consequences of free will: good actions and evil actions. Evil actions entail a set of potential actions of particular concern to the POE. Thus far, this set of evil actions has been referred to as intense evil. The non-theistic claim that there are intense evils that are gratuitous (i.e., have no compensating good) represent a direct attack on the theistic claim of G's existence and character. What then could be a justifying reason for why G would allow intense evil? One argument that could be made makes use of free will: all moral evil is the result of human choices. This statement, simple though it may be, speaks directly to the heart of the matter. G does not make or coerce people to perform intense evil; people are responsible for their own actions. However, this observation, though important and foundational, only pushes the question back one step farther. As C. S. Lewis states, "Even if all suffering were man-made, we should like to know the reason for the enormous permission to torture their fellows which God gives to the worst of men."[24] So, even though people are responsible for the evils they

---

24. Lewis, *Problem of Pain*, 601.

commit, because of their free will, the question of G's duplicity/complacency remains. Perhaps ironically, the solution to this conundrum can be found within the claim of non-theists.

Without free will there would be no criticism of moral (or natural) evil. Reacting to a sense of moral obligation, a person questions the rightness of a situation and the those who would allow it to happen. If it were not for free will such an outcry (which is itself an act of free will) would not be possible, or perhaps more accurately, any outcry that occurred outside of free will would merely be a causal reaction and not bear the gravitas implied in its words. For, by proclaiming the POE one hopes to elicit a thoughtful response from others. To question the value of free will while expecting others to make a choice toward one's argument is to have a double standard regarding the value of free will. All people, regardless of their philosophical bent, live their lives with a respect for the importance of free will.[25] The claim that G should override an individual's free will in order to prevent intense evil is a claim that does not necessarily negate the goodness of free will, but it does lessen the quality of goodness inherent in free will. Furthermore, just as the use of free will to object to the value of free will does in fact affirm the value of free will, so too does the call for more goodness in the face of evil affirm free will.

Observing and questioning the existence of intense evil contains an interesting quality. Desiring good over evil denotes a sense of moral obligation and the value of what is good. An action is good, in part, because someone made a choice contra evil. If one were to restrict free will (beyond the free systems that exist in this world) to the point of altering another's choices one effectively devalues good at the same time. The praiseworthiness of a good deed is directly proportional to the potential for evil. A child chooses to put their dishes in the sink after dinner. This demonstrates obedience and solidarity with the family; it is a praiseworthy deed. However, when the child is tempted to start a fight at school, but does not do so, the child has done good, and the praiseworthiness of the later is far greater than that of the former. Any action that lowers the free will of the child also lowers the praiseworthiness (i.e., goodness) of an act. The same free will that allows good also allows

---

25. There are, of course, determinists and oppressors. As to the determinists, while they do not believe free will exists, they nevertheless live out their lives as if they do have free will. As to the oppressors, the very act(s) of oppression they commit reflect a high regard for free will, one that is bent toward selfishness and greed (they value free will so much as to wish to horde the free will of others). In short, even those who would seem to not value the importance of free will affirm its value by nature of how they live their lives.

evil. Someone's free will can only be altered toward decreasing the potential for evil by devaluing the potential for good.

Does there exist a valid reason(s) for why G would allow intense moral evil? Assuming for the moment that it would be within G's character to oppress an individual's free will in at least one instance, G could only do so at the expense of the good of free will for all of humanity. Either the implicit value of individual free will would be diminished or the systems which govern free will for all of humanity would need to be altered. Regardless of the method chosen, the result would be a free will that does not contain the value it had before, and the potential goods that would result would also be lessened. As it is, for G to act in such a way is contrary to his nature, and the potential for good that arises from free will, and the free systems which allow free will to be actualized, would suffer if moral evil were prevented by G through a means that violated free will. If there is to be any consistency in this world, and it has already been argued that regularity is a valuable good, then free will and free systems also need to be regular and regularly upheld/respected by G.

Free will denotes personal responsibility. G has created a world with great potential for good as well as evil, but the resultant goods/evils are a result of free will choices. This section has also made frequent references to the relationship between free will and free systems. In short, free systems entail the regularity of natural laws which work toward providing an environment where free will can be actualized. It has been implicitly argued that the relationship between free systems and free will results in a world where G is severely restricted in terms of interaction with that world. Specific to this section, the value of free systems and free will restricts G's involvement in cases of intense evil. While this does lay a foundation for a response to ME1 and FW1, the theism argued for here affirms the ability of G to interact with humanity. Does the FSC, which is irrevocably tied to the relationship between free will and free systems, negate the possibility of G's interaction with humanity? The answer to that question is a resounding, "No!" How then can G interact with humanity without violating free will and the regularity of free systems? The answer to that question, as least in part, can be found in an act of free will known as prayer.

Prayer as an Act of Free Will

Prayer is communication between humanity and G. As such, prayer entails some qualities that make it invaluable in understanding the relationship between humanity, G, and the in/actions of both. Prayer can take on many forms, such as worship and penitence, but of particular concern here are the types of prayers that involve a petition for G to act within this physical world (and it is with this understanding that the word "prayer" will be used here). Although the goal of prayer is a desire to see G act in a certain way, prayer is an action. What is more, prayer comes as a result of a conscious choice made by free agents. In other words, prayer is an act of free will.

The implications of this observation are simple yet profound: in a world governed by the regularity of free systems prayer equates to permission for G to interact directly with a system that may otherwise inhibit such action. Since prayer results from a free will choice to ask G for intervention in this world, prayer provides a potential means by which G can affect change without violating either free systems or free will. Prayer works within the rules of regularity and free will thereby allowing G to act. While this may seem to answer the aforementioned question about the possibility of G's interaction with humanity, this observation raises at least one further question: Why do prayers asked on behalf of those suffering go unanswered? Given the great number of people professing to pray for those in need and O, this is a question that theism must be able to address if it has any hope of answering the APOE.

There are many factors involved with prayer. For example, the intent/motivation of the petitioner can have a great impact on prayer. If the prayer is motivated by selfishness, even though on the surface it could appear to be altruistic, it is likely that G, who epitomizes moral virtue, would not answer that prayer in the affirmative. Furthermore, there is the possibility that G would choose to not answer a prayer as a means of testing/building the faith of the petitioner. However, the primary prayer of concern here are those which are genuinely well intentioned and aimed at the good but are still unanswered. Why is it that prayers such as peace on earth often seem to go unanswered (at least in accord with the wishes of the petitioner) by G? Hasker touches upon this very issue when he states, "We must confess that peace on earth . . . and the doing of God's will are rather the exception than the general rule. The reason, of course, lies squarely in the will of creatures such as ourselves, who in the very many cases are far from desiring what God desires and from willing to do God's will."[26] Hasker argues that in a great many prayers there are more parties involved than G and the petitioner. Other parties can include a person being prayed for and those who may also being involved with the object of the prayer (doctors, nurses, lawyers, police officers, etc.). In short, G does not grant the wish of any worthy prayer for at least two reasons: G is not an automaton and the free will of others still needs

---

26. Hasker, "Is Free-Will Theism Religiously Inadequate," 439.

to be respected. It is entirely possible for a prayer to be worthy (such as world peace) but violate either G's plan/will (e.g., for all that is known a tragic example of suffering may be required for there to be a resultant greater number of goods) or another's free will (e.g., a child may pray for their mother to quit smoking, but if the mother does not want to it could be a violation of free will for G to suddenly make her addiction cease). Indeed, it appears that the simple concept of prayer is at once a means for allowing G to operate in this world and an ineffectual tool stymied by the slightest unforeseen variable. Is prayer truly a satisfactory answer for how it is that G can operate in this world? At the very least, the FSC can answer this question in the affirmative and offer some hope to those petitioning G for action.

In applying the FSC to this latest question, consider the example of a child requesting that G would make it so her mother would quit smoking. Furthermore, the child has been praying for three years for her mother to quit but instead of an answered prayer her mother's addiction has become worse. Surely, this is a worthy prayer born out of a child's (Molly's) love for her mother's (Bettie's) well-being. Molly has acted in free will by petitioning G for his help. This act of free will effectively gives G permission to intervene in this world designed to preserve the free will of humans, yet it appears that G does nothing. Perhaps the most obvious observation to be made here entails G's respect of Bettie's free will. If Bettie does not wish to quit G will not make her, for if he did he would become an oppressor, which is contrary to his nature. While this is an accurate observation the non-theist could easily make an abductive claim that at the very least it is possible (perhaps even probable given G's good nature) that he could speak to Bettie on a basic level and use his omniscience to speak to her in a way that would motivate her to make the right choice. In short, the non-theist could claim that if G exists then he could still positively influence Bettie without violating her free will.[27] Of course, taken too far this tact could still result in oppression, but assume for the moment that the non-theist's claim has warrant. After all, it does seem that the inference to the best explanation for how G would act in this situation would be to do everything in his power that did not violate free will to help Bettie. However, the non-theist's abduction only stands as the most probable if there are no other competing explanations that more fully account for the evidence at hand. Enter the FSC.

---

27. The line of argumentation the non-theist takes here is an anticipation of how non-theists would react to what has been argued thus far in this paper. So, instead of arguing for a justified overriding of free will the argument here is that G's goodness and omniscience would compel him and provide the means for him to influence someone toward a desired end.

Assume that the above information about Molly's request is accurate. The FSC, with its emphasis on theodical suggestions born from free will and free systems, helps to guide observation toward a more complete picture of a situation. One question that has not been asked is, "Why is Bettie addicted to cigarettes?" Likely there were social pressures involved at first (and there still may be, few people like to admit that they have made a mistake and quitting would be admitting to the mistake of smoking) but there are also physiological conditions. G made human minds and bodies with incredible means of maintaining a regular state of health. Outside factors can influence health, but the function of the human body is so regular that when a body functions differently it is considered something to be fixed. Bettie made a choice to smoke, and in making that choice she introduced toxins into her body that were not part of the nutrients the body needed. Thus, a physical addiction occurred, and along with this physical condition comes mental habit. In short, the regular workings of Bettie's body were negatively influenced by the tobacco resulting in strong influences on her decisions to quit smoking. Even if G was "allowed" to alter the physical condition of her body, Bettie still has strong psychological motivations for continuing her habit. It is entirely possible that G did act as the non-theist claims he should but because of how free systems are influencing her free will Bettie decides to not quit smoking (i.e., she gives into temptation). This theodical suggestion, this explanation for why it appears Molly's prayers have been unanswered, may not be true but it is possible. Indeed, given what is known about addictions it is probable. What makes this theistic conclusion more probable than the non-theist's resides in the foundation for the conclusion.

The objection raised by non-theists here plays the attributes of G against an apparent example of G's inaction. The FSC, on the other hand, in looking for the implications of free will and free systems working together, not only accounts for the observations of the non-theists but includes additional observations which raises the probability of theism over the non-theistic objections. Prayer does involve an act of free will on the part of the petitioner, but G still must be true to his nature (which includes honoring free will) and this includes his interactions with those who are the object of prayer. Admittedly, there is much that is beyond human ken; the full set of circumstances surrounding Molly and Bettie (and any actual persons) are likely to be unknown. However, the FSC enables the observer to gather more data, observe more circumstances that are in play, for a given situation. Prayer may appear to go unanswered, but that does not mean that G is incapable of acting. The more the complexities of a situation are revealed the more intricately woven the lines of free will and free systems are found to be. This means that there may be times G cannot act without becoming an oppressor, but it can also mean that there may be times when G can act in un/subtle ways but the person involved shuns G's advances.[28]

In sum, prayer is an act of free will that can allow G to interact with this world, but those same standards of free will and free systems can also result in an apparent noninvolvement of G despite the presence of prayer. As was seen in the example of Molly and Bettie, the FSC draws observations regarding nature and free will. The ability for free systems and free will to provide theodical suggestions for addressing the APOE will likewise need to be able to be applied to natural and moral evils. Therefore, the implications of the FSC for natural evil and moral evil will be considered.

What Should Be Expected

This world experiences no shortage of natural evil. Tornadoes, earthquakes, tsunamis, blizzards, and hurricanes represent only a partial list of mortal dangers found in nature. Each of these are responsible for human and/or animal deaths every year. A fundamental question in the POE, as it relates to natural evil, states, "If G is truly loving and omnipotent, why would he make a world in which natural evils occur?" Of course, this is not a new question and as such there have been many theistic responses over the years. This section briefly examines theistic responses to natural evil and then offers the perspective of the FSC. For, there exists a question prior to the above question in the POE: "Given one's understanding of the universe, what should be expected?" The answer to this later question will greatly impact the impetus behind the former.

In general, there seems to be two types of theistic responses to natural evil: (NE1) gratuitous evils exist but are not contradictory to G and (NE2) there are spiritual causes for natural evil. NE1 attempts to account for seemingly pointless intense evil via regularity; NE2 takes seriously the spiritual side of theistic belief. Each of these offers a helpful perspective in addressing the POE but ultimately falls short in adequately addressing the APOE.

An example of NE1 can be found in Bruce Reichenbach. In addressing a hypothetical fawn suffering in a forest fire (an example commonly used by nontheists which will be specifically addressed in the next chapter), Reichenbach states, "A world operating with regularity according to natural laws is a necessary condition for the greater good of the realization of moral values. . . . The suffering fawn may be pointless or gratuitous,

---

28. It is possible that G can act and effect changes in more pronounced (i.e., miraculous) ways. The implications of miracles and regularity will be discussed later in this chapter.

but the possibility of it is a necessary condition of there being that greater good."[29] While Reichenbach does not use the term "seemingly" as a descriptor of the gratuitousness of the fawn's suffering it does seem to be implied given that he views said suffering to be allowed as part of a greater purpose for creation. Therefore, it is not truly gratuitous since it does serve a function (even if that function is one of by-product rather than intent). The main goal of Reichenbach's argument here can be found in absolving G of all blameworthiness for natural evils because of the necessity of the potential for such instances in the design of a creation containing free will. Elsewhere, Reichenbach states, "God cannot be held morally accountable or blameworthy for the existence of a world run by natural laws. But evils are a necessary consequence of natural objects acting according to natural laws upon sentient, natural creatures. Hence, God cannot be held morally accountable or blameworthy for natural evils."[30] Reichenbach asserts that G is on logically solid ground in creating a world not sustained by miraculous intervention (i.e., it is self-sustaining) and that a natural consequence of this is the potential for natural evil. In short, the existence of regular natural laws (which are logically necessary for there to be a world not sustained by miracles) will contain examples of intense suffering as a result of nature acting as it should. There is much similarity here between Reichenbach and van Inwagen's EFWD. As was discussed in chapter 5, van Inwagen was responding to the pain and suffering resulting from evolution and the charge that regularity is a good that cannot be compromised. Though Reichenbach and van Inwagen approach the topic from different angles, in the end they represent a methodology of accounting for natural evil that takes seriously the logical ramifications of regularity as it relates to acts of nature. However, it is the theistic position that the spiritual world exists, and Alvin Plantinga offers a perspective on natural evil that makes use of the spiritual and the limits of human ken.

As was discussed in chapter 4, Plantinga asserts that it is possible for natural evils to be caused by the actions of spiritual beings operating beyond human perception. This class of defense has been here referred to as NE2, and while it may not be popular to account for natural evil by looking to the supernatural, Plantinga insists that this has no bearing the rational possibility of supernatural free agents influencing natural evil.[31] Though Plantinga's FWD allows for other possible answers, it is this pointing to nonhuman free agents that seems to be the focus of Plantinga's FWD in relation to natural

---

29. Reichenbach, "Inductive Argument from Evil," 226.
30. Reichenbach, "Natural Evils and Natural Law," 189.
31. Plantinga, *God, Freedom, and Evil*, 62.

evil. Perhaps this is due to wanting to affirm the supernatural considering those, such as J. L. Mackie (discussed in chapter 4), who favor a causal worldview which makes no allowance for free will or the supernatural, including G. Regardless of Plantinga's motivations for focusing on nonhuman causes of natural evil this is an important point in the FWD against natural evil. The FWD has resiliency in its ability to withstand scrutiny of the kind that would wish to disprove it entirely. As it stands, the FWD (specifically regarding nonhuman agents and natural evil) cannot be disproven as such, but that is not qualitatively the same as being convincing. It would seem that for many people, especially non-theists, the charge that spiritual beings are responsible for natural evil is absurd. Granted, in the FWD this accounting of natural evil comes after argumentation for warranted belief in G, but despite the logical nature of Plantinga's arguments the FWD accounting of natural evils faces strong abductive push back.

Though there is much unknown about the workings of the universe there are many things that are known. For example, weather formations contain a lot of unknowns but what is known are relationships between times of year, bodies of water/land, etc., that influence weather patterns and offer a degree of predictability. That April showers bring May flowers constitutes a concept of regularity in relation to weather. Though drought or excess rainfall may inhibit May flowers, the norm of this pattern is predictable. Therefore, one may state that the inference to the best explanation for why flowers come in May is a result of the regular rain in April. While this is an example of a good that derives from April rain it would be a mistake to overlook the motor accidents that result from rainfall or the potential for sickness and suffering from exposure to the elements during this time. To Plantinga's point, these instances of evil are a deviation from the norm of good, therefore, spiritual beings may be the cause of these abnormalities. However, for someone who does not believe in the spiritual, the regular conditions of the weather provide enough of an answer for why things are the way they are. In short, for natural evil the FWD is not abductively strong; it still may be correct, but it can be difficult to accept as an inference to the best explanation for natural evil.

It is the conclusion here that NE1 is superior to NE2 for its potential to speak in terms that are more readily identifiable with non-theists. As such, NE1 can serve as a foundation for addressing examples of natural evil in a manner that is abductive. Defenses, such as the EFWD, are effective in logically drawing conclusions regarding natural evil, but they do seem to be lacking in their abductive appeal. The reason for this resides not in any logical inconsistency/oversight but rather in the hesitancy for such defenses to speak to specific examples. Such hesitation is understandable; in moving toward specific examples a defense runs the risk of becoming a theodicy, and if just one application of a theodicy can be proven incorrect the whole of the project becomes endangered. The FSC, making serious use of the importance of regularity, aids defenses such as these because of its tandem emphasis on theodical suggestions.

What should be expected in nature are systems of regularity that conflict. A tree, governed by regular physical laws, grows properly for the conditions of its environment. Likewise, the atmosphere behaves as it should, which also includes the creation of storms. The FSC anticipate the regularity of the tree growth and weather formations, and it also anticipates the likelihood that these systems may/will intersect. When this happens there may be undesirable consequences, but a constant avoidance of these consequences can only come at the expense of regularity. The FSC also anticipates that within natural evil it may be possible to ascertain some possible reason for why G chose not to intervene. Due to limits of human knowledge it is quite possible that in many cases the conclusion may resound with the importance of regularity, but in seeking for plausible reasons the FSC keeps an attentive ear open for additional reasons for intense suffering being allowed. When such reasons present themselves, they work together with the good of regularity to offer a more complete telling of a situation; a more complete telling which may speak to that part of human consciousness which thinks abductively. Furthermore, since humans live in this natural world it stands to reason that this world can have an influence on moral evil as well as natural evil.

It is a simple matter, and indeed seems to comes quite naturally to many, if not most, people to think of nature and humanity in separate terms. The sentience of humanity affords some understanding for this conceived dichotomy; when one has higher reasoning of a form far superior to all other life and forces in this world a feeling of separateness can be expected. However, despite any legitimate, and/or inflated, perceptions of one's uniqueness in this world the fact remains that humanity operates within not only nature but the free systems which govern it as well. Free systems have a significant impact upon moral action. The rules that provide structure by which free will deeds can be regularly performed also help to define the morality of a given deed. For example, if randomly punching someone in the nose resulted in good fortune for the defender then punching someone in the nose could be deemed a morally good thing to do. However, given the parameters that the laws of physics and biology dictate, randomly punching someone in the nose causes pain and suffering. Thus, it is not a morally good act. While someone may have the free will ability to randomly punch someone in the nose, the regular way in which the aforementioned laws guide human physiology give cause for viewing such an act as morally wrong. Without free systems people would not be able to make moral judgments about a given situation with any degree of certainty. As was discussed in chapters 2 and 3, there are natural indicators of how things are to be, and the existence of a strong sense of moral obligation speaks to this. Without free systems and free will, moral obligation would never have a hope of being fulfilled. As was also discussed, it is the theistic position that G alone can help humanity to cross the moral gap, the distance between moral ought and moral capability, but even if a person never chooses to accept G's help, the free will that person possesses affords them the opportunity to perform significantly good moral actions. Without the opportunity to do otherwise a good act would not smell as sweet. This potential for good or evil action, known as free will, finds itself actualized while surrounded by the web of regular laws known here as free systems. The FSC expects an interplay between free will and free systems in moral actions. To ignore the potential implications of free systems is to wear a pair of glasses which restrict one's vision. Additionally, to view moral potential as anything but an intricate/vital aspect of human identity is to be in denial about the human condition.

Chapters 2 and 3 discussed moral obligation and natural law. While space would be wasted in fully repeating their content here, this present discussion will benefit from some insight from their topics. In addressing the human ability to alter its perception of what is good and bad, C. S. Lewis states, "The real objection is that if man chooses to treat himself as raw material, raw material he will be: not raw material to be manipulated, as he fondly imagined, by himself, but by mere appetite, that is, mere Nature, in the person of his de-humanized Conditioners."[32] Here, Lewis highlights the ability of humanity to use its power of reason to justify whatever it wants. In short, in viewing itself as merely a set of properties that can be applied toward whatever is desired humanity becomes less human. The problem, as Lewis sees it, resides in a denial of nature. Specifically, he observes that the more relative morality appears the more one loses one's human identity. Lewis states, "It is no use trying to 'see through' first principles. If you see through everything, then everything is transparent. But a wholly transparent world is an invisible world. To 'see through' all things is the same as not to see."[33] In other words, when someone questions the existence of moral obligation one has laid the foundation to question the truth of anything.

Moral obligation is a fundamental aspect of human identity. The FSC recognizes this and the relationship that human free will has with free systems.

32. Lewis, *Abolition of Man*, 726.
33. Lewis, *Abolition of Man*, 730.

Without free systems free will becomes a desire with no outlet. In thinking of free will *and* free systems, one begins to see interrelated connections that not only help to explain why an act is right/wrong but also the forces of regularity which allow those choices to come to fruition. Once one considers G at these intersections of free will and free systems one begins to see theodical suggestions which provide possible explanations for why G may have chosen to not intervene. By virtue of his nature, G is respectful of the free systems he created as well as the free will he bestowed upon humanity. In short, the more information that is gleaned the more reasonable it becomes that G would not act in observations of intense evil. G is not only the creator of a universe made to sustain free will, but he is its caretaker as well.

Challenges to the Free System Corollary

Before the FSC is applied to two cases of intense evil and evaluated for its abductive power over non-theism, there are some challenges to the FSC that should be considered. First, given the strong reliance of the FSC on the good of regularity, and its assertion that G can still operate within free systems, the compatibility of miracles and regularity will be considered. Second, also foundational to the FSC is the truth of free will. Therefore, the implications of this linchpin should be discussed. Third, the FSC also relies upon limits of epistemic knowledge. Yes, the FSC does seek to illuminate one's knowledge of a situation, but theodical suggestions are, ultimately, a plea to one's ignorance compared to G's omniscience of a situation. Therefore, it will be seen if the FSC affords a way to counter William Rowe's critique of skeptical theism.

Miracles and Regularity

Given the emphasis thus far on the good of regularity for the operation of the world and the fulfillment of free will, it could be said that any claims as to G's ability to operate proactively in this world are little more than hollow words, an empty sentiment born of religious duty more than logical consistency. Does the good of regularity negate the possibility of G working directly in the affairs of this world? Are miracles incompatible with regularity? The answer to both questions is negative, for not only are miracles and regularity compatible but they should be anticipated.

An example of the compatibility with regularity and divine intervention can be seen in the world of computers. Programs depend upon regularity. In fact, programs never make mistakes. They work within and upon the parameters given to them by their creators. Any appearance of a malfunctioning program is due to a flaw in design, not because the program decides to act other than how it was made. In fact, programs are the epitome of regularity. They have no independent thought. Yes, there can be randomizing generators and algorithms which attempt to anticipate responses thus giving a scant appearance of intelligence/free will, but in the end, all computers and computer programs, from IBM's Watson to solitaire, are governed by regularity. This does not mean, however, that once a program is created that it cannot be altered. Programmers have the capability of creating backdoors into a program. These backdoors allow for changes to be made to the program. The computer language being used does not change, nor does the intent of the program (e.g., an accounting program will remain an accounting program), but changes can be made that benefit the performance of that same program.[34] Computer programs cannot function if they do not have a dependable (i.e., regular) system which consistently allows for actions to be accomplished, yet the programmer retains the capability of altering that program without it losing its purpose.

If finite humans possess the skill to enact and make use of backdoors to their programming how much more likely is it that G should be able to do the same with his creation? As was discussed earlier in this chapter, prayer, as an act of free will, provides one means by which G can operate in this world without violating the terms of regularity which are so vital for its functionality. Given that G created this world, there remains a very probable likelihood that a backdoor was built into this system so that G could interact with his creation without violating regularity. Again, if humans have the wherewithal to create backdoors into their programs it becomes highly improbable that an infinite/omniscient divine being would not think to do the same with his creation. To make use of a backdoor is to make use of a system that is within the bounds of the systems of regularity of the created world. In other words, were G to make use of the backdoor of this creation it would not be a violation of the good of regularity.[35] Surely, prayer represents a kind of backdoor, but given the limits of human ken there exists a likely possibility that G has created backdoors of kinds unimagined by finite

---

34. Interestingly, this same line of argument can be used to support Plantinga's argument for the relationship between natural evil and nonhuman spiritual entities. For, the presence of a backdoor could also allow someone with ill intensions to harm the program. That is not the argument being made here, but this does highlight the logical (if not abductive) resilience of Plantinga's argument.

35. Perhaps it should be said that "it would not necessarily be a violation," as the possibility remains that a backdoor can be used for evil. However, given the character of G this should not be a concern for humanity.

beings. Of course, any use of a backdoor by G would be consistent with his character, and this implies that action by G will not produce evil. So, regularity remains a guideline, created by G, which he honors, otherwise he would become an oppressor which is contrary to his nature.

Regularity and the possibility of a backdoor work together to create a balance. G can operate in this world, miracles can happen, but a balance/ respect for regularity needs to be maintained for the world to retain its cohesion. This at once explains how it is that G can operate in this world and why he may choose / not be able to intercede to prevent an act of natural or moral evil. In speaking against those who claim miracles cannot happen, theist Craig Keener references theist and physicist John Polkinghorne when he states, "God is consistent with the patterns that God established in nature, but 'consistency is not the same as dreary uniformity. In unprecedented circumstances, God can do unexpected things.' The 'unexpected things' are not the predictable stuff of science, but neither are they inimical to the normal, predictable stuff of science."[36] Consistency/regularity is not synonymous with unwavering repetitiveness. One can be consistently good but enact that goodness in a variety of ways. Similarly, G possesses the capability of respecting regularity while proactively working with/in his creation.

The concept of a backdoor not only demonstrates the potential for G being able to perform miracles within a world governed by regularity but its very existence also allows humanity to anticipate its potential use by G. If finite humanity is capable of deriving a means of altering a program run by regularity without violating that regularity, then it should be anticipated that G could think of doing the same thing with his creation. While miracles may be a hard concept to accept, especially for those who need convincing that the spiritual exists, the coexistence of miracles and systems of regularity remains possible. Thus, the good of regularity, a vital component of the FSC, does not contradict the theistic belief in the possibility of miracles. Of course, the counterpart to regularity in the FSC is free will as the intersection of these two concepts provides the basis for theodical suggestions. While miracles may not be inherently contradictory to regularity, the value of free will in the FSC remains an unwavering necessity in its operation and is thus open to scrutiny.

The Linchpin of Free Will

Admittedly, the single most important component to the FSC is free will. Were either the good of regularity or regularity itself proven false, the theist

---

36. Keener, *Miracles*, 127.

would still be capable of addressing the APOE using free will as a launching pad. However, remove free will, prove it an ill-conceived notion, and regularity becomes solely a tool of determinism. Eliminate free will and the FSC becomes useless. However, denouncing free will is not only difficult but it comes at a high cost as well.

The existence of free will has already been discussed in chapter 2 and was briefly defended in light of Mackie in chapter 4. Discussions on the nature/reality of free will have a rich history in philosophy, and there does not appear to be any signs of it stopping any time soon. Indeed, this discussion has exemplified brevity in its treatment of free will as a necessity of moving the conversation toward the POE, and the APOE specifically. However, in the interest of critiquing the FSC the topic of free will arises again. Furthermore, the FSC makes no apology for its dependence upon free will. In fact, a curiosity exists in discussing free will versus determinism which points toward the strength of acknowledging/proclaiming the existence free will. One cannot speak of determinism without the need to explain away free will. As has been argued here, free will does not require a complete absence of causality in nature for existence, but determinism does require an absence of free will for its survival.

The problem of free will for determinism can been seen in the natural human inclination toward believing in its existence. Of course, determinists such as Mackie have their arguments for why this is an illusion, but as was argued in chapter 4 it is possible that determinists are in fact the ones suffering from Metaphysical Double Vision. If free will is an illusion it comes as an illusion that is powerful and persistent. So resilient are conceptions of free will that the burden of proof resides with determinists to prove it an illusion. In discussing the importance of free will (though he himself opposes libertarian free will), philosopher Robert Kane states, "This is one of the many ironies of the modern history of debates about free will: libertarian free will has been under attack in the modern era as a premodern and outdated conception, while the values associated with libertarian free will have becomes the defining values of post Enlightenment modernity."[37] Even as philosophers refine and reproduce deterministic arguments the importance of free will becomes more pronounced within society. The value of free will has an element of intractability in human ideals. Therefore, the FSC, while dependent upon the existence of free will, finds itself abductively sound in its use of free will. Adding to the abductive appeal of free will is the cost of the nonexistence of free will.

---

37. Kane, *Significance of Free Will*, 212.

A natural implication of a purely deterministic world (i.e., a world where no free will exists) is the absence of choice. With no choice comes further implications for daily life. For example, if all actions are determined then no responsibility can be attributed for said action. A murderer did not choose to murder someone, they had no choice. How can someone be held responsible for a crime if they had no responsibility in the matter? It could be said that the judicial system results from causality, which is to say that it could eventually change, and these are the motions involved with certain actions for this stage of humanity. However, this does not track with human conceptions of reality. Personal responsibility for actions is a concept that manifests with the first stages of life. Even children understand that if they do not eat the food they are given they will be hungry. Some children choose not to eat and go hungry. Others choose to eat the food they do not like and are not hungry. While causality can be seen here so too can choice (i.e., free will) be seen. To espouse a deterministic view is to tell people that the many choices they make every day are an illusion. Not only does this fail abductively but it undermines virtually, if not all, concepts of justice. Indeed, this is a high price to pay for asserting that free will does not exist despite ubiquitous natural inclinations to the contrary. This also bears an interesting implication for the deterministic philosopher.

Anytime someone writes they are attempting communication. In philosophy, and academics in general, the communicator, more often than not, attempts to prove a particular concept. Whether the author writes to prove an ideal discussed in class or is attempting to argue for the illusion of free will, the written word has the intent of convincing the other as to the truth of its proposition. Authors hope to persuade the reader to their point of view, to urge them to choose their argument over another's. In other words, the very words espoused by determinists, such as Mackie, are dependent upon the truth of free will's existence. If free will is an illusion, no purpose exists for the words being written aside from compulsively succumbing to the momentum of the universe. For a philosophical paper to have any meaning it needs to have the power/potential to persuade. The cost of the belief of determinism results in the pointlessness of arguing for the truth of determinism.

Undoubtedly, free will is the linchpin of the FSC. However, free will is not such a fragile thing as to cause concern for its use in theistic defenses. Free will persists in human conception with a tenacity that calls for acceptance. Even if one could disprove the existence of free will it would come at a high cost. Not only would personal responsibility disappear but with an absence of free will comes an ineffectual academic cause. To write to persuade someone of the truth of determinism assumes that the reader can make a choice to accept the philosophy, but if determinism is true then the reader can no more choose to embrace determinism than a dog can stop being a dog. It would seem that the truth of free will has an abductive quality to it which places the burden of proof on those who would espouse its falsehood. Therefore, the FSC accepts free will as its linchpin and moves forward with addressing the APOE. However, at least one more critique of the FSC requires attention before its application to specific cases of intense evil.

Are We Still on Rowe's Trolley?

In the FSC, free will and free systems work together to discover theodical suggestions. The good of regularity and free will are clear catalysts in this defense. However, these aspects of the FSC, if left unchecked, could easily be used to create a theodicy. Theodical suggestions are more modest, and therefore more defendable, than a theodicy, for they make claims of possibility rather than claims of necessity. The governor which works within the FSC to maintain its status as a defense, and not a theodicy, is skeptical theism. As was discussed in chapter 7, skeptical theism calls into question the extent of human ken. For all that is known, G could very well have a justifying reason for allowing a specific example within O to occur. Therefore, given the limits of human knowledge, no one can rightly say, with absolute certainty, that an instance of intense evil is gratuitous. Skeptical theism reminds the practitioner of the FSC that the limits of human ken also mean that the apparent explanation for a given instance of intense evil may or may not be correct. Thus, any observation regarding the non/action of G which results in a possible explanation is only one among any number of possible solutions known to G but undetected by humanity. In short, skeptical theism provides humility as a governor for applications of the FSC. However, there remains a critique of skeptical theism which, if true, not only threatens the use of skeptical theism but that of the FSC as well.

Also, discussed in chapter 7 was Rowe's Trolley. In sum, William Rowe observes that skeptical theism causes as much doubt for potential evils as it does for potential goods. In other words, that which makes skeptical theism effective in doubting the human ability to ascertain the potential good of a situation also makes it unlikely that humanity can ascertain potential evils. Those who board the trolley car of skeptical theism will find that it has no brakes to save it from crashing into an ocean of epistemic relativism. This is a lethal critique of skeptical theism and, given the importance of skeptical theism to the FSC, should be addressed if any use of skeptical theism is to be taken seriously.

Hasker too recognizes this potential for moral skepticism and thinks it should be addressed, but rather than argue more stridently for the value of skeptical theism he highlights what he sees to be the cornerstone of the difficulty for Wykstra's project. After a discussion on how skeptical theism can be taken toward moral skepticism, even though humanity should have some confidence in recognizing good and evil, Hasker states, "Awareness of our cognitive limitations may reduce to some extent our confidences that a given instance of evil is gratuitous but will not and should not eliminate entirely the evidential force of apparently gratuitous evil."[38] Part one of his argument acknowledges the potential for skeptical theism to work in addressing an instance of apparently gratuitous evil, but Hasker also points out that the non-theist will still have abduction to fall back on. For, even the logical strength of an argument cannot completely dispel the seemingness of a situation. Hasker goes on to note that the focus should be on what he calls Rowe's Requirement, which claims that G cannot coexist with gratuitous evil.[39] By focusing on non-theistic conceptions, such as Rowe's Requirement, the need for the epistemic arguments of skeptical theism become unnecessary. While Hasker's strategy is viable in addressing Rowe's Requirement, there is no need to throw the baby out with the bath water. Skeptical theism is a useful concept, but possible resolutions to the moral skepticism critique should be addressed before it is abandoned.

Stephen Wykstra, aware of the critique of moral relativism, does offer some rebuttal in defense of skeptical theism. In addressing a thought experiment designed to highlight the moral ambiguities in skeptical theism, Wykstra considers the plight of Hiker Sally (a psychopath forest ranger who finds someone tied to railroad tracks) who must decide between amputating someone to save their life (which she knows how to do) or making a fifteen-hour trek to gain help. Since she is a psychopath she has no intrinsic motivators to guide her. In essence, Hiker Sally is epistemically unclear as to what are the greater potential goods or evils in the situation (like Rowe's Trolley, Hiker Sally finds herself in a relativistic quandary). Wykstra states, "When we are properly functioning, there's usually a pretty good correspondence between our subjective duty in the situation . . . and the action that, objectively, 'ought to be done.' . . . The existential despair of Hiker Sally suggests that some such correspondence presumptions are embedded in the epistemology of moral common sense."[40] Here, Wykstra makes a twofold argument. First, he highlights the term "properly functioning." The

---

38. Hasker, *Triumph of God over Evil*, 185.
39. Hasker, *Triumph of God over Evil*, 185.
40. Wykstra, "Does Skeptical Theism Force Moral Skepticism," 37.

existence of a psychopath is an abnormality in humanity, an exception that proves the rule. To not have a sense of morality, to feel no pull toward right or wrong, is an extreme that does not apply to humanity in general, but this also leads to his second point: the existence of moral common sense. Even within a psychopathic mindset there remains evidence of which actions would work toward the good. For example, though Hiker Sally may not feel any remorse, guilt, pleasure, etc., regarding the person in need she still retains the cognitive ability to recognize the value of human life over no human life. This reality, when conjoined with theism, diminishes the worry of moral skepticism.[41] The theistic position affords a means by which moral skepticism can be avoided, for one can only be agnostic about goods/evils when one is agnostic about G. To be a theist is to look at O and to see if O conflicts with G. Skeptical theism shows that it does not conflict and the existence of G's goodness saves skeptical theism from moral ambiguity. While this line of argumentation does address moral skepticism, it does not appear to avoid/answer Hasker's concern of (to use this paper's terms) abductive force in non-theistic arguments. However, there remains a means of answering both Hasker and moral skepticism, and its foundation can be seen in the words of Rowe himself.

Rowe was a staunch non-theist who desired to live amicably with theists. Thus, some of his projects involved discussing the POE in a manner that encouraged other non-theists to have compassion on well-intentioned theists. It is in this context that Rowe states, "What counts most in human life, in my judgment, is one's effort to live a morally good life. And given that there are necessary moral truths, just as there are necessary mathematical truths, one can do so whether one is a theist, atheist, or an agnostic."[42] It is Rowe's comment regarding necessary moral truths that stands out here. As was discussed in chapter 2, MO has such a strong presence so as to be difficult to account for in naturalistic terms. Thus, it is fitting that MO should be present in discussing Rowe's Trolley.

As was stated at the beginning of this section, Rowe asserts that skeptical theism is a trolley with no epistemic brake to stop it from crashing into moral relativism. However, any discussion of human epistemic limits should also be willing to include foundational truths of human existence, such as MO. A curious aspect of MO can be seen in its striving for the good. Even if these goods are only the necessary goods to which Rowe refers to, there is still a call toward the good which is ever present with humanity. Though the rider may climb into the trolley and begin to panic as doubt creeps in from

---

41. Wykstra, "Does Skeptical Theism Force Moral Skepticism," 37.
42 .Rowe, "Friendly Atheism Revisited," 13.

every corner, if that same rider will survey his surroundings, he will find a lever labeled "Moral Obligation," and once that lever is pulled Rowe's Trolley will stop. For, in the goodness of MO one finds weighty evidence which unbalances the epistemic scales in favor of the good. MO provides a means of restraining skeptical theism from becoming moral skepticism without relying upon the inclusion of the existence of G. That is not to say that this argument would not be made even stronger/probable when considering the theistic position. Indeed, the goodness of G reinforces MO's call toward the good as evidence which favors a skeptical assumption toward unknown goods. Furthermore, the significance of this observation is its translatability/potential acceptability by non-theists. In other words, because this use of MO does not hinge upon theistic presuppositions, skeptical theism can avoid moral relativism in a way more readily accessible to those non-theists to whom the skeptical theist is addressing. MO as a governor for skeptical theism allows it to be used effectively; no abandonment required.

The most dangerous arguments for skeptical theism are those such as Rowe's Trolley which observe the potential for skeptical theism to resolve itself into moral skepticism.[43] The ubiquitous presence of MO serves as a braking system for Rowe's' Trolley. When the rider begins to feel lost in an epistemic stalemate of good and evil it is MO that turns the tide. MO serves as evidence toward the good on a basic human level. Furthermore, MO serves as a reminder that, when considering the limits of human ken in relation to potential goods and evils, G will act toward the good.

Conclusions

The Free System Corollary is a theistic defense which makes use of theodical suggestions that arise from the intersections/interactions of free will and free systems. By observing (i.e., actively looking) for the systems of regularity that are in play for a given instance of intense evil, and how these systems interact/influence free will, one begins to see a world of intricate relationships. For, there does not exist only one regular good in this world. Gravity, inertia, momentum, biology, and many more are all strands which come together to form a web of regularity which allows people to act freely. Tug/break one strand and the effects can be felt throughout the web. These systems of

---

43. Admittedly, as was discussed in chapter 7, Rowe was not comfortable with ascribing goodness to a basic understanding of the divine. Therefore, he would likely have challenged this conclusion on that point. However, the strong presence of MO provides a properly basic belief in the goodness of G. Rowe himself believed in necessary moral truths, and if there is a creator he created humanity with MO. Therefore, it is reasonable to ascribe goodness as a basic quality of the divine.

regularity provide a consistent means by which choices can be actualized. Disrupting free systems and/or free will could have disastrous effects on this world. G created this complex world of regularity and free will, and if G does not honor/respect his creation he ceases to be good.

The FSC anticipates there to be natural and moral evils. Natural evils can occur when free systems intersect (such as the growth of a tree with a storm), and moral evils are a natural consequence of having free will. Free will entails choice, choices for good and/or evil. G can only prevent all instances of natural and moral evil by violating the free will and free systems he established, which would make him an oppressor. However, this does not mean that it is impossible for G to interact with creation. Prayer constitutes an act of free will which allows G to work. Also, just as a programmer can leave a backdoor to a program so too could G have created this world with a backdoor. In short, miracles are possible, but the intricate workings of this world conjoin to provide plausible reasons for why G may not act in a given situation (i.e., theodical suggestions). There are, of course, counter arguments to be made. Aside from the aforementioned miracles (how are miracles consistent with regularity), free will, and moral skepticism stand as serious threats to the FSC. However, the burden of proof for the denial of free will rests squarely on the shoulders of determinists (free will is not just a fragile thing as to not be able to support the FSC). Additionally, moral obligation serves as a foundational evidence for good which acts as a governor for the FSC's use of skeptical theism, keeping it from moral skepticism.

As with any assertion/thought/project there are and will continue to be counter arguments/thoughts/projects, but in addressing these concerns here the FSC stands ready to test itself for its abductive quality. The FSC makes a bold claim in being able to account for specific instances of intense evil in an abductively plausible manner, all while remaining a defense and not a theodicy. It is toward this end that the next chapter is dedicated.

9

Applying the Free System Corollary

When it comes to making abductive arguments, non-theists, it would seem, have an advantage over theists. To prove, or at the very least make a case for, the nonexistence of G, non-theists only need to show one case which is incompatible with what theists recognize G to be. Thus, theists tend to eschew theodicies for defenses. However, while defenses provide sound logical explanations for the compatibility of G with the general states of affairs with which humanity finds itself, theistic defenses are hesitant to provide explanations for specific cases. Indeed, doing so would turn the defense into a theodicy, and non-theists would then have the much easier task of showing how such a theodicy fails in at least one case. The theist, then, seems to be in a difficult situation. Either take the less defendable position and make a theodicy or maintain a more secure defense and forgo direct explanation for specific instances. Logically, a defense would seem to be the best course of action, but the tact employed by non-theists does not rely on logic alone.

A by-product of arguing for the gratuitousness of specific instances of intense evil, non-theists not only seek to make a logical argument but they also make an abductive one. There are two basic stages to this abductive strategy: (1) empathy and (2) authority. The ubiquitous nature of intense evils in this world means that nearly, if not every, person has experienced it. Therefore, upon hearing of a specific case of intense evil a person can easily identify/empathize with the given case. Empathy does not necessarily equate to agreement, but with non-theists being willing to engage directly with said cases, and theists hesitant to do so, the non-theists can appear to be more authoritative. This is the goal of the non-theistic abductive arguments from the POE: make non-theism appear to be the inference to the best explanation by touching upon human empathy in ways which theists are hesitant to approach. Essentially a game of chicken, non-theists make their abductive case with specific instances of intense evil. If the theists stay within their defenses, they run the risk of losing the abductive challenge. If theists engage directly with these specific instances, they open themselves up to the vulnerabilities of a theodicy. Theism may be logically sound but to answer the challenge of the non-theists it needs to be abductively strong as well.

It has been the contention throughout this book that there does exist a means by which theism can make an abductive argument without becoming a theodicy. In the previous chapter, the FSC was introduced as a solution to the above dilemma. The claim: by making use of theodical suggestions born from the intersections of free will and free systems an abductive case for theism can be made in specific instances of intense evil. Here, the FSC will be evaluated for its ability to engage with non-theists in this manner.

While there are many more examples of intense evil than can be accounted for in one paper, there are two examples of intense evil that are commonly touted by non-theists as being defeaters for theism. Therefore, the FSC will be evaluated directly with these cases. The non-theistic case is perhaps best summed up by William Rowe when he states, "P: No good we know of justifies an omnipotent, omniscient, perfectly good being in permitting E1 [a fawn caught in a fire] and E2 [the abuse/rape/murder of a 5-year-old girl], Q: no good at all justifies an omnipotent, omniscient, perfectly good being in permitting E1 and E2; therefore, not-G: there is no omnipotent, omniscient, perfectly good being."[1] Here, Rowe outlines the APOE: gratuitous evil is not compatible with G and since there are at least two cases of gratuitous evil G must not exist. The admittedly tragic (i.e., intense) cases of the fawn and little girl provide a case of natural evil and a case of moral evil for consideration. Given the accepted use of these examples in discussions of the APOE, these instances will be examined in light of the FSC. If successful, the FSC will provide an abductive argument for theism that is theodically compelling and defensively sound.

Addressing a Particular Case of Natural Evil

A Free System Corollary Account of an Instance of Natural Evil

Consider a potential case of natural evil: a fawn (Bambi) finds itself trapped in a forest fire caused by lightning and dies. If G is good, why did he not save Bambi? Is this a commentary on G's goodness and/or omnipotence? What possible greater goods could come from allowing an innocent animal to suffer and die? Furthermore, how could intervention have possibly hurt the regularity of nature and/or free will since there were no people around to

---

1. Rowe, "Evidential Argument from Evil: A Second Look," 263.

be impacted by Bambi's rescue? Though Bambi's predicament can be easily stated its simplicity belies a much larger undercurrent of issues that nontheists hold theists accountable for answering. In sum, why would G create a world which could cause such intense evil in the life of a creature that does not have the capacity to rebel against G?

Vital to any discussion of an instance of evil is information, and this includes unknown as well as known information. In the case of Bambi, there is much unknown. For example, what does the state of the balance of regularity look like? Has G intervened elsewhere in nature so that one more interjection would have compromised regularity as a good? If so, why did G choose to intervene elsewhere but not here? While regularity will be discussed in light of what is known, the point here remains that human ken suffers from severe limitation when it comes to comprehensive knowledge of global events. However, limits of human ken are evident before making global considerations. Despite the best efforts of zoologists, biologists, veterinarians, and animal-loving people in general, no one knows what it is like to burn in a fire from Bambi's perspective. Is a deer fearful when separated from others? Would the smoke have incapacitated Bambi before any experience of pain? Although humanity does have such limits of knowledge, given that animals do sense pain, it remains a possibility that Bambi did truly suffer. The word "possibility" here refers to potential. By virtue of the premise, there can be no outside observer of Bambi's demise. Therefore, E1, Bambi's fiery death, is speculative. However, given the existence of forest fires (naturally occurring in this case) and the habitation of forests by deer it remains a plausible possibility. In sum, there exists much that is unknown. There are questions of the balance of goods/regularity and what the experience would be like for a deer that does not possess higher cognitive function. These unknowns, and what they entail, are beyond human ken, but there yet remains much that is attainable.

In discussing what is known of Bambi's death, there are three general principle players: weather, animal life, and the forest. Weather possesses two innate abilities which can appear to be antithetical to each other. Patterns of rain, temperature fluctuations, etc., promote life but they can also be very destructive. Interestingly, weather seems to be considered a good thing until it runs afoul of something of concern to humans. For example, rains that bring growth to a garden are considered good, but the same rains can cause traffic accidents. What is the difference? In one case the rain was helpful but on the other side of town it was detrimental. The value and/or rightness/wrongness of the rain is completely a function of human interpretation. Weather, it would seem, is amoral, moving about in its patterns day after day.[2] Indeed, E1 may not have even been considered a problem for theism if it were not for the affection many people seem to have for cute, young animals. This leads to some interesting observations regarding the forest.

The focus of the challenge of E1 is the fate of Bambi, but what of the other living things in the forest? The scenario makes it clear that the other deer have fled, but there are many more living things in the forest than deer. Birds, trees, plants, insects, and rodents all reside within a tinderbox waiting for a lightning strike. This observation impacts the discussion in two ways. First, it highlights the emotive aspect of E1. Deer, fawns especially, are more visually appealing to most people than, say, a beetle. By evoking the image of Bambi, rather than any other number of innocent creatures potentially trapped by that fire, E1 draws emotions of compassion to the surface. The result, the audience hearing of E1 feels saddened at the loss of such an adorable creature, and this sadness yearns for resolution. The nontheistic response is quick, and in its brevity, it affords an answer that can be swiftly digested. However, recognizing the cleverness behind E1 does not defeat it, rather this makes the task even more significant for the theist. For, not only does the theist need to account for the death of one innocent fawn but the potential deaths of many more innocent creatures. The limitations of knowledge discussed above apply to these beings as well, but there is something else that is known which should be considered.

Animals have free will. Granted, the free will animals have does not compare to the free will possessed by humanity, and within the animal kingdom there can be great variation in the manifestation of free will. For example, worms are not known for their trainability, but not only can a dog be trained it also can ignore its master. Likewise, a deer can choose to do or not do many tasks, although one does not commonly hear of moral worth being ascribed to the actions chosen by a deer. Of course, it can be debated as to how much this sort of behavior is a degree of free will versus pure instinct, but the point here highlights the possibility of there being some freedom of choice in the animal kingdom even if it cannot come close to the moral responsibility exhibited by human free will.

In applying the FSC to E1, it is important to remember that while there are no humans directly involved, the free systems which are needed for the application of free will are the same systems of regularity present here. Weather does not behave differently when people are around than when they are not. The laws of physics which guide weather patterns are good in

---

2. For a brief discussion of Alvin Plantinga's proposal that natural evils are caused by supernatural forces, please see chapter 4.

their regularity. Also present are the physical and botanical/biological laws which provide regularity for nature. Significant here is the role of fire. While fire can be a very destructive force it can also be a catalyst. Trees such as pines and aspens are not only capable of surviving fires, but fires can foster their growth. It is possible that the "destruction" of the forest in E1 could result in a thicker forest better able to provide shelter to more creatures. What is observed here are systems of regularity (physics, botany, biology, cosmology, etc.) which sustain the environment of this world. The only fly in the ointment, so to speak, is the presence of Bambi amid the conflagration. Were it not for Bambi, the fire would be of little consequence and may even be seen as useful for the development of the forest, but the presence of a single fawn casts the good of upholding these free systems in a shadow of doubt. How can G not be capable of rescuing Bambi? Rather than inferring that G must not exist because of the presence of one fawn in a naturally occurring event, perhaps the question should be, "What is the cost of G intervening on Bambi's behalf?"

Weather patterns are not isolated events. For example, a blizzard in Illinois can/will result in cooler temperatures in North Texas. To interrupt/modify the weather pattern in E1 would be to affect weather on a much larger scale. What if G had stopped the lightening from striking? As storm patterns develop, they build up energy. The energy needs to be spent somewhere/how. The lightning could have struck elsewhere (but there could have been many more innocents there), or the force of the storm could have worsened and negatively impacted other innocents. Perhaps, G could have moved Bambi to another location, but just as there are weather patterns there are migration patterns as well. Deer are a part of the ecosystem of the forest. To force a deer to move could disrupt that pattern resulting in overpopulation and diminished food resources. Overpopulation of deer can result in a slow and agonizing death by starvation for many deer. Everything involved in E1, Bambi, the forest, the weather, has a role to play in the free systems which universally exist so that free will can be lived out. To ask G to intervene in E1 is to ask G to disrupt those very free systems which were created for the actualization free will. This brings with it a potential cost of abuse of power resulting in the oppression of free will. Such an act does not align with the character of G. However, "potential" was utilized here for two significant reasons.

The use of "potential" here reflects the theodical suggestion aspect of the FSC and of the limits of human ken. It is the contention here that the intersection of free will and free systems in E1 show the real possibility of complications arising should G intervene. However, that is not to say that G would choose to not save Bambi. While complications in nature may arise, the creator of the universe does have the capability of interacting with creation. There exists the real possibility that G would have attempted to save Bambi by working within free systems and honoring what little bit of free will Bambi possessed. Perhaps G did provide some warning, or unusual sound to alert the animals to run, but Bambi ignored it.

To assume that G's working within a situation to avoid evil will always result in the avoidance of evil is to forget about the logical restrictions G has placed upon himself in this world. Yes, G has the raw power to make anything happen, but G's character prevents him from doing evil acts, and this includes acts that would undermine the free will of creatures. Although Bambi does not have the same level of free will as humanity, Bambi is still G's creation. Anyone who would compromise a creature in this fashion would not possess the level of character entailed with G. Therefore, this provides a plausible/possible explanation for how G would allow Bambi to be caught in a forest fire.

The Free System Corollary in Comparison with Naturalism, Part 1

While the FSC posits a theodical suggestion for Bambi's fate, non-theists look at the same situation but come to a different conclusion. Notable among arguments that seek to advance the non-theist position of G's nonexistence is that of William Rowe.

The foundation for Rowe's argument that the plight of Bambi is a defeater for theism consists of three stages. Given that there exists a great amount of animal (and human) suffering in the world, Rowe states:

> 1. There exist instances of intense suffering which an omnipotent, omniscient being could have prevented without thereby losing some greater good or permitting some evil equally bad or worse. 2. An omniscient, wholly good being would prevent the occurrence of any intense suffering it could, unless it could not do so without thereby losing some greater good or permitting some evil equally bad or worse. 3. There does not exist an omnipotent, omniscient, wholly good being.[3]

Rowe's point (3), the conclusion that G cannot exist, is dependent upon the relationship between (1) and (2). Although the theist may have a temptation to reject the entirety of Rowe's argument because of its conclusion, theists should have no problem with (2). For, (2) merely asserts that G can/will help those in need so long as no greater good will be prevented

---

3. Rowe, "Problem of Evil and Some Varieties of Atheism," 2.

as a result, or some greater evil come about as a consequence of intervening. Indeed, (2) reflects the concept behind the good of regularity and the character of G supported by the FSC. However, the coupling of (2) with (1) does cause problems for theism. (1) asserts the existence of gratuitous evil; evil which could/should have been prevented by G, given his character. Per Rowe, the observations of gratuitous evils (1) are incompatible with G's good character (2), and since gratuitous evils can be readily observed there must be a problem with the conception of G, therefore G does not exist (3). Here, the theist could rightly raise an objection by pointing out that it would be very difficult to prove the accuracy of (1). Nevertheless, as Rowe is readily able to point out, though (1) may be challenging to prove conclusively it is another matter altogether to show its plausibility.

The defense of (1), rather than doubling down on proving it to be true, is a strategic move which preserves the message of (1) without the need for proving its absolute correctness. Rowe states, "The truth is that we are not in a position to prove that (1) is true. We cannot know with certainty that instances of suffering of the sort described in (1) do occur in our world. But it is one thing to *know* or *prove* that (1) is true and quite another thing to have *rational grounds* for believing (1) to be true."[4] In addressing the weakness of (1), Rowe makes a shift from an inductive to an abductive style argument. If one can infer that the best explanation for the existence of intense evil resides with it being of a gratuitous nature, one alleviates oneself of the necessity of proving that gratuitous evils do in fact exist. Rowe states, "It seems quite unlikely that *all* the instances of intense suffering occurring daily in our world are intimately related to the occurrence of a greater good or the prevention of evils at least as bad . . . our experience and knowledge . . . provides *rational support* for the first premise . . . we have *rational support* for atheism."[5] Essentially, Rowe is making a rational appeal to emotion to support the notion of gratuitous evil. Rational in that it makes use of available information; emotional in that has as its goal the comforting reassurance of being able to explain the truth about instances of intense evil. By Rowe's own admission, (1) cannot be conclusively/absolutely proven. His use of abduction then becomes a means for supporting (3). For, rationally one will/can arrive to questions that evoke the memory of Skeptical Theism: for all that is known, perhaps G is real and has legitimate reasons for allowing evil. Rowe's argument curtails any chain of thought that would lead down that path and stops it at the moment of evil. There must be at least one instance of evil that is pointless. Surely, a little fawn could not even hurt a fly, so why would G, if

---

4. Rowe, "Problem of Evil and Some Varieties of Atheism," 4.
5. Rowe, "Problem of Evil and Some Varieties of Atheism," 5.

he exists, allow such a thing? Nothing comes immediately to mind, therefore abduction: G does not exist. Admittedly, Rowe does not seem to be trying to appeal to emotions through his rationality, but whether or not he intended it the result remains. That result is a powerful abductive argument against theism. Rowe does see a potential theistic counter to his argument, but his response to that is rooted in abduction as well.

Rowe asserts that the theist's best course of action would be to apply the G. E. Moore Shift against (1). In short, the theist would argue (not-3): there is rational belief for the existence of G. Given (2), (not-3) and (2) result in (not-1): there do not exist cases where G could have prevented some evil but did not do so.[6] By beginning with a revised version of premise (3), the theist can arrive at a conclusion that does not support Rowe's atheistic argument. Rowe's counter to this? He then argues for a friendly atheism, an atheism which can accept that some theists can have rational grounds for their belief, even if they are in error.[7] In other words, theists are working with broken calculators, so atheists should have respect for them even if theists are wrong through no fault of their own.[8] So, even if the theist attempts to rationally make a case for G, Rowe asserts that the inference to the best explanation is not-G and any arguments to the contrary are rooted in something that is at fault with the ability of theists to think rationally. This amounts to an abductive argument that defends itself by clinging onto what is immediately known while attacking theists for their attempt to look beyond the foremost concerns on the minds of those contemplating intense evil. The question that now presents itself is, "Can the FSC provide an abductively strong argument in the case of Bambi?"

The application of the FSC in the previous section resulted in a theodical suggestion for Bambi's death: it is possible that Bambi ignored G's warnings and that the fire was allowed for the betterment of the forest and its future inhabitants.[9] From a theistic perspective, this theodical suggestion aligns with G's character while accounting for the preservation of free systems. This theodical suggestion is a theistically plausible explanation for E1. From a non-theistic perspective, Rowe's account of E1 is also plausible. The nonexistence of G explains why such things may happen. One could even say that both accounts of E1 are equally sound. However, these are mutually exclusive tellings of E1. As was stated above, Rowe believes that theists use

6. Rowe, "Problem of Evil and Some Varieties of Atheism," 7–8.
7. Rowe, "Problem of Evil and Some Varieties of Atheism," 8–9.
8. Rowe, "Problem of Evil and Some Varieties of Atheism," 11n7.
9. To be clear, it is not the position of this paper that this theodical suggestion is the only one that can be found with the FSC. Indeed, more information and/or other perspectives may yield additional theodical suggestions.

reason but are working with broken calculators. Undoubtedly, theists would claim that the depravity of humanity results in the non-theist working with a broken calculator. What then, are theists and non-theists to be locked in an eternal argument with no clear resolution in sight? While motivational factors that influence an individual's preference for non/theism will vary from person to person, the order of logical progression in each argument can illuminate the logical probability of one over the other.

Rowe's case for E1 being a defeater for G is well thought out but it does suffer from an *a priori* inclination toward non-theism. From the very beginning with (1), Rowe's argument has an antagonistic tone toward G by assuming gratuitous evil. As was mentioned above, Rowe does admit that (1) cannot be proven to be true, but he sees rational grounds for believing it to be true. Nevertheless, from the beginning non-theism serves as a standard by which the rest of the argument is aligned to. There is significance in the FSC's approach in addressing Rowe and E1. The initial concern of the FSC entail an examination of the interactions between free will and free systems. Then these observations are used to identify theodical suggestions that correlate with G. Free will serves as a launching point as it has been identified as a defining characteristic of humanity. This process is significant, for it places an examination of the situation prior to any dialogue concerning G. Yes, G's character is not one of oppression, so G will value the preservation of free systems and honor free will, but that criterion is a tool in developing a theodical suggestion; the tool works with the raw materials of free will and free systems. In other words, the FSC engages with observable phenomenon to gather as much information as possible, regardless of one's theistic position, and then compares the compatibility of said observations with conceptions of deity. Rowe's (1) reflects a position of non-theism and as such it colors the remainder of his argument. While the FSC is unashamedly theistic in its conclusions, the initial steps guiding the FSC are neutral. In the endless merry-go-round that exemplifies accusations of broken calculators, the FSC stands out for the uniqueness of its starting position. It is the contention here that this starting position, which results in a plausible theodical suggestion, allows the FSC the possibility to present theism as being more probable than non-theism in answering examples of natural evil from the APOE.

Addressing a Particular Case of Moral Evil

A Free System Corollary Account of an Instance of Moral Evil

E1 represents a case of natural evil, an intense evil that occurs in nature. In contrast, E2 entails a case of moral evil, an intense evil done at the hands of a free agent. What is more, unlike the theoretical, though arguably probable, Bambi, E2 represents a real-life situation involving a five-year-old girl. For the purposes here, the girl will be referred to as Sally and the other players will have alternative names as well.

Sally lived in an apartment with her mother (Marge), the mother's boyfriend (Vince), an unemployed man (Earl), and two other children, one of whom was an infant. The three adults went to a bar, and while there Vince was asked to leave around 8 p.m. (he had been drinking and doing drugs). Vince tried to reenter several times but gave up around 9:30 p.m. Around 2 a.m. the Marge and Earl left the bar; Marge went home and Earl went to another party. Vince attacked Marge when she entered the home. Marge's brother (Joe) was there and knocked him out. With Vince incapacitated, Joe left. Later, Vince again attacked Marge, but Marge knocked Vince unconscious again. After looking in on her children, Marge went to bed. At 3:45 a.m., Earl came home and found Sally beaten head to toe, raped, and strangled to death by Vince.[10]

Undeniably, this event is offensive and emotionally stirring. To think of what Sally went through, without doubt, qualifies as intense evil. Furthermore, one can easily see how non-theists, such as Rowe and Russell, would want to use this as an example of gratuitous evil. However, before a verdict is reached this case should be examined to see if the evidence does favor the non-theist's claim that Sally's death serves as grounds for denying the existence of G.

As was done with E1, E2 will be evaluated first by looking at the intersections of free will and free systems. Unlike the case of Bambi, the free systems of nature are not responsible for Sally's death, but they are still important for the good of regularity. Although there does not appear to be any environmental concerns in terms of weather, there are human made environments. The apartment, the bar, the location Earl went to, and also the layout of the apartment plays a part in the regular lives of these people. Of course, foremost on the minds of those reading of E2 are the actions of Vince, a free will agent, but Vince was not the only exemplar of free will. Marge, Earl, Sally, the bartender, the bouncer, and Joe are all part of this story.

---

10. Russell, "Persistent Problem of Evil," 123.

While Sally can hardly be faulted for waking up in the middle of the night, there are many more instances of free will action than Vince's crime. Vince was caught doing drugs and drinking too much, as was evidenced by his expulsion from the bar. It is not clear here who noticed his drug use, but eventually the proprietors of the bar noticed his behavior. Truly, he deserved to be kicked out, but they (as well as Marge and Earl) also chose to not call the police. Hindsight is 20/20, and perhaps the bouncer, and other employees, followed standard procedure, but that was a choice nonetheless. More remarkable than this are the choices made by Marge and Joe. Vince attacks Marge and is put down by Joe . . . who then leaves. Granted, Vince lived there, but he had also just shown violent tendencies. Joe then chooses to leave Marge alone with someone who had just wanted to do harm to her. Then, for a second time Vince tries to hurt Marge. Even though she won that fight she chose to leave him in the apartment. Perhaps Vince was too heavy, or she was afraid to touch him. Regardless, Marge could have called the police and had Vince removed. Marge then chooses to go to sleep. She is understandably tired, but she chose to leave the violent man unattended.[11] Finally, there is Vince's choice to abuse and murder Sally. Each violent act committed by Vince was an act of free will. Even in the end, and throughout the ordeal, Vince continued to exercise free will in violation of the sanctity of another.

As with many things in life, what is seen here entails more complexity than may be immediately construed. Why did G allow this to happen? Or, perhaps more accurately, how does this align with G's power and character? First, it should be noted that the above analysis of free will in E2 reveals more than one party involved in free will acts that directly affected Sally. The repeated rejections at the bar, two reactions to two separate violent acts, and a final decision to leave Vince in the apartment amount to at least five choices made by others that allowed Vince to continue interaction with Marge and her family. In other words, before Vince chose to assault Sally, other free agents had an opportunity to remove him from their presence. Admittedly, it is unlikely that Marge, Earl, or anyone else could have predicted Vince's behavior (based on the information provided), but his continued violence/threat should have been easy to predict.[12] The result of these free will acts? Sally died a horrible death and Vince became known as a molester/murderer.

---

11. Given Marge's lack of police involvement with Vince's violence, this does make one wonder if Vince had beaten her before. This would have some interesting implications for analyzing this case, but as there is no direct mentioning of this in the account it remains speculation and will not be further considered here.

12. It is perhaps possible that the alcohol consumed by Marge impeded her judgment, but drinking was a free will act in and of itself.

With the consideration of free will, and the necessity of free systems, what was at first a relatively simple (albeit tragic) tale of jealously and rage becomes more complicated. Vince is not the only person contributing to the narrative; multiple people (five at minimum) had free will involvement. Though the responsibility of some was greater than others, the fact remains that if G had overruled the choices made here much was at stake. It has already been discussed in this paper of the sanctity of one person's free will. How much more five people's? This observation is not meant to be a theodical suggestion for E2. Rather, it highlights the complexity of the situation. Complexity is part of the puzzle, but it is not the entirety of the puzzle. If G had overridden Marge, Earl, Vince, or anyone else's free will it would make G an oppressor. Furthermore, to alter the physical layout of the apartment (so Sally remained unseen) or some other alteration of free systems could have negative repercussions for many more people. "But," the non-theist says, "why couldn't G, at the very least, have made Vince temporarily paralyzed? Surely that would not have disrupted free systems or free will enough to not allow the saving of Sally?" This question is not only valid it speaks to the heart of the matter. Theists believe in the omniscience and omnipotence of G. In the Bible, people are made temporarily mute and/or blind, why could not have G done something similar here? Even though it may seem as if the FSC has done nothing but push the question back a little farther, the intersection of free will and free systems still has at least one other insight to give.

As was mentioned above, Vince was violent, and he chose to exercise that violence at least three times in this case. The two cases of Vince attacking Marge offer a window into Vince. Someone cannot do that which they do not already have the capacity for doing. Someone may do something for the first time, but the ability for them to do that thing existed before they attempted it. A true act of charity is a reflection of the good will within that person. They would not have been able to give if they did not possess the capacity/inclination for altruism. Similarly, Vince was able to harm Sally because he already possessed the capacity for committing such crimes. The implications of this observation are staggering. If Vince had not assaulted Sally, he would have walked away with the same potential for violence living inside of him. In this case, Vince was identified, but if G did not allow this to happen it is possible that Vince would have attacked someone else in the same manner, and perhaps he would not have been caught. Painful though it is to consider, it is possible that G allowed Sally to die for the benefit of many others who may have been harmed before Vince got caught.

The Free System Corollary in Comparison with Naturalism, Part 2

Since E2 involves actual, as opposed to hypothetical, people, emotions run much higher when considering this case. Not only does the involvement of humanity contribute to this emotional state but the young age of the victim makes it even more poignant as age is often equated/related to innocence. Therefore, the stakes are higher with E2 than with E1. Although non-theistic arguments from E2 can take on varied forms, non-theists such as Bruce Russell and William Rowe tend to focus on the implications of G's omniscience, and Russell is particularly concerned with the tolerances of regularity.

The question, "How can G allow this to happen," takes a different tact in the hands of Russell. Rather than pondering the motivation/circumstances surrounding the apparent inaction of G, Russell chooses to compare G's behavior with that of humanity. Russell states, "I am arguing that if we are not justified in believing that no reason would justify god in allowing the brutal rape and murder, then we are not justified in believing that no reason would justify the onlooker in allowing that same act."[13] If a human would be held accountable if they stood by and did nothing as Sally was assaulted how much more should G be held accountable? Implied here is the concept that someone who was unable to assist Sally, whether by restraint or lack of knowledge, would not bear responsibility for not coming to Sally's aid. Since G is omnipotent and omniscient, Russell asserts that G should be held accountable for his lack of involvement in Sally's fate, should he exist. Of course, if there did exist any justifying evidence for why G did not intervene this point would be mute. Russell does not believe such evidence exists, and Rowe believes that the evidence that does exist points to a reasonable non-belief in G.

Rowe strives for pragmatism when weighing the evidence for theistic belief. For Rowe, any evidence that can be used for the support of a universal deity will be common to all people. However, Rowe does not believe that such evidence exists. Rowe states, "Given our common knowledge of the evils and goods in our world . . . it is *irrational* to believe in theism unless we possess or discover strong evidence in its behalf."[14] So, Rowe is looking for evidence relating to G's in/actions in the world and concludes that none exist. What would count as evidence? The above statement references common knowledge of goods and evils. In other words, Rowe makes use of the experiences (i.e., testimonies) of people who have either experienced first hand or have observed intense evil and goods (which for Rowe does not outweigh the

---

13. Russell, "Defenseless," 198.
14. Rowe, "Evidential Argument from Evil: A Second Look," 282.

evils). Interestingly, Rowe calls upon common knowledge, but he is selective about what knowledge he is willing to entertain. Prior to the above statement (where k represents background knowledge of goods and evils with no presuppositions about G), Rowe states, "Will k include the information that ordinary religious experiences and mystical religious experiences occur? Insofar as the inclusion of such information raises the probability of G on k above 0.5 we will have to exclude it."[15] Rowe expresses a desire to make use of common knowledge/experiences but is unwilling to entertain those very testimonies which support the working of G in this world because they are significant enough to shift the evidence in favor of believe in G. While this reflects a significant *a priori* leaning toward non-theism, and does color the evidence, some understanding for Rowe's dismissal of theistic evidence can be seen in his critique of a common theodicy used to explain instances of intense evil: soul making.[16]

Soul making, the theodicy which argues for eternal compensation for wrongs suffered in this world, is not uncommon in the history of Christianity. Per soul making, any intense evil, such as Sally's, will result in an overall balance toward the good because of the spiritual growth that will occur as a result of a given trial as well as spending eternity with G. Rowe references this concept when he states, "No good involving God, such as the little girl's enjoying eternal felicity in the presence of God or (Plantinga's suggestion) the little girl's enjoying God's gratitude in eternal felicity, is even a candidate for consideration, since such a good is actual only if God does exist."[17] Here, Rowe recognizes the logical consistency of soul-making with belief in G, but since it is dependent upon belief in G, and the existence of G is the question of the hour, Rowe does not accept soul-making as a viable explanation for intense evil. On one hand, Rowe may be guilty of begging the question since soul-making does provide a balance of good for intense evils that is logically consistent with G. Therefore, soul-making places the ball back into the non-theist's court and asked them to find new evidence that disproves G's existence. On the other hand, soul-making does require a belief in G for its plausibility which can make it a hard pill to swallow for someone who does not believe in G's existence. Furthermore, what evidence is there within an instance of intense evil that lends itself toward a soul-making theodicy? Russell suggests there is none. Russell states, "No one would give up striving to perfect himself because someone like the little girl in Flint [Sally]

---

15. Rowe, "Evidential Argument from Evil: A Second Look," 266.

16. It is not the intent here to imply that Rowe's observations regarding soul-making justify his rejection of theistic testimony.

17. Rowe, "Reply to Plantinga," 550.

was saved. People are not encouraged to make themselves better because they have observed what seems to be a case of gratuitous suffering, nor discouraged from perfecting themselves if some such suffering is prevented."[18] Here, Russell is expressing his belief in the unlikeliness that the suffering of Sally would result in anyone's betterment. Of course, Russell's comment here does not address any blessings that Sally would receive in the presence of G, but Russell and Rowe highlight an important aspect of soul-making that is relevant for this discussion of the APOE: the benefits soul-making are difficult to see in this present world.

As was mentioned above, soul-making has a long history in Christianity. It has been acknowledged that it has a logical consistency with belief in G, but no more defense of soul-making will be here. While Rowe and Russell display something of their presuppositions in their treatment of soul making, they also offer valuable critiques in terms of what is observable from this existence. In other words, soul making, while logical, is not abductively strong to a non-theistic audience. Additionally, though personal growth through trials is a biblical concept, soul-making as a primary justification for intense evil does not necessarily follow.[19] This brief discussion on soul-making highlights an important aspect of E2: non-theists are concerned with the instance at hand and what it means for belief in G. Reflective of this observation is Russell's conclusion: "A world with on less instance of a brutal beating, rape and murder of a little girl is morally better than one with such an instance."[20] In short, when it comes to instances of intense evil, such as E2, the non-theistic argument can be boiled down to an objection of observable goods resulting/being allowed from said evil. For Rowe, this manifests in questions of knowability, and for Russell knowability gives birth to questions of the limits of regularity as a good.[21] In either case, the non-theistic claim focuses on the act of intense evil itself. The FSC, however, looks at the act, the foundations that made the act possible, and the potential repercussions.

In the previous section, the FSC was applied to E2 and a theodical suggestion was found. The FSC kept in mind the value of regularity as a good and the many number of free will agents involved in the situation. It also recognized the relationship between potential and action. While all people have the potential to do great evil, as well as great good, the actions of Vince revealed a potential for evil of such quality as to be of great concern. If Vince

18. Russell, "Persistent Problem of Evil," 128–29.

19. Discussions on the primacy or tertiary nature of soul-making is a polemical discussion best suited for another paper.

20. Russell, "Defenseless," 201.

21. For a more detailed discussion of Russell's "just one more" argument, and van Inwagen's sound response, see chapter 5.

had walked away from Sally that evil aspect of his character very well could have been directed toward others. In the case of Sally, the perpetrator was known thereby giving the police the tools they needed to find and arrest Vince. Given the good of regularity, the many opportunities free will agents had to prevent the situation, and the real capacity for violence within Vince, it is possible that G allowed E2 not because he wanted Sally to suffer but because free will needs to be respected, and a violent person needed to be taken off the streets. Though it is not a comfortable concept, by allowing E2, G may have prevented more instances of intense evil at the hands of Vince. Admittedly, any analysis of E2 will be uncomfortable. Either one will conclude, like Rowe and Russell, that G does not exist or one will accept that G would allow E2 to happen. Regardless of the reasons for allowing E2, should humanity ever be privileged enough to know them, the fact remains that intense evil occurred. The emotion of a situation cannot be avoided.

The FSC theodical suggestion presented here (indeed, there may be more to be found) is plausible over and against non-theism for at least two basic reasons. First, it gives a more complete telling of E2 by examining the details that present themselves when looking at the intersection of free will and free systems. Second, though the conclusion is logically consistent with G it is not dependent upon a prior belief about G to be true. Though it may not be of much comfort to those experiencing E2, the silver lining of Vince being identified for the crime remains regardless of one's view of G. What makes it a theodical suggestion here is its compatibility with G. So, the FSC produces a theodical suggestion that can be argued for by the evidence. However, does this equate to abductive superiority over and against non-theists such as Rowe and Russell?

Several times throughout this chapter the presence of emotions has been mentioned. Emotion is an important factor in any abductive account. Ultimately, abductive arguments are at the mercy of the sensibilities of the individual. Indeed, the abductive power of Rowe's non-theistic argument can be found in its target audience. Rowe states, "It is the lack of any direct sense of God's presence in one's own life that, I suspect, makes it difficult for an enormous number of rational human beings to sustain a belief [in G] . . . it was a keen sense of the lack of God's presence in my life, along with the horrible evils in our world, that let me slowly to move away from being a committed theist to being a friendly atheist."[22] Rowe's audience are those like him who want answers but because of a lack of experience with G doubt his existence. Therefore, Rowe's argument will have appeal to some. However, the FSC has been shown capable of producing a defense

---

22. Rowe, "Friendly Atheism Revisited," 11.

that is abductively strong for its ability to plausibly account for evil in light of observable reality.

Conclusions

As a test of the FSC's ability to speak abductively to the POE it has been applied to E1, a hypothetical fawn's death in a forest fire, and E2, the real-life abuse and murder of a little girl. Both E1 and E2 are representative of the kinds of intense evils used by non-theists to argue against the existence of G. As was discussed in chapter 8, an examination of the intersection of free will and free systems resulted in theodical suggestions. It has been the contention here that the FSC is abductively plausible for its ability to apply theistic defenses to specific instances of intense evil through a means which seeks to maximize the available data.

An examination of E1 resulted in a theodical suggestion that G would/could have tried to warn/startle the fawn into running away, but the fawn did not respond. This reflects a respect of the good of regularity as well as how could have interacted with the fawn without violating what little free will the fawn possessed. The examination of E2 brought forth a theodical suggestion highlighting the possibility that by allowing Vince to act more atrocities may have been avoided. In each case, the FSC demonstrates abductive ability in its attention to the details which affect free agents and free systems. Non-theistic arguments, while they are detailed in their analysis of the intense event, do not seem to pay as much attention to the nuts and bolts, as it were, of those observable underpinnings of life in action. However, having abductive power is not the same as being abductively stronger.

A critical aspect of abductive arguments is that they rely upon experience. The inference to the best explanation is not a purely logical exercise. If someone has experienced four out of five times a chair breaking that person is not likely to care to hear of the overwhelming majority of positive chair sitting experiences in the world. For them the abductive conclusion is that chairs are dangerous. This is not to say that one's abductive thoughts are a slave to one's experience, but there is a correlation. Additionally, experiences can often bring emotions into play. These factors of experience and emotion are not unique to abductive thought. The same people who have experienced and felt are the same people who use logic and reason. While abduction attempts to make use of this reality, all theistic and non-theistic arguments, whether deductive, inductive, or abductive, are aimed at people living with experiences and emotions that can, and often will, guide their judgments.

It has been the goal of this chapter to utilize the FSC toward making an abductively plausible argument for theism in light of E1 and E2. Admittedly, the persuasive power of the abductive theistic accounts provided here will vary from person to person since their personal experiences (and corresponding emotions) will vary. Nevertheless, it is the contention here that the FSC has been demonstrated as capable of agility in approaching instances of intense evil. It has the potential to seek out theodical suggestions among the intricate fabric of free will and free systems that impact all human life.

10

Conclusion

THE IMPORTANCE OF THE POE has not diminished over the centuries. Philosophers, theistic and non-theistic alike, have been engaged in dialogue regarding the compatibility of a wholly good, loving, omniscient, and omnipotent deity with intense evil and how such a being could allow atrocities to happen. In recent times, the focus of the discussion has shifted away from the logical compatibility of G with evil toward inductive arguments. In recounting specific instances of intense natural and moral evil non-theists argue for a rational non-belief in G. In short, the argument asserts the rationality of acting/believing based on what can be known, and if no good can be seen for allowing evil to happen it becomes rational to have non-belief in G. These arguments, though they begin inductively, are abductive in nature since they coax out an inference to the best explanation for the existence of evil based on personal experience. Here, this has been known as the abductive problem of evil (APOE).

Theists have made excellent use of defenses in answering the POE. Since a defense does not commit itself to a specific reason for an instance of intense evil, choosing instead to offer a meta-narrative which can account for the existence of intense evil in general. Hence, it is more strategically secure compared to theodicies, which seek to give specific reasons for intense evils. However, the APOE makes an appeal to personal experience/knowledge for its claim of justified non-belief in G. Since people think abductively on a daily basis (e.g., trusting in the safety of a vehicle), theism needs to be able to answer the APOE in abductive terms if it is to fully address the aforementioned non-theistic arguments. What is needed is a theistic strategy that can make use of theistic defenses while offering assistance in making abductive applications to specific cases of intense evils. Toward that end, this book has argued for the value of the FSC in providing just such an application. Since the FSC depends heavily upon free will it was fitting to examine the relationship between morality and free will and the use of free will in existing theistic defenses.

Chapter 2 saw a discussion on the existence of MO and its ubiquitous presence in human life. The assertiveness of MO was argued to be an indicator of the existence of G since humanity is incapable of achieving the ideals of MO on their own; one cannot cross the moral gap without G's help. Non-theists provide explanations for the existence of MO, but ultimately naturalism cannot account for the persistence of MO as well as theism. Of course, MO entails a calling toward the good which in turn implies that there is choice in moral affairs. This choice implies the reality of free will in human life. The recognition of free will as actual is essential for theistic defenses such as the FWD, EFWD, and FSC. Interestingly, Rowe makes a provocative claim that the perfect goodness of G would override his free will. In other words, if G exists, he could only do what is good; he could not do otherwise. Therefore, G would not be worthy of any praise/worship. However, supererogatory action is a class of unnecessary good needs that would not be required to be performed by a morally perfect being. The person and work of Jesus Christ serves as a prime example of divine supererogatory action. Therefore, it is on the level of supererogatory actions, at the very least, that G is praiseworthy for his good deeds. The morally good G who gave humanity MO not only expects humanity to live up to his moral standards but he himself is worthy of praise for his good actions.

The supererogatory deeds of G also find importance in discussions of natural law. As was discussed in chapter 3, any act performed by G in this world is an act of humility. G has no obligation to rescue humanity from the just consequences of its actions. This makes the supererogatory work of Christ even more poignant. Furthermore, G can use human emotion to draw people out of a spirit of complacency. This chapter built upon the previous chapter by highlighting how it is that G can make use of creation to call people back toward a proper relationship with him. Like a frantic man drowning in a sea who cannot see or hear the rescuers nearby, humanity, complacent in its sin, may need something to grab their attention. The creator of the universe has, at his disposal, the entirety of a rationally constructed creation to gain said attention. Though this paper takes small issue with the idea of suffering being necessary (preferring to use the phrase "necessary potential"), what is clear is that suffering can contain a silver lining in a world that is rational. Ironically, the rationality of the universe is used by some to argue against the existence of G.

Non-theist J. L. Mackie serves as an example of the use of rationality in an argument against G's existence. He views this world through a causal lens which understands beliefs in G to be little more than evolutionary

CONCLUSION

happenstance, the result of one's tendency to mistake temporal and geographical perspective in understanding the universe. Mackie refers to this tendency as metaphysical double vision (MDV). As was discussed in chapter 4, the principles of MDV can also be applied to non-theistic understandings of the universe. Nevertheless, Mackie provides much for theists to ponder, as Alvin Plantinga has done. Plantinga, being a theist, naturally disagrees with Mackie's non-theistic position, and in his endeavor to provide a theistic defense of the POE, he pursues the logical limits that coexist with G's omnipotence. Transworld depravity (TWD) is put forth as a possible condition which all free will agents possess. Therefore, if G were to make people with free will (which is necessary for there to be significantly good moral actions) then it is possible that those people will go wrong with regards to moral actions at least once. Plantinga's Free Will Defense (FWD) makes use of TWD, and G's logical constraint of not overriding free will, to explain the logical coexistence of G and moral evil. However, Plantinga's explanation for natural evil relies heavily upon the possibility that supernatural forces are responsible for natural evil. Although this view is logically consistent with theism it lacks in its explanatory power from an abductive perspective. However, Plantinga's FWD is largely responsible for the shift in non-theistic argumentation from logical contradiction between G and evil toward inductive evidential arguments.

Though not alone in making evidential arguments from the POE, Bruce Russell stands out for his persistently implied question of, "Why not just one more?" Russell's argument attempts to account for the amounts and kinds of goods and evils present in a given instance of intense evil. He consistently cannot find a greater good that results from an allowance of evil. Furthermore, Russell argues that one less abuse of a little girl (e.g., Sally) would not cause any harm to the overall balance of goods in this world. Since G is supposed to be omnipotent, wholly good, and omniscient, Russell concludes that G must not exist, for if he did exist surely there would be at least one less instance of intense evil in this world. Thus, Chapter 5 brings an evidential argument that attempts to appeal to one's sensibilities about the operation of this world. This example of the APOE finds a theistic responder in Peter van Inwagen. In his EFWD, van Inwagen argues for the good of regularity. Though this does have as its foundation a response to the natural evil found in evolution, van Inwagen does apply this to Russell as well. He notes that arbitrary lines must exist or there would be an overriding of free will. Van Inwagen offers thought experiments such as rescuing survivors of Atlantis: only one more ferry trip but the odds of success proportionately decrease with each new refugee on board. At some point a determination must be made as to when to stop allowing people aboard. For van Inwagen, a massively irregular world is not a good world. Although the EFWD provides a more compelling account of natural evil than the FWD, and it does address Russell's wanting of "just one more" intervention by G, should he exist, in the end van Inwagen seems reluctant to engage in specific instances of intense evil. It has been the understanding here that this is due to a concern of the EFWD becoming a theodicy. This is strategically sound from a logical standpoint, but a reluctance to engage in specific instances of intense evil while non-theists are willing to do so affords non-theists with a degree of abductive advantage.

The non-theism of Paul Draper runs a course different from Russell and Mackie yet contains similarities. Draper considers himself an agnostic because of how he views the POE through the lens of the hypothesis of indifference (HI). HI, with its plea to conflicting evidence for and against theism, calls into question the need for making a/theistic claims regarding reality. Draper's claim of the existence of inscrutable evil gives theism pause to explain why it is that G would allow people to experience gratuitous pain. As was briefly considered in chapter 6, HI and inscrutable evil are open to the critique of the logical limits of G's intervention in creation, but not all theists are willing to reject the existence of inscrutable evil. Breaking from theists such as Plantinga and van Inwagen, Daniel Howard-Snyder admits to the existence of inscrutable evil, but instead at arriving at an agnostic position he derives what he calls divine hiddenness (DH). When inscrutable evil is conjoined with the reality that G does not always make himself clearly visible to humanity (DH) it gives rise to inculpable nonbelief. For Howard-Snyder, the evidences used by Draper do not give support to HI but they do provide a justification for why some people do not believe in G. However, the theological cost of Howard-Snyder's position is high. Theism can account for DH without soteriological castration, as was briefly discussed with C. S. Lewis's account of a drowning man flailing and not receiving available help. One's own uncontrolled cries for help may drown out G's voice, but it does not mean that G is not there or that there is a valid excuse for not noticing the evidences of G's existence.

Throughout this paper, questions of the ability/limits of human ken have been a recurring theme. From moral obligation to the existence of free will to the logical constraints of a given argument, the question of what can be known is ever present. Responding to evidential arguments from the POE, Stephen Wykstra proposed Skeptical Theism as a counter argument which calls into question the human ability to doubt the wisdom of G's goodness in cases of intense evils. Contra Wykstra, Rowe responds with what is perhaps the most strident critique of Skeptical Theism: the danger of moral relativism.

CONCLUSION

Chapter 7 presented Wykstra's core concept CORNEA (Condition of Reasonable Epistemic Access) which serves as a foundational principle for Skeptical Theism, urging one to think in terms of what can be expected in a given situation. In relation to the POE, an application of CORNEA results in skepticism regarding the capability of human ken to know divine levels of knowledge in instances of intense evil. If G is actual, a certain level of human ignorance relative to divine knowledge should be expected. However, Rowe presents a serious challenge to Skeptical Theism. Rowe defines the divine void of any goodness and then pushes Skeptical Theism to its logical limits. He then concludes that Skeptical Theism gives one cause to be doubtful of one's ability to know all potential/actual evils as well as goods. Rowe contends that siding with Skeptical Theism is akin to boarding a trolley car that does not stop. For all that can be known, there are a greater amount of evils than goods, and the goods that are seen may not be the best possible goods. However, as was argued in chapter 7, the existence of MO, specifically its call toward what is good, brings goodness back into considerations of the divine and serves as a governor on Rowe's Trolley. Rowe's critique serves as a valuable warning against relativism, but when considered in light of MO this critique becomes less lethal and more cautionary. The FSC, while it seeks to uncover more of the intricacies of this world than may be immediately considered, finds good company in Skeptical Theism. For, with greater understanding of the world often entails a recognition of how much more there is not known.

Chapter 8 saw the formulation of the FSC. Based upon the utilization of the intersection of free will and free systems toward developing theodical suggestions, the FSC is a theistic defense, but it is unique to other defenses in at least two fundamental ways. First, the word "corollary" was chosen carefully. The FSC is not an extension of another defense, nor is it a completely independent defense. Rather, the FSC works alongside (correlates with) any number of defenses with a goal of providing additional information. Second, the use of this additional information allows the FSC to make theistic defenses abductively plausible. The more information that is known the greater the intricacies become revealed. Non-theistic arguments in the APOE speak to shared experiences of intense evil. This additional information allows theistic defenses to posit theodical suggestions which serve as possible reasons for G's in/action in a given case. In other words, the FSC provides a means of attaining information which can shed light on a given instance of evil, and in so doing theistic defenses can reach across the divide of meta narrative and real/personal applications. If finite humanity can find a plausible reason for a specific case of natural and/or moral evil there could be many more beyond human ken. In addressing specific instances of intense evil, as described above and in chapter 8, theism becomes capable of addressing the APOE.

The FSC anticipates there to be natural and moral evils. Natural evils can occur when free systems intersect (such as the growth of a tree with a storm), and moral evils are a natural consequence of having free will. Free will entails choice, choices for good and/or evil. G can only prevent all instances of natural and moral evil by violating the free will and free systems he established. However, this does not mean that it is impossible for G to interact with creation. Prayer constitutes an act of free will which allows G to work. Also, just as a programmer can leave a backdoor to a program so too could G have created this world with a backdoor. In short, miracles are possible, but the intricate workings of this world conjoin to provide plausible reasons for why G may not act in a given situation (e.g., theodical suggestions). There are, of course, counter arguments to be made. Aside from the aforementioned miracles (how are miracles consistent with regularity), the existence of free will, and moral skepticism stand as serious threats to the FSC. However, the burden of proof for the denial of free will rests squarely on the shoulders of determinists (free will is not just a fragile thing as to not be able to support the FSC). Additionally, moral obligation serves as foundational evidence for good which acts as a governor for the FSC's use of skeptical theism, keeping it from moral skepticism.

The common use of E_1 and E_2 by non-theists in the APOE made them the ideal test beds for evaluating the usefulness of the FSC. In chapter 9 the FSC was applied to E_1 and E_2 and arrived at a plausible theodical suggestion for both. In each case, the abductive plausibility for theism was a result of the process of utilizing the FSC. For E_1, it is possible that G would have attempted to warn/startle Bambi resulting in Bambi running from the fire, but it is also possible that Bambi could have ignored that warning. For E_2, that part of Vince that enabled him to act out his horrendous deeds would not have disappeared if Sally had not been his victim. It is possible that through Sally's death many more girls were saved from being abused by Vince. These theodical suggestions began with a recognition of free will and the inherent good/value of free systems. The FSC seeks first to uncover what can be humanly known of the intricacies in a specific case of intense evil. Only then may a theodical suggestion be derived. Since the FSC does not ask the theistic question first it affords a level of accountability in not presupposing not/G. Whereas, non-theists, such as Rowe, were shown to have an *a priori* disposition toward not-G. Furthermore, if the FSC is able to discover theodical suggestions by examining the intersection of free will and free systems, how many more reasons may there be beyond human ken for allowing E_1 and E_2, or some other instance of evil? It is here that at least two objections to the FSC could be made, one non-theistic in nature and the other theistic.

The claim that the FSC offers accountability in avoiding *a priori* assumptions about the divine is likely to draw criticism. One can almost hear the non-theist say, "Clearly you were a theist before using the FSC, so if our *a priori* assumptions affect an analysis of intense evil yours do too." The non-theist raises a valid concern. A theist should take precautions against bias in evaluating evidence. This is true for all theists, regardless of type, and all non-theists, regardless of type. All people have a belief/inclination toward a certain view of G; this is unescapable. However, this reality is not a defeater for discussions of the APOE. Through dialogue and careful critique ideas and thoughts can be examined and refined, put to the fire so the dross can be skimmed from the top. The accountability afforded by the FSC is one that exists because of its starting point of two basic goods in human life: free will and free systems. Yes, the definition of the FSC states that it makes use of theodical suggestions, but those theodical suggestions only arise after consideration of the intersection of free will and free systems. In short, it is the assertion here that the conclusion of theodical suggestions naturally follows from the evidence provided from free will and free systems. The non-theist is, of course, free to counter and attempt to utilize the FSC in an effort to find non-theodical suggestions. Such a dialogue would be welcome, for the methodology of the FSC, properly applied, will help to govern the bias of all involved. The complaint of the theist, however, is likely to take on a different tact.

A concept that has been utilized throughout this project, and especially in the FSC, is the good of regularity. Indeed, this concept has been unapologetically adopted from van Inwagen's analysis in his EFWD. Therefore, the theist could say, "The FSC is nothing more than an application of the EFWD. Nothing original can be found here." While the FSC does not claim to be a completely from-the-ground-up original theistic framework, it is designed to be used alongside other defenses (hence the use of the term "corollary"), it does claim to be unique in its approach and focus. Specifically, the FSC seeks to answer the APOE whereas the EFWD has a different task in mind. In summarizing the EFWD van Inwagen states, "The purpose of the story [EFWD] is to raise doubts in the minds of the agnostics about one of the premises of the argument from evil: namely, the conditional premise, 'If there were a God, we should not find vast amounts of horrendous evil in the world.'"[1] In short, the purpose of the EFWD entails the explanation for why the amounts and kinds of evils in this world are not incompatible with G. Specifically, van

---

1. Van Inwagen, "Global Argument Continued," 91.

Inwagen is concerned with accounting for the amounts and kinds of suffering in this world that results from the evolutionary process.

The EFWD has three basic parts which argue for a possible explanation of suffering. First, evolution constitutes a law of regularity which accounts for the existence of pain and suffering.[2] Second, intrinsic good results from the aforementioned suffering as manifested in the existence of higher-level sentient creatures (which could not have come about if not for evolution).[3] Third, anything that is massively irregular is a defect at least morally as great as any suffering found in this world.[4] While the FSC does depend upon the good of regularity its focus is different than that of the EFWD. Van Inwagen was concerned with addressing the specific challenge of evolution to theistic responses to the POE. As a result, the EFWD identifies the good that comes as a result of regularity, even if that regularity entails suffering, whereas the FSC identifies potential theodical suggestions for specific instances of intense evil. The EFWD and the FSC may share some commonalities but their focus/intent is different.

The EFWD is not concerned with the APOE. Its task is to provide a metanarrative explanation for how there still can be greater amounts of good in this world despite the existence of the amounts and kinds of sufferings that exist. As was discussed in chapter 5, van Inwagen appears reluctant to address specific instances of intense evils with the EFWD, and there is good reason for that. The EFWD does not have the built-in capability of crossing from metanarrative to individual cases without becoming a theodicy. The FSC, however, can due to its difference in focus and intent for answering the APOE. Perhaps it could be said that the FSC is a set of specialized tires that allow the vehicle of free will defenses to perform better over certain kinds of terrain.

There are, of course, many more avenues this discussion may take, and challenges not anticipated in this paper are likely to arise from theists and non-theists alike. These challenges are welcome. It has been the goal here to introduce the FSC and present it as a viable tool in answering the APOE. It may be impossible to say if any particular theodical suggestion is more abductively appealing, in a universal sense, than a non-theistic claim, but what can be said is that, one way or another, the FSC strives to advance theistic discussions on the abductive problem of evil.

2. Van Inwagen, "Problem of Evil, the Problem of Air," 159–60.
3. Van Inwagen, "Problem of Evil, the Problem of Air," 160.
4. Van Inwagen, "Problem of Evil, the Problem of Air," 161.

Bibliography

Adams, Robert Merrihew. *Finite and Infinite Goods: A Framework for Ethics*. New York: Oxford University Press, 1999.

Alston, William P. "The Inductive Argument from Evil and the Human Cognitive Condition." In Howard-Snyder, *Evidential Argument from Evil*, 97–125.

Baggett, David, and Jerry L. Walls. *God & Cosmos: Moral Truth and Human Meaning*. New York: Oxford University Press, 2016.

———. *Good God: The Theistic Foundations of Morality*. New York: Oxford University Press, 2011.

Berthold, Fred. *God, Evil, and Human Learning: A Critique and Revision of the Free Will Defense in Theodicy*. Albany: State University of New York Press, 2004.

Caruso, Gregg D. *Exploring the Illusion of Free Will and Moral Responsibility*. Lanham, MD: Lexington, 2013.

Dougherty, Trent, and Justin P. McBrayer, eds. *Skeptical Theism: New Essays*. Oxford: Oxford University Press: 2014.

Draper, Paul. "Comments on 'The Problem of Evil and the History of Peoples.'" In *Divine Evil? The Moral Character of the God of Abraham*, edited by Michael Bergmann et al., 198–203. Oxford: Oxford University Press, 2010.

———. "Confirmation Theory and the Core of CORNEA." In Dougherty and McBrayer, *Skeptical Theism*, 132–41.

———. "Cosmic Fine-Tuning and Terrestrial Suffering: Parallel Problems for Naturalism and Theism." *American Philosophical Quarterly* 41 (2004) 311–21.

———. "Evil and the Proper Basicality of Belief in God." *Faith and Philosophy* 8 (1991) 135–47.

———. "God and Perceptual Evidence." *International Journal for Philosophy of Religion* 32 (1992) 149–65.

———. "God, Science, and Naturalism." In *The Oxford Handbook of Philosophy of Religion*, edited by William J. Wainwright, 272–300. Oxford University Press, 2005.

———. "Meet the New Skeptical Theism, Same as the Old Skeptical Theism." In Dougherty and McBrayer, *Skeptical Theism*, 164–77.

———. "Pain and Pleasure: An Evidential Problem for Theists." *Noûs* 23 (1989) 331–50.

———. "Pain and Pleasure: An Evidential Problem for Theists." In Howard-Snyder, *Evidential Argument from Evil* (1996), 12–29.

———. "Probabilistic Arguments from Evil." *Religious Studies* 28 (1992) 303–17.

———. "Richard Swinburne, Providence and the Problem of Evil." *Noûs* 35 (2001) 456–74.
———. "Seeking but Not Believing: Confessions of a Practicing Agnostic." In *Divine Hiddenness: New Essays*, edited by Daniel Howard-Snyder and Paul K. Moser, 197–214. Cambridge: Cambridge University Press, 2001.
———. "The Skeptical Theist." In Howard-Snyder, *Evidential Argument from Evil*, 175–92.
Draper, Paul, and Ryan Nichols. "Diagnosing Bias in Philosophy of Religion." *Monist* 96 (2013) 420–46.
Evans, C. Stephen. *God and Moral Obligation*. Oxford: Oxford University Press, 2013.
Hare, John E. *God and Morality: A Philosophical History*. Malden, MA: Wiley-Blackwell, 2009.
———. *The Moral Gap: Kantian Ethics, Human Limits, and God's Assistance*. Oxford: Clarendon, 1997.
Hasker, William. "All Too Skeptical Theism." *International Journal for Philosophy of Religion* 68 (2010) 15–29.
———. "Can God Be Free? Rowe's Dilemma for Theology." *Religious Studies* 41 (2005) 453–62.
———. "Defining 'Gratuitous Evil': A Response to Alan R. Rhoda." *Religious Studies* 46 (2010) 303–9.
———. "The Foreknowledge Conundrum." *International Journal for Philosophy of Religion* 50 (2001) 97–114.
———. "Is Christianity Probable? Swinburne's Apologetic Programme." *Religious Studies* 38 (2002) 253–64.
———. "Is Free-Will Theism Religiously Inadequate? A Reply to Ciocchi." *Religious Studies* 39 (2003) 431–40.
———. *The Triumph of God over Evil: Theodicy for a World of Suffering*. Downers Grove: InterVarsity, 2008.
Howard-Snyder, Daniel. "Agnosticism, the Moral Skepticism Objection, and Commonsense Morality." In Dougherty and McBrayer, *Skeptical Theism*, 293–305.
———. "The Argument from Divine Hiddenness." *Canadian Journal of Philosophy* 26 (1996) 433–53.
———. "The Argument from Inscrutable Evil." In Howard-Snyder, *Evidential Argument from Evil*, 286–310.
———, ed. *The Evidential Argument from Evil*. Bloomington: Indiana University Press, 1996.
———. "Foundationalism and Arbitrariness." *Pacific Philosophical Quarterly* 86 (2005) 18–24.
———. "Hiddenness of God." In *Encyclopedia of Philosophy*, vol. 4, edited by Donald M. Borchert, 352–57. Detroit: Macmillan Reference USA, 2006.
———. "How *Not* to Render an Explanatory Version of the Evidential Argument from Evil Immune to Skeptical Theism." *International Journal for Philosophy of Religion* 78 (2014) 1–8.
———. "Seeing through CORNEA." *International Journal for Philosophy of Religion* 32 (1992) 25–49.
———. "Theism, the Hypothesis of Indifference, and the Biological Role of Pain and Pleasure." *Faith and Philosophy* 11 (1994) 452–66.

Howard-Snyder, Daniel, and E. J. Coffman. "Three Arguments Against Foundationalism: Arbitrariness, Epistemic Regress, and Existential Support." *Canadian Journal of Philosophy* 36 (2006) 535–64.

Howard-Snyder, Daniel, and Frances Howard-Snyder. "The Christian Theodicist's Appeal to Love." *Religious Studies* 29 (1993) 185–92.

———. "How an Unsurpassable Being Can Create a Surpassable World." *Faith and Philosophy* 11 (1994) 260–68.

———. "Is Theism Compatible with Gratuitous Evil?" *American Philosophical Quarterly* 36 (1999) 115–30.

Howard-Snyder, Daniel, and Paul K. Moser. "The Hiddenness of God." Introduction to *Divine Hiddenness: New Essays*, edited by Daniel Howard-Snyder and Paul K. Moser, 1–23. Cambridge: Cambridge University Press, 2002.

Howard-Snyder, Daniel, and John O'Leary-Hawthorne. "Transworld Sanctity and Plantinga's Free Will Defense." *International Journal for Philosophy of Religion* 44 (1998) 1–21.

Joyce, Richard. *The Evolution of Morality*. Cambridge: MIT Press, 2007.

———. *The Myth of Morality*. New York: Cambridge University Press, 2001.

Kane, Robert. *The Significance of Free Will*. New York: Oxford University Press, 1996.

Keener, Craig S. *Miracles: The Credibility of the New Testament Accounts*. Grand Rapids: Baker Academic, 2011.

Lewis, C. S. *The Abolition of Man*. In *The Complete C. S. Lewis Signature Classics*, 689–732. New York: HarperOne, 2007.

———. *A Grief Observed*. In *The Complete C. S. Lewis Signature Classics*, 647–88. New York: HarperOne, 2007.

———. *Mere Christianity*. New York: HarperSanFrancisco, 2001.

———. *The Problem of Pain*. In *The Complete C. S. Lewis Signature Classics*, 543–646. New York: HarperOne, 2007.

Mackie. J. L. "Causal Priority and the Direction of Conditionality." *Analysis* 41 (1981) 84–86.

———. "Causes and Conditions." *American Philosophical Quarterly* 2 (1965) 245–64.

———. *The Cement of the Universe: A Study of Causation*. Oxford: Oxford University Press, 1980.

———. "The Direction of Causation." *Philosophical Review* 75 (1966) 441–66.

———. "Dispositions, Ground, and Causes." *Synthesis* 34 (1977) 361–69.

———. "Genes and Egoism." *Philosophy* 56 (1981) 553–55.

———. "The Law of the Jungle: Moral Alternatives and Principles of Evolution." *Philosophy* 53 (1978) 455–64.

———. "Metaphysical Common Sense." *British Journal for the Philosophy of Science* 23 (1972) 247–52.

———. "Miller's So-Called Paradox of Information." *British Journal for the Philosophy of Science* 17 (1966) 144–47.

———. "Morality and the Retributive Emotions." *Criminal Justice Ethics* 1 (1982) 3–10.

———. "Newcomb's Paradox and the Direction of Causation." *Canadian Journal of Philosophy* 7 (1977) 213–25.

———. "Omnipotence and Evil." In *The Problem of Evil*, edited by M. M. Adams and R. M. Adams. New York: Oxford University Press, 1990.

———. "The Paradox of Confirmation." *British Journal for the Philosophy of Science* 13 (1963) 265–77.

———. *Problems from Locke*. Oxford: Oxford University Press, 1976.

———. "The Relevance Criterion of Confirmation." *British Journal for the Philosophy of Science* 20 (1969) 27–40.

———. "Responsibility and Language." *Australasian Journal of Philosophy* 33 (1955) 143–59.

———. "Simple Truth." *Philosophical Quarterly* 20 (1970) 321–33.

———. "The Transitivity of Counterfactuals and Causation." *Analysis* 40 (1980) 53–54.

———. "Truth and Knowability." *Analysis* 40 (1980) 90–92.

———. "What Can We Learn from the Paradoxes? Part I." *Crítica: Revista Hispanoamericana De Filosofía* 5 (1971) 85–108.

———. "What Can We Learn from the Paradoxes? Part II." *Crítica: Revista Hispanoamericana De Filosofía* 5 (1971) 35–54.

Morriston, Wes, and Daniel Howard-Snyder. "Is Faith in the Ultimate Rationally Required? Taking Issue with Some Arguments in the Will to Imagine." *Religious Studies* 49 (2013) 209–20.

O'Leary-Hawthorne, John, and Daniel Howard-Snyder. "God, Schmod and Gratuitous Evil." *Philosophy and Phenomenological Research* 53 (1993) 861–74.

Palmer, David, ed. *Libertarian Free Will: Contemporary Debates*. New York: Oxford University Press, 2014.

Peterson, Michael L. "The Logical Problem of Evil." In Taliaferro et al., *Companion to Philosophy of Religion*, 491–99.

Plantinga, Alvin. "Content and Natural Selection." *Philosophy & Phenomenological Research* 83 (2011) 435–58.

———. *Does God Have a Nature?* Milwaukee: Marquette University Press, 1980.

———. "Epistemic Justification." *Noûs* 20 (1986) 3–18.

———. "Epistemic Probability and Evil." In Howard-Snyder, *Evidential Argument from Evil*, 69–96.

———. "Evolution, Epiphenomenalism, Reductionism." *Philosophy and Phenomenological Research* 68 (2004) 602–19.

———. "God, Freedom, and Evil." In *The Problem of Evil*, edited by M. M. Adams and R. M. Adams, 7–64. New York: Oxford University Press, 1990.

———. "Is Belief in God Properly Basic?" *Noûs* 15 (1981) 41–52.

———. "Justification in the 20th Century." *Philosophical Issues* 2 (1992) 43–77.

———. *Nature of Necessity*. Oxford: Oxford University Press, 1978.

———. "The Nature of Necessity." In *The Problem of Evil*, edited by M. M. Adams and R. M. Adams, 83–109. New York: Oxford University Press, 1990.

———. "On 'Proper Basicality.'" *Philosophy & Phenomenological Research* 75 (2007) 612–21.

———. "Positive Epistemic Status and Proper Function." *Philosophical Perspectives* 2, Epistemology (1988) 1–50.

———. "The Probabilistic Argument from Evil." *Philosophical Studies: An International Journal for Philosophy in the Analytic Tradition* 35 (1979) 1–53.

———. "Probability and Defeaters." *Pacific Philosophical Quarterly* 84 (2003) 291–98.

———. "The Prospects for Natural Theology." *Philosophical Perspectives* 5, Philosophy of Religion (1991) 287–315.

———. "Reformed Epistemology." In Taliaferro et al., *Companion to Philosophy of Religion*, 674–80.

———. "Transworld Depravity, Transworld Sanctity, & Uncooperative Essences." *Philosophy and Phenomenological Research* 78 (2009) 178–91.
———. "Two Concepts of Modality: Modal Realism and Modal Reductionism." *Philosophical Perspectives* 1, Metaphysics (1987) 189–231.
———. "Warrant and Accidentally True Belief." *Analysis* 57 (1997) 140–45.
———. *Warranted Christian Belief*. New York: Oxford University Press, 2000.
———. *Where the Conflict Really Lies: Science, Religion, and Naturalism*. New York: Oxford University Press, 2011.
———. "Which Worlds Could God Have Created?" *Journal of Philosophy* 70 (1973) 539–52.
———. "World and Essence." *Philosophical Review* 79 (1970) 461–92.
Reichenbach, Bruce R. "The Cosmological Argument and the Causal Principle." *International Journal for Philosophy of Religion* 6 (1975) 185–90.
———. "Divine Necessity and the Cosmological Argument." *Monist* 54 (1970) 401–15.
———. *Epistemic Obligations: Truth, Individualism, and the Limits of Belief*. Waco, TX: Baylor University Press, 2012.
———. *Evil and a Good God*. New York: Oxford University Press, 1982.
———. "Fatalism and Freedom." *International Philosophical Quarterly* 28 (1988) 271–85.
———. "The Inductive Argument from Evil." *American Philosophical Quarterly* 17 (1980) 221–27.
———. "Karma, Causation, and Divine Intervention." *Philosophy East and West* 39 (1989) 135–49.
———. "The Law of Karma and the Principle of Causation." *Philosophy East and West* 38 (1988) 399–410.
———. "Natural Evils and Natural Law: A Theodicy for Natural Evils." *International Philosophical Quarterly* 16 (1976) 179–96.
———. "Omniscience and Deliberation." *International Journal for Philosophy of Religion* 16 (1984) 225–36.
———. "Why Is God Good?" *Journal of Religion* 60 (1980) 51–66.
Ritchie, Angus. *From Morality to Metaphysics: The Theistic Implications of Our Ethical Commitments*. Oxford: Oxford University Press, 2012.
Rowe, William L. "Alvin Plantinga on the Ontological Argument." *International Journal for Philosophy of Religion* 65 (2009) 87–92.
———. *Can God Be Free?* Oxford: Clarendon, 2006.
———. "Causing and Being Responsible for What Is Inevitable." *American Philosophical Quarterly* 26 (1989) 153–59.
———. "In Defense of 'The Free Will Defense.'" *International Journal for Philosophy of Religion* 44 (1998) 115–20.
———. "The Evidential Argument from Evil: A Second Look." In Howard-Snyder, *Evidential Argument from Evil*, 262–85.
———. "Evil and the Theistic Hypothesis: A Response to Wykstra." In *The Problem of Evil*, edited by Marilyn McCord Adams and Robert Merrihew Adams, 161–67. New York: Oxford University Press, 1990.
———. "Free Will, Moral Responsibility, and the Problem of 'Oomph.'" *Journal of Ethics* 10 (2006) 295–313.
———. "Friendly Atheism Revisited." *International Journal for Philosophy of Religion* 68 (2010) 7–13.

———. "Friendly Atheism, Skeptical Theism, and the Problem of Evil." *International Journal for Philosophy of Religion* 59 (2006) 79–92.

———. "The Problem of Evil and Some Varieties of Atheism." In Howard-Snyder, *Evidential Argument from Evil*, 1–11.

———. "The Problem of No Best World." *Faith and Philosophy* 11 (1994) 269–71.

———. "Religion within the Bounds of Naturalism: Dewey and Wieman." *International Journal for Philosophy of Religion* 38 (1995) 17–36.

———. "Reply to Plantinga." *Noûs* 32 (1998) 545–52.

———. "Response to: Divine Responsibility without Divine Freedom." *International Journal for Philosophy of Religion* 67 (2010) 37–48.

———. "Responsibility, Agent-Causation, and Freedom: An Eighteenth-Century View." *Ethics* 101 (1991) 237–57.

———. "Ruminations about Evil." *Philosophical Perspectives* 5 (1991) 69–88.

———. "Two Concepts of Freedom." *Proceedings and Addresses of the American Philosophical Association* 61 (1987) 43–64.

Russell, Bruce. "ASA Conference 2009: The New Politics of Community." *Humanity & Society* 34 (2010) 189–213.

———. "Contextualism on a Pragmatic, Not a Skeptical, Footing." *Acta Analytica* 20 (2005) 26–37.

———. "Defenseless." In Howard-Snyder, *Evidential Argument from Evil*, 193–205.

———. "Epistemic and Moral Duty." In *Knowledge, Truth, and Duty*, edited by Matthias Steup, 34–47. Oxford: Oxford University Press, 2001.

———. "Exploring the Realm of Rights." *Philosophy and Phenomenological Research* 53 (1993) 169–72.

———. "How to Be an Anti-Skeptic and a Noncontextualist." *Erkenntnis* 61 (2004) 245–55.

———. "Moral Relativism and Moral Realism." *Monist* 67 (1984) 435–51.

———. "On the Relation between Psychological and Ethical Egoism." *Philosophical Studies: An International Journal for Philosophy in the Analytic Tradition* 42 (1982) 91–99.

———. "On the Relative Strictness of Negative and Positive Duties." *American Philosophical Quarterly* 14 (1977) 87–97.

———. "The Persistent Problem of Evil." *Faith and Philosophy* 6 (1989) 121–39.

———. "Rock Bottom: Coherentism's Soft Spot." *Southern Journal of Philosophy* 50 (2012) 94–111.

Russell, Bruce, and Stephen Wykstra. "The 'Inductive' Argument from Evil: A Dialogue." *Philosophical Topics* 16 (1988) 133–60.

Schellenberg, J. L. "Divine Hiddenness." In Taliaferro et al., *Companion to Philosophy of Religion*, 509–18.

Suarez, Antoine, and Peter Adams. *Is Science Compatible with Free Will? Exploring Free Will and Consciousness in the Light of Quantum Physics and Neuroscience*. New York: Springer, 2013.

Swinburne, Richard. *Mind, Brain, and Free Will*. Oxford: Oxford University Press, 2013.

Taliaferro, Charles, et al., eds. *A Companion to Philosophy of Religion*. Blackwell Companions to Philosophy. Oxford: Wiley-Blackwell, 2010.

Van Inwagen, Peter. "Ability and Responsibility." *Philosophical Review* 87 (1978) 201–24.

———. "Causation and the Mental." In *Reason, Metaphysics, and Mind: New Essays on the Philosophy of Alvin Plantinga*, edited by Kelly James Clark and Michael Rea, 152–70. Oxford: Oxford University Press, 2012.

———. "Comments on 'the God of Abraham, Isaac, and Jacob.'" In *Divine Evil? The Moral Character of the God of Abraham*, edited by Michael Bergmann et al., 79–84. Oxford: Oxford University Press, 2010.

———. "Creatures of Fiction." *American Philosophical Quarterly* 14 (1977) 299–308.

———. "Fiction and Metaphysics." *Philosophy and Literature* 7 (1983) 67–77.

———. "The Global Argument Continued." In *The Problem of Evil: The Gifford Lectures Delivered in the University of St Andrews in 2003*, 75–94. Oxford: Oxford University Press, 2006.

———. "The Global Argument from Evil." In *The Problem of Evil: The Gifford Lectures Delivered in the University of St Andrews in 2003*, 56–75. Oxford: Oxford University Press, 2006.

———. "How to Think about the Problem of Free Will." *Journal of Ethics* 12 (2008) 327–41.

———. "Laws and Counterfactuals." *Noûs* 13 (1979) 439–53.

———. "The Local Argument from Evil." In *The Problem of Evil: The Gifford Lectures Delivered in the University of St Andrews in 2003*, 95–113. Oxford: Oxford University Press, 2006.

———. "The Magnitude, Duration, and Distribution of Evil: A Theodicy." *Philosophical Topics* 16 (1988) 161–88.

———. "Meta-Ontology." *Erkenntnis* 48 (1998) 233–50.

———. "Moral Responsibility, Determinism, and the Ability to Do Otherwise." *Journal of Ethics* 3 (1999) 343–51.

———. "Ontological Arguments." *Noûs* (1977) 375–95.

———. "Plantinga's Replacement Argument." In *Alvin Plantinga*, edited by Deane-Peter Baker, 188–202. New York: Cambridge University Press, 2007.

———. *The Problem of Evil*. Great Britain: Oxford University Press, 2006.

———. "The Problem of Evil and the Argument from Evil." In *The Problem of Evil: The Gifford Lectures Delivered in the University of St Andrews in 2003*, 1–17. Oxford: Oxford University Press, 2006.

———. "The Problem of Evil, the Problem of Air, and the Problem of Silence." In Howard-Snyder, *Evidential Argument from Evil*, 151–74.

———. "Reflections on the Chapters by Draper, Russell, and Gale." In Howard-Snyder, *Evidential Argument from Evil*, 219–43.

———. "Relational vs. Constituent Ontologies." *Philosophical Perspectives* 25 (2011) 389–405.

———. "We're Right. They're Wrong." In *Disagreement*, edited by Richard Feldman and Ted A. Warfield, 10–29. Oxford: Oxford University Press, 2010.

———. "When Is the Will Free?" *Philosophical Perspectives* 3 (1989) 399–422.

Van Inwagen, Peter, and Dean W. Zimmerman. *Persons: Human and Divine*. Oxford: Clarendon, 2007.

Vihvelin, Kadri. *Causes, Laws, and Free Will: Why Determinism Doesn't Matter*. New York: Oxford University Press, 2013.

Wielenberg, Erik. "Divine Deception." In Dougherty and McBrayer, *Skeptical Theism*, 236–49.

———. "God and the Reach of Reason. Great Britain: Cambridge University Press, 2006.
———. *God and the Reach of Reason: C. S. Lewis, David Hume, and Bertrand Russell.* Cambridge: Cambridge University Press, 2007.
———. "Goodness without Qualification." *Journal of Value Inquiry* 32 (1998) 93–104.
———. "How to Be an Alethically Rational Naturalist." *Synthese* 131 (2002) 81–98.
———. "Many Are Culled but Few Are Chosen." *Religious Studies* 36 (2000) 81–93.
———. "On the Evolutionary Debunking of Morality." *Ethics* 120 (2010) 441–64.
———. "The Parent-Child Analogy and the Limits of Skeptical Theism." *International Journal for Philosophy of Religion* 78 (2015) 301–14.
———. "Pleasure as a Sign of Moral Virtue in the Nicomachean Ethics." *Journal of Value Inquiry* 34 (2000) 439–49.
———. "Pleasure, Pain, and Moral Character and Development." *Pacific Philosophical Quarterly* 83 (2002) 282–99.
———. *Robust Ethics: The Metaphysics and Epistemology of Godless Normative Realism.* Oxford: Oxford University Press, 2014.
———. "Saving Character." *Ethical Theory and Moral Practice* 9 (2006) 461–91.
———. "Sceptical Theism and Divine Lies." *Religious Studies* 46 (2010) 509–23.
Wykstra, Stephen. "Does Skeptical Theism Force Moral Skepticism? Hesitations over Bergmann's Defense." In *Reason, Metaphysics, and Mind: New Essays on the Philosophy of Alvin Plantinga*, edited by Kelly James Clark and Michael Rea, 30–37. Oxford: Oxford University Press, 2012.
———. "The Humean Obstacle to Evidential Arguments from Suffering: On Avoiding the Evils of 'Appearance.'" In *The Problem of Evil*, edited by Marilyn McCord Adams and Robert Merrihew Adams, 138–60. New York: Oxford University Press, 1990.
———. "Rowe's Noseeum Arguments from Evil." In Howard-Snyder, *Evidential Argument from Evil*, 126–50.
Wykstra, Stephen, and Timothy Perrine. "Skeptical Theism, Abductive Atheology, and Theory Versioning." In Dougherty and McBrayer, *Skeptical Theism*, 142–63.

www.ingramcontent.com/pod-product-compliance
Lightning Source LLC
Chambersburg PA
CBHW070922180426
43192CB00037B/1706